P9-CQV-536

Patterns of Racial Discrimination

Volume II: Employment and Income

Patterns of Racial Discrimination

Volume II: Employment and Income

Edited by

George M. von Furstenberg
Ann R. Horowitz
Bennett Harrison

Lexington Books
D.C. Heath and Company
Lexington, Massachusetts
Toronto   London

Library of Congress Cataloging in Publication Data

Main entry under title:

Patterns of racial discrimination.

    Papers of a conference on racial discrimination in housing and employ-
ment held at Indiana University, May 11, 1973.
    Includes bibliographical references.
    CONTENTS: v. 1. Housing.—v. 2. Employment and income.
    1. Discrimination in housing—United States—Addresses, essays, lectures.
2. Discrimination in employment—United States—Addresses, essays, lec-
tures. I. Von Furstenberg, George M., 1941—   ed. II. Horowitz, Ann
R., ed. III. Harrison, Bennett, ed.
HD7293.P345   301.45'19'6073   73-19594
ISBN 0-669-92460-1

Published simultaneously in Canada.

Printed in the United States of America.

International Standard Book Number, set: 0-669-92460-1

International Standard Book Number, Vol. 2: 0-669-91918-7

Library of Congress Catalog Card Number: 73-19594

Contents

List of Figures

List of Tables

Preface

Pursuant to an OEO contract, a conference on racial discrimination in housing and employment was held at Indiana University on May 11, 1973. Leading researchers of all aspects of discrimination, among them John Kain, Bennett Harrison, Richard Muth, Peter Mieszkowski, Joseph Stiglitz, Barbara Bergmann, Marcus Alexis, and Finis Welch, assembled at Bloomington to take stock and to give new directions. Extensive correlation and confrontation of the papers presented at the conference led to substantial rethinking and revisions. As a result, these chapters, all previously unpublished, represent the best reasoned analyses and policy statements several of the leading economists are capable of rendering after they have interacted with each other.

Patterns of Racial Discrimination is published in two volumes, Vol. I: *Housing*, and Vol. II: *Employment and Income*. The studies in the first volume cover (1) the debate over the consequences on black incomes and employment of the decentralization of urban jobs and (2) the conflict between disequilibrium and equilibrium theories of the housing market in interpreting the empirical evidence on the housing prices and dwelling expenditures of blacks. The chapters in the second volume cover (1) the role of collective and individual preference theories of discrimination in explaining the actual and potential impacts of governments, employers, and employees on observed patterns of discrimination in the labor market and (2) the measurement of the most recent trends in racial income inequality by isolating the factors that have historically affected the economic status of blacks. Interdependencies among the various studies of discrimination are stressed throughout.

Each part of this volume is organized similarly. After the introductory summary, a "state-of-the-art" survey or review chapter follows. The middle chapters present original research, and statements on appropriate policies conclude each part. The written and oral comments which the conference participants have contributed to each other have generally been used to revise the original papers, so that only a few far-reaching comments are published separately.

The editors are grateful to the participants for cooperating splendidly in the revision process. Part 1 was edited by George von Furstenberg of Indiana University who was also the recipient of the OEO contract and conference organizer. Ann Horowitz of the University of Florida edited Part 2. Bennett Harrison of the Massachusetts Institute of Technology participated throughout. Substantive editorial help from Joseph Stiglitz is also gratefully acknowledged. Ruth Fishel typed several drafts of the manuscript at Indiana University and assisted in the style editing with exemplary competence and dedication. Florence Setzer monitored the project for OEO and provided continuing help and advice as an economist and administrator.

In preparation for this study, two bibliographies have been prepared by George M. von Furstenberg with the assistance of William S. Cartwright. They have been published by the Council of Planning Librarians, as *Discrimination in Employment: A Selected Bibliography*, No. 297, and *Discrimination in Housing: A Selected Bibliography*, No. 298, in July 1972 (Mary Vance, ed., Monticello, Ill., 61856). In addition, extended references to the current literature are given at the end of many of the fourteen chapters in this volume.

The resulting two volumes of readings provide a comprehensive review of the major issues of racial discrimination and several empirical and theoretical thrusts beyond past frontiers of knowledge and perception in this field. It is hoped that they will be received as a fitting testimonial to one of the significant concerns of OEO and as a resource strong enough to succor some of the economic trials of blacks where they occur in American society.

George M. von Furstenberg
Ann R. Horowitz
Bennett Harrison

Part 1:
Racial Discrimination in
Employment

Part 1A: Theories and
Policies for the Labor
Market

Part 1B: Extensions of the
Formal Theories

Introduction to Part 1A: Theories and Policies for the Labor Market

The chapters in this part provide a sampling of some of the most insightful new theories that may explain the historical pattern of wage and employment discrimination as well as the prospective impact of a number of policy measures. In Chapters 1 and 3, Joseph Stiglitz and Richard Freeman review the atomistic competitive models which relate income inequality to differences in endowments and to differences in tastes. Both authors find that the competitive models are incompatible with significant long-run differences in wages received by individuals of the *same* productivity. The discriminatory preferences of individuals may produce segregated work forces but they cannot sustain price differences in equilibrium, except under implausible conditions.

The burden of accounting for the lasting racial income differences in the real world thus shifts to the theories which can explain why productivity remains *unequal* between the races. Stiglitz shows that this may be due to a number of interlocking factors: (1) individuals' preferences (demand) for education may be a function of their parents' education and other factors perpetuating a particular milieu, (2) the resulting differences in education and background lead to differential expectations and differential uncertainty regarding the qualifications of particular groups of workers and the payoffs from training them, with the effect that (3) multiple equilibria exist in the labor market which may lock different groups into different positions in the income distribution.

Freeman, on the other hand, places most of the blame for maintaining differences in education and productivity on the policies of governments and provides empirical support for his position. Government, he argues, is free from the competitive pressures that undercut the ability of individuals to discriminate effectively in the unorganized private market. The policy remedy this implies is simple: Remove the inequality in educational expenditures and provide the human capital and legal prerequisites for equal employment opportunity, and the competitive market will tend to eliminate discrimination.

Stiglitz sees more ingrained obstacles in the way. Not only may governments and unions activate collective discriminatory preferences and impose the median discrimination preference on the individual agents, but past discrimination may have such lasting effects on the preferences and job choices of the discriminated that compensatory, though transitory, shocks of reverse discrimination may well be necessary to break the persistence of differential employability.

Stiglitz is also acutely aware that in certain states of the labor market—for instance, when productivity depends on the wage or the wage does not depend on the productivity of the marginal worker in a given skill class (as under minimum wage legislation)—there may be persistent excess supply of low-skilled grades of labor. With queuing, employers can then indulge their (or their other workers') discriminatory preferences at no cost to themselves simply by picking or rejecting workers from the pool as they see fit. Though there need be no discrimination in the wages paid to workers of given productivity, those who are hired miss the on-the-job training of the others and do not follow their chain to advancement. Hence, employment discrimination in hiring without wage discrimination among those hired can explain systematic income inequality between the races over time.

Barbara Bergmann reinforces this point in Chapter 2 by furnishing a model in which the unemployment and vacancy rates and the duration of unemployment for the different races can be simulated systematically from specified employer notions of differential employability and from the common disposition of workers and employers to become increasingly inclined to accept job offers the longer the duration of unemployment or vacancies.

From the theory of voting behavior, we have long learned that the order in which issues are put to a vote affects the ultimate outcome of the vote under certain voting rules. The chapters in this part show that a similar process may be operating in employment. The order of call is much more important than the hoary issue of equal pay for equal work, defined narrowly. As Stiglitz puts it, "We can think in terms of a hierarchy of jobs by 'productivity' requirements: individuals of the discriminated groups may be assigned systematically to lower jobs in this hierarchy than individuals of the same productivity belonging to the discriminating group. Thus the 'discriminatory preferences' result in differences in status and in advancement opportunities, which may be far more important to the individual—and to our sense of equal economic opportunity—than the simple differences in wages." Freeman provides evidence that when excess supply of labor develops in the cyclical context, earnings inequality between the races mounts, giving some credence to the last-hired first-fired hypothesis, particularly in the upper-level jobs.

The fourth and last chapter in this part, by Jerolyn Lyle, provides a valuable assessment of the guidelines and enforcement practices adopted by government agencies charged with implementing the objectives of civil rights legislation. It shows how agonizingly slow most of these agencies have been to formulate, to agree on, and eventually to enforce policies that take account of the total impact pattern on minorities of the activities of federal contractors and of institutions receiving federal grants or other types of government benefits. With few splendid exceptions, the isolated-incident approach—making a case here and there, often after lengthy delays and for the narrowest possible remedies—still appears to be the order of the day.

1

Theories of Discrimination and Economic Policy

Joseph E. Stiglitz *

It is now well established that different groups of workers—blacks and whites, men and women, those with college education and those with less than college education—receive different incomes. It is probably also true that in other categorizations of the population (e.g., by religion or ethnic origin), differences in incomes would be observed. The question is, How can we explain these differences?

To answer this question, we must have a theory of the determination of individuals' incomes. The theory which economists have generally accepted—and which will underly the discussion of this chapter—is the marginal productivity theory of distribution: factors get paid according to their marginal products. Differences in income can then be attributed to two sources: (1) Differences in endowments. Some individuals have more innate ability, or skills which are valued by the market, than do others. Some individuals inherit more capital than do others. Finally, some individuals receive—either as a gift of their parents or of the government—more human capital, more education, than do others. (2) Differences in tastes. Some individuals have a stronger relative preference for leisure over consumption goods than do others. Some individuals value certain non-pecuniary advantages associated with certain jobs more than do others. Some individuals have a greater aversion to risk than do others. And some individuals have a higher rate of time preference than do others (and hence save less for later years of their life than do others).

A number of the characteristics which we have mentioned as being potentially important in explaining differences in incomes are difficult to quantify, for example, the nonpecuniary characteristics associated with any job. Accordingly, it is perhaps not too surprising that attempts to use the "productivity model" to explain differences in income have met with only limited success.

The question in which we are interested here, however, is differences in incomes among groups of individuals. One's first inclination is to see how much of the difference in income can be attributed to differences in productivity. Unfortunately, we have few direct measures of productivity (apart from Rapping's study in the baseball industry) and accordingly we must use indirect methods. Specifically, we will attempt to see how much of the differences in income can be explained by differences in education and ability, as measured by

*Professor of economics, Yale University.

test scores. Of course such an approach fails to take into account some of the important explanations of differences in income discussed above, and for the most part, the data used provides only a crude measure of the variables in which we are really interested. The underlying hypothesis, then, is that although such omissions limit the ability of the model to explain individual differences, there is no reason to believe that the groups under examination differ systematically with respect to those characteristics which affect productivity but which were not included in the analysis.

This hypothesis might, on the face of it, seem rather plausible; yet one might still be disturbed by the size of the unexplained income differences. These unexplained differences are so large that many individuals have concluded that individuals of equal productivity but belonging to different groups receive systematically different wages.

We have thus broken the problem of differences in income among groups into two parts: differences in productivity and differences in wage payments at the same productivity. We then face two further questions: (1) How is it possible in a competitive economy for individuals of the same productivity to receive different wages? Why will all competitive firms not hire only the worker with the lower wage, thereby bidding up his wage until wages are equalized? (2) If there are differences in productivity, how can we explain these differences?

The resolution of these issues is of some importance, for the policies which are appropriate to reduce such income differences depend critically on the answers.

The Conditions That Make Wage Discrimination Possible

We turn first to the question of the circumstances under which individuals of the same productivity might receive different wages.

The most extensively discussed theory is that originally due to Becker. Individuals have a preference for working with or employing members of a particular group; these preferences are sufficiently strong that individuals are willing to sacrifice income in order to work with individuals of their own group. I shall argue that this does not provide a very plausible explanation of differences in income. Assume we have two classes of labor, skilled and unskilled. We first need to distinguish between within-factor (intrafactor) discrimination, for example, preferences of unskilled workers to work with members of their own group, and across-factor (interfactor) discrimination, for example, preferences of skilled workers for working with unskilled workers of their own group.[1]

Assume first that employers or skilled workers are indifferent with respect to the group identity of their employees (of the unskilled workers with whom they work). It is clear that if unskilled workers prefer working with members of their own group, then they will insist on receiving higher wages if they are put in a mixed work force than if they are put in a work force consisting only of members of their own group; equivalently, they would be willing to work for lower wages for an employer who had only members of their own group in the labor force.

This is clearly an argument for segregation of labor forces, but it provides no explanation of wage differences.

Consider now the case of between-factor discrimination. Consider the most extreme case, where the skilled individuals have an infinite aversion to working with unskilled members of the other group. Then establishments will consist only of members of a single group. But this does not necessarily imply that there will be differences in factor prices, even if the ratio of skilled to unskilled workers differs in the two groups, because the group with a relatively high proportion of skilled workers will specialize in skilled-worker-intensive industries, and the group with a relatively high proportion of unskilled workers will specialize in unskilled-worker-intensive industries. As is well known from international trade theory, trade in commodities may be a perfect substitute for movements of factors. The Becker-Arrow analysis essentially assumes a single sector (or equivalently, that all sectors have the same factor intensities). It is obvious that with infinite aversion, differences in factor supplies must then result in differences in factor incomes.

We may, of course, not have complete factor-price equalization,[2] for example, if the differences in factor supplies (relative proportions of skilled and unskilled workers) in the two groups are sufficiently large. This will provide an incentive for those individuals who are less than infinitely averse to working with members of the other group to do so. There will be some "integration" of establishments, and factor-price differences will be reduced. If there are enough individuals who are indifferent with respect to the group with whom they work, there will again be complete factor-price equalization. Only a limited amount of factor movements is required to equalize factor prices.[3]

If we do not have complete factor-price equalization, the theory predicts that the scarce factor ought to receive a relatively high income; indeed, if in one group there is a relative scarcity of skilled workers, not only should the skilled/unskilled factor price ratio be higher, but the absolute income of skilled workers should be higher. This prediction of the theory suggests that it is probably not the appropriate explanation of differences in income in the United States between blacks and whites. It may also be the wrong model since it is difficult even to observe the salaries of white or black skilled working solely with black unskilled.

To guarantee factor-price equalization, we need to assume constant returns to scale production functions, no factor-intensity reversals, and at least two commodities which are freely traded. The latter assumption is probably not unreasonable, for although there may not be "free trade" in the service sector, the composition of the work force for most manufactured commodities is unknown and of no concern to the purchaser of the commodity. Our point is that even with *infinite* aversion to working with members of other groups, there may be complete factor-price equalization.

The model admits of considerable generalization. Assume we now have three factors, capital, skilled labor, and unskilled labor. If capital is freely mobile between groups the analysis follows as above. (Note it is only the white capital that need move.) Even if capital is not freely mobile, as long as some of it is (some of it is "unprejudiced") it will move, and again if factor endowments are close enough, there will be complete factor-price equalization. If they differ too much, we can still make predictions—somewhat weaker than before—about relative factor prices in relationship to factor scarcities.

Assume now that only the workers have an aversion to working with members of the other group, but capital and skilled laborers do not. We have then a conventional "regional" trade model with mobile factors. As long as all but one of the factors are mobile, there will be complete factor-price equalization even in the absence of any trade. We would find all firms having completely segregated work forces, but there would be no wage discrimination. As we said earlier, wage discrimination requires interfactor prejudices, not intrafactor prejudices. The latter can only explain segregation.[4]

This analysis is sometimes extended to a dynamic context, in two different directions.

First, it has been argued by Arrow that if there are costs of adjustment, and initially all firms are all white, then even asymptotically wage discrimination may persist.[5] For instance, if white workers dislike working with black workers and require higher wages to compensate them for doing so, and there are specific training costs associated with any job, then even if a firm could hire a black worker at lower wages, it will not do so, unless the wage is sufficiently low that it pays the firm either to pay the white workers the higher wage they demand for working with black workers or to let the white workers quit and hire an all-black labor force, paying for the additional training costs.

This analysis assumes that there are fairly high specific training and hiring costs. Moreover, it implies that, contrary to economic reality, no new plants, shops, departments, and so forth, are established. Otherwise, the new production units (establishments) will hire only the workers in the lower-wage group, and this will continue until equality is attained presumably in a fairly short time. Secondly, it is argued that since the nondiscriminatory firms are making higher profits, they will drive the discriminatory firms out of business, so in the long-run steady state, only nondiscriminatory firms will survive. Although there is some presumption for this, this is not necessarily the case. It must be remembered that discriminatory firms are willing to accept a lower return to satisfy their prejudices. If both kinds of firms save the same percentage out of profits, and if (as in the Rosa Luxemburg model) all savings are internal to the firm, then the nondiscriminatory firms will expand more rapidly, so that asymptotically they dominate the market, but this will not be true even asymptotically, if the discriminatory firms compensate for their lower returns by increasing their savings rate.[6]

The policy implications of the competitive model are interesting, and some of them contrast markedly with those of the models to be presented later. First, the elimination of wage discrimination (if it exists), will result in more hiring discrimination, and in unemployment of the group of workers that was formerly discriminated against,[7] since it is only the fact that these workers are less expensive which induces the prejudiced firms to hire them. Second, if guidelines or quotas are imposed to ensure that job discrimination has not occurred, then national output may increase, but there are complex distributional effects.

In the two-factor model, if skilled labor is the scarce factor among the discriminated group, they will be worse off, although the unskilled workers will be better off; conversely, the income of skilled workers of the "discriminating" group, will rise (although if they are the ones with "discrimination preferences," their welfare may decrease), and that of the unskilled will fall. The dollar gains of the "discriminating" skilled and "discriminated" unskilled workers will not in general be enough to compensate the welfare losses of the other workers.[8]

Noncompetitive Forces

So far, we have argued against the plausibility of the competitive models in explaining significant differences in wages received by individuals of the same productivity. Alternatively, it is argued that there are noncompetitive forces which result in differential pay.

Most widely discussed are the exclusionary practices of certain unions. Whether these practices themselves result in wage differentials is a moot question. It depends on two factors : (1) Are unions able to obtain higher wages for their own members? The answer is probably yes, although the magnitude of the gains is open to some question. The standard estimates are too small to explain much of the wage differential between blacks and whites.(2) Even if unions do not raise their own workers' wages by much, exclusionary practices could lower the wages of the excluded group. This depends on the importance of "differential rents" to specific skills—that is, if a large fraction of the income of plumbers or carpenters is a "rent" to an innate skill and or a skill which these individuals have an absolute advantage in acquiring, then exclusion will lower the rents received by individuals of the excluded group with these skills. On the other hand, if the income of carpenters or plumbers can be thought of as simply a return to "raw labor" and to "human capital" (training for the specific craft), then the differential rent to a carpenter's or plumber's skill is zero. Exclusion from carpentry simply diverts the "specific training" into other uses.

Government actions provide an alternative mechanism by which the competitive forces which would lead to equal pay for equal productivity are limited. This is probably usually an unintentional consequence of government actions aimed at other objectives. Most notable in this respect is minimum-wage legislation. If the minimum wage is effective, it means that the number of applicants for unskilled jobs exceeds the supply. The employer must select among these applicants. If he prefers hiring workers of a given group, he can do this at no economic cost to himself. If a worker is hired, he, of course, receives the same wage, but because fewer members of one group are hired than of another, the average wage of one group is lower than that of the other. Moreover, if the individual acquires skills while he is on the job which enable him to eventually obtain a higher-paying job, the exclusion from the lowest-paying jobs reduces the opportunity for obtaining higher-paying jobs in the future.

Supporters of minimum-wage legislation might argue, on the contrary, that minimum-wage legislation reduces wage discrimination. For it is exactly the unskilled workers of groups discriminated against which are in the weakest bargaining position vis-à-vis their employers, and who, in the absence of minimum-wage legislation, would receive the lowest wages. The two views are based on different assumptions concerning the degree of competitiveness in the labor market for unskilled workers.

There are certain situations where the latter view is perhaps correct: individuals located in one company town who, for one reason or another, face large costs in moving to another town. Overall, however, the former view seems far more descriptive of labor markets in the United States. This provides just one more reason why minimum-wage legislation is the inappropriate mechanism for attacking the problems associated with low incomes; general instruments such as wage subsidies or negative income taxes seem far more desirable.

Other government actions may be deliberately aimed at either excluding entry into a given occupation by members of a particular group, or at least securing advantages for individuals who are already in a given occupation—for example, licensing requirements to practice in certain professions which may not be directly related to ability to perform that occupation. Alternatively, the government could impose certain training or education requirements, and then, by controlling the educational system, limit the ability of individuals of a particular group to acquire the requisite credentials. To the extent that these are still important, the policy implications are clear; the government should reexamine such requirements, making sure that they are justified in terms of the performance of the particular function for which they are designed.

Disequilibrium

Some economists have objected to the equilibrium framework implicit in the above analysis. The presence of queues means that firms can select among applicants and that wages do not—for one reason or another—adjust very quickly. In this world, it is hypothesized, the market forces leading to equalization of factor prices would not be present; that is, if there are two applicants for the same job, and they both receive the same wage, then there is no market pressure for the firm not to exercise its prejudices. If, however, there is any flexibility in factor prices, then the group discriminated against would have its wage lowered, and all the market pressures of the kind described earlier would be brought to bear.

As in the earlier model, policies designed to ensure no wage discrimination (i.e., requiring firms to pay individuals of the same ability doing the same job the same wage) may result in employment discrimination, because they reduce the competitive forces, which might have led to its disappearance. For instance, we can imagine white employers having a very strong preference for higher profits over lower profits and a very weak preference for white employees over blacks. Then, a slight adjustment of the relative wages would eliminate all occupational discrimination. The blacks as a group are better off in the situation where wage discrimination is allowed. Admittedly, we have no evidence concerning the speed with which the economy converges to equilibrium. There are lags in the adjustment of firms and imperfect mobility of factors: it is possible that there be no discrimination in competitive equilibrium and yet discrimination persists for a long time.[9] Most observers, however, seem to feel that without government intervention, discrimination would not be simply a transitory phenomenon. In particular, disequilibrium (and political intervention) in the housing and transportation markets may be important in restricting access to some jobs located out of the urban center.

The basic argument of this section was that competitive forces strongly limit the extent to which individuals of the same productivity may receive different wages. The fact that "discriminatory preferences" cannot explain significant wage differences does not mean that the consequences of discriminatory preferences are any the less invidious. This is particularly important because the form in which the wage differentials are likely to show up is not in different wages for performing the same job, but rather in the assignment of individuals to different jobs. We can think in terms of a hierarchy of jobs by "productivity" requirements: individuals of the discriminated groups may be assigned systematically to lower jobs in this hierarchy than individuals of the same productivity belonging to the discriminating group.

Thus the discriminatory preferences result in differences in status and in advancement opportunities, which may be far more important to the individual—and to our sense of equal economic opportunity—than the simple differences in wages.

Lasting Inequalities in Productivity

We now turn to the question of how we can explain differences in productivities among groups. There may be many explanations of such differences, but from an analytic point of view, the interesting case is that where the groups are, in some sense, "innately" the same. Is it possible that, in long-run equilibrium,[10] they have different productivities nonetheless? We shall argue that the answer is affirmative.

In the discussion below, we shall discuss a number of factors leading to differences in productivities. Most of these will be related to considerations usually omitted from conventional economic analyses; for example, endogenous preferences, imperfect information, and the dependence of productivity on wages. Since several of the arguments have a common mathematical structure, it is worthwhile to call attention to it here. Consider an economy with a single group of individuals. Under certain circumstances, it is clearly possible that there may be several long-run equilibria for this economy (with different levels of per capita income) which we denote by Equilibrium 1, Equilibrium 2, . . . Assume that the given economy is in equilibrium in Equilibrium 1, and there is another economy in equilibrium in Equilibrium 2. Under certain circumstances it is possible that when they merge, the members of the first group remain distinct from members of the second group.

Education

That there are differences in educational attainment among different groups in the population seems well established. These differences could be attributable to differences in demand or to differences in supply. Since education is primarily supplied by the government, a deliberate government policy in some states to provide differential education to blacks and whites would clearly result in differences in educational attainment and this may be an important determinant of income differences. Numerous econometric studies have attempted to determine exactly how important these educational differences are in explaining income inequalities. Why don't educational differences appear to be more important than they are, and why, at least until recent years, was the white/black wage ratio higher for the more educated than for the less educated?

The most obvious answer, of course, is that the education variables commonly used do not appropriately measure the "quality" of education. The "real output" is likely to be a function not only of the resources supplied by the school but also of the "effort" and other resources—difficult to observe directly—supplied by the individual and his family.[11] It is also a function of the inputs supplied to other children attending the same school (the externalities effect) and the homogeneity of the students (a kind of "returns to scale" effect).[12] If E is the expenditure on formal education, I the level of "informal" education, $\overline{I}$ the mean level of informal education in the school,[13] and σ_I a measure of heterogeneity, then we postulate[14] (in simplified form)

$$Q_i = F(E, I_i, \bar{I}, \sigma_I).\tag{1.1}$$

The question of whether efficiency implies that we should allocate more or less resources to students with lower I_i hinges on whether E and I are substitutes or complements, that is, whether an increase in informal education increases or decreases the marginal returns to formal education. The question of whether students should (on "efficiency" grounds) be grouped homogeneously or heterogeneously depends on whether an individual's informal training is a complement or substitute for that of his peers (i.e., whether a high level of informal training in music is likely to increase or decrease the return to having a peer group with a high level of musical appreciation) and if a substitute, whether this spillover effect is stronger than the reduction in the "scale" effect produced by heterogeneity. The allocation of resources to education and of students to schools has important and obvious implications for the distribution of income as well. It should also be noted that the efficiency and equity effects differ depending on whether private education is an alternative to public education. A policy of uniform allocation of students (regardless of the value of I_i) might increase national output and redistribute income from whites to blacks if there were no private schools; with private schools, it may lower national output and increase the disparity of income between the groups (since the $\bar{I}$ of the students remaining in public schools could well be lower without much compensating reduction in σ_I).

There is, however, another aspect to education: not all education is skill acquisition; some of it is "screening," that is, identifying individuals' abilities. One of the aspects in which poorer quality education is in fact poorer is that it screens less well. Thus very able students are classified with students who are less able, and accordingly receive lower wages. The private returns to education of students with given abilities will be lower in a system with less screening at any given level of inputs on the part of the students. Accordingly, they will invest less of their own inputs in their education. (Even if no resources of their own were required, and even if the educational system had no effect on productivities, the "finer" screening system will tend to have wages rise more upon each stage of screening,[15] so those who manage to pass through the "screen" obtain a larger return to their "luck"; this private return is not directly related to any social return to education.[16])

Endogenous Preferences

There is no doubt that many of our attitudes (preferences) are culturally determined: the food we eat, the clothes we wear, the design of the house we live in, all differ from country to country, and to a lesser extent, from group to group within a country. From our point of view, what is important are differences in attitudes which result in differences in incomes: differences in attitudes toward education, in the need for achievement, in attitudes toward job mobility, in intertemporal time preferences, in attitudes toward risks. These attitudes are likely to depend critically on the attitudes (income, socioeconomic status) of one's parents. Consider the following simple example. The percentage of one's income spent on education (a_t) depends on the current rate of return (ρ_t) and on the percentage of one's parents' income spent on education (a_{t-1}):

$$a_t = \phi (a_{t-1}, \rho_t). \tag{1.2}$$

(The excess of expenditure on education over that required to obtain the market rate of return may be thought of as "consumption.") Long-run equilibrium requires that

$$a_t = a_{t-1} . \tag{1.3}$$

Multiple equilibria are clearly possible, as illustrated in Figure 1-1. Consider a group which is discriminated against in such a way as to increase the return to education (by lowering the wages in activities not requiring high levels of education more than in activities requiring high levels). This shifts the ϕ curve upwards. Assume initially everyone is in the middle stable equilibrium. Then, the introduction of discrimination will move the group toward the upper equilibrium point E'''. If the discrimination is later removed, the historical effect remains: the group continues to obtain a high level of education E' and the associated high level of income. Conversely, if a group is discriminated against in such a way as to lower the return to education, and then subsequently the discrimination is removed, the group may now be in the lower equilibrium (E'').

Note that policies aimed at eliminating wage discrimination or job discrimination will not affect this outcome; reverse discrimination, raising temporarily the return to education leading to an increased consumption of it, may.

Imperfect Information of Employer
Concerning Employees

Individuals have different skills, work habits, and so forth, and it is important to firms to place individuals in the appropriate jobs. Unfortunately, there do not exist any perfect predictors of job performance, and so firms must use whatever evidence they can bring to bear. If "race" or "sex" is correlated with the productive characteristics with which the firm is concerned, then efficient job allocation—and competitive market forces—require the use of this information in the allocation of jobs. Under certain circumstances, these differences in economic treatment are themselves the cause of the differences in productive

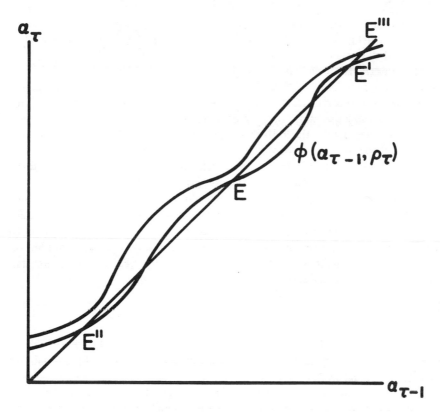

Figure 1-1. Endogenous Preferences and the Demand for Education

characteristics, that is, the difference in economic treatment on the basis of productivity characteristics is self-confirming. More precisely, we make the following assumptions: (1) There is, for any given vector of characteristics of the individual, a "best job" for the individual; at other jobs, he has a lower productivity. (2) Some elements of the vector are (a) not perfectly observable before the job placement and (b) can be "purchased" at a cost (e.g., foregone leisure). (3) Individuals are not perfectly certain of their vector and are risk averse. (4) There are specific training costs associated with each job and/or observation of productivity on the job is costly and imperfect. Then, if firms believe individuals of two groups have different distributions of the imperfectly observable characteristics, then they will in general use the group membership in job placements and hence in the determination of wages; and given that firms use group membership in job placement, the groups will have different incentives for acquiring the given characteristics and so will in fact differ in the distribution of these characteristics. There may exist a statistical discriminating equilibrium, where the distributions of partial observable characteristics assumed by the firms correspond to the actual distributions.

The importance of all but the third assumption should be obvious. The third assumption is required in order to avoid the possibility of the individual coming to the firm and offering to absorb the risk associated with hiring him (i.e., with the specific training costs). There are other reasons, particularly those associated with moral hazard, why the individual might not be willing to offer to insure the firm against the risk that he or she does not have the requisite skills.

We now consider an example,[17] in which, for analytic simplicity, individuals are assumed to be risk neutral, perfectly informed about their abilities, but unable to insure firms against the loss involved in training them if they do not have the requisite skills. The argument can be extended to the more general case. Assume we have two classes of jobs: the better job requires the individual to have acquired a value of productivity, P, at least equal to $\hat{P}$, and in addition demands an investment of T by the firm.[18] We assume the firm is risk neutral, and requires an expected return r on its investment, so that

$$r = \pi \left(M_2 - w_2 \right) / T \tag{1.4}$$

where M_2 is the marginal return of an extra worker on the better job (which we shall assume to be constant), w_2 is the wage on the job, and π is the probability that the individual's value of $P \geqslant \hat{P}$.[19]

Assume now that the individual is risk neutral. The cost of acquiring the given level of productivity $\hat{P}$ is a function of the individual's ability, $C(A)$, so if the return on the investment in acquiring P

$$(w_2 - w_1) / C(A) \tag{1.5}$$

(where w_1 is the wage in the lower job) is greater than say ϕ, then the individual undertakes the investment. For simplicity, we let $C(A) = 1/cA$, that is, costs are inversely related to A. Define $1/\hat{A} = A$. Let $F(\hat{A})$ be the distribution of $\hat{A}$, and $f(\hat{A})$ the density function. Then π, the proportion of individuals undertaking the investment, is defined as

$$\hat{\pi} = F\left[\frac{c}{\phi} \left(w_2 - w_1 \right) \right], \text{ and} \tag{1.6}$$

$$\frac{d\hat{\pi}}{dw_2} = \frac{fc}{\phi}$$

$$\frac{d^2\hat{\pi}}{dw_2^2} = f'\left(\frac{c}{\phi} \right)^2 .$$

An equilibrium is where $\hat{\pi} = \pi$, and as Figure 1-2 makes clear, there may be multiple equilibria, so that one group could be in equilibrium at E and another at E''.[20] But from (1.4), if E is different, the wages received will be different.[21]

These models have several interesting implications:

1. If firms are required to pay individuals the same wage, regardless of the group to which they belong, there will be hiring discrimination (just as in most of the other models examined).

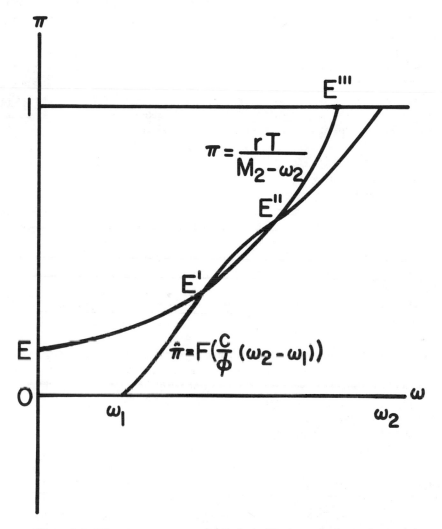

Figure 1-2. The Proportion of Skilled Workers (π) under Skill Uncertainty

2. If both hiring and wage discrimination are prohibited then, in the short run (in the first model at least), national output will be lowered, since the allocation of labor will not be performed as efficiently as before. Indeed, as a result, it is even possible that the group that was relatively worse off in the discriminatory equilibrium would be made absolutely worse off by the switch to the nondiscriminatory equilibrium.

3. If firms are not allowed to differentiate between individuals according to the group to which they belong, firms may rely more heavily on other indices for the prediction of performance, for example, on test scores. This may result in little change in the job opportunities facing workers of different groups, compared to the original situation.

4. In the new, long-run equilibrium without discrimination, national output may be lower or higher, depending on the relative proportions of the two groups in the population. For instance, in Figure 1-2, if the aggregate proportion of those with $P \geqslant \hat{P}$ is greater (less) than A' (the value of A corresponding to E'), then the economy converges to E'' (E).[22] Moreover, in the new, long-run equilibrium, quantitative restrictions will be unnecessary.[23]

*Productivity Depending on
Factor Payments*

Conventional economic theory takes the productivity of the individual as given. Yet managers of firms have often recognized that individuals may work harder and the labor force may have a lower turnover if the firm pays higher wages. Net productivity (productivity after paying for turnover costs) may be an increasing function of the wage.

Thus the argument that individuals belonging to certain groups receive low wages because they have a low productivity is turned on its head: the reason that they have low productivity is that they have low wages.

The discussion of the preceding section provided an argument of why a wage schedule with a low return to increases in productivity will result in low productivity. But here we are concerned not with the wage schedule but with the level of wages. The argument must be put carefully, since in at least one of its common versions it is incorrect.

We shall first present an argument that, if the relationship between productivity and wages takes on a particular shape, then even without minimum-wage legislation there may be unemployment among the very unskilled even in equilibrium, and this unemployment allows firms to discriminate (without cost) among different workers.

Assume that workers' productivity is an increasing initially convex and then concave function of his wage.[24] This increased productivity may, as perhaps in some LDCs, be due to nutrition, but in the more developed countries, it is likely to be associated with psychological factors of the kind that Henry Ford recognized: Pay a worker more and he feels he ought to work harder. Then if a worker who receives a wage of w has an efficiency index of $\lambda(w)$, and the efficiency wage curve appears as in Figure 1-3, the firm minimizes labor costs

$$\min w/\lambda(w) \qquad\qquad (1.7)$$

by setting $\lambda' = \lambda/w$. Firms then hire laborers up to the point where the marginal productivity of labor equals the wage.

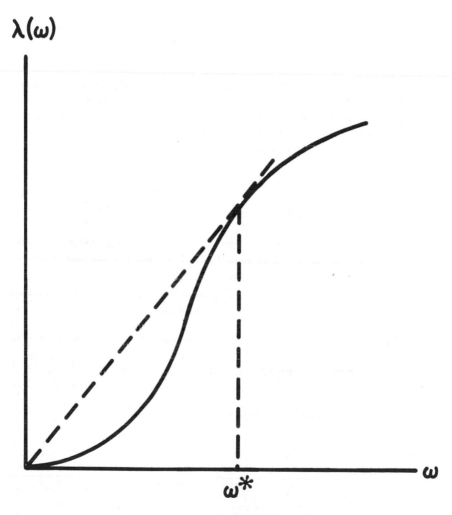

Figure 1-3. The Efficiency Wage Curve as a Function of the Wage Level

The equilibrium, that is, the cost minimizing wage, may be set at a level above that which assures full employment; although all those working have a positive marginal product, there is no competitive pressure to lower the wage. In this world, firms can exercise their prejudices in selecting among the applicants with impunity. The model may be more appropriate to discrimination in earlier stages of development, but it may have some applicability to individuals who are very unskilled. Their "norms" concerning a reasonable wage are defined largely by the norms for the population as a whole and may not be very dependent on the distribution of wages for other individuals performing work requiring skills comparable to their own.

Behavior of Job Seekers

So far, we have considered differences between groups related to their productivity on the job. But differences in behavior with respect to seeking jobs may also be important in explaining differences in income. We focus here on two aspects of job-seeking: differential information with respect to the availability of different jobs and the role of self-selection mechanisms in choosing among alternative jobs.

Differential Information of Job Seekers

Although economists have not been particularly successful in explaining differences in wages between different groups within the population, they have not been much more successful in explaining differences in wages received within any group. Typically, regressions using education, IQ, and related variables explain a relatively small part of the dispersion in wages. Recent attempts to explain dispersion in prices of factors (or goods) have focused on the absence of perfect information. In particular, it has been shown that in a market like that of labor, where there are continually new individuals entering with imperfect information about the wages being offered by different firms, there exist equilibrium wage distributions such that individuals who have identical productivities receive different wages simply depending on their luck in sampling firms.[25] (It is an equilibrium in the sense that given the quit rate functions—which in turn depend on the wage distribution—the firms are all maximizing their profits at a zero level and individuals are pursuing optimal search strategies given their information.) It has also been established that there are multiple equilibria, that is, numerous alternative wage distributions are consistent with equilibrium.

Thus, if we had completely segregated job markets, there is no reason to expect that the equilibrium arrived at in each of these markets will be the same.

Some of these equilibria involve lower average wages but higher average turnover costs than other equilibria, so that total costs of production remain the same.[26] The only reason that this is an equilibrium, that is, the only reason that the arguments of the first section are not applicable, is that these markets are assumed to be completely segregated.

But differential information on the part of entrants to the labor force has very much the same effect. This appears in two different ways. Assume that children only sample among the firms that employ their parents and the friends of their parents, and that there is some relationship between the distribution of jobs of the parent group and the distribution of initial jobs of the children. Assume we have two kinds of jobs, low-training, low-wage jobs, and high-training, high-wage jobs. Then if all the members of one group hold only high-training cost, high-wage jobs, the children all go to those firms, and the high wages are perpetuated. But if some of the other group go initially to the low-wage job, their children will as well, and this equilibrium may be perpetuated.

Secondly, because of limited information, each firm has a limited amount of monopsony power, that is, it obtains workers even though there are other firms which pay higher wages. Assume that information about high-paying firms spreads imperfectly, so that the number of applicants is a function of the wage. Then the firm will choose w to maximize

$$F(K,L(w)) - [w + q(w)TL(w)], \qquad (1.8)$$

assuming total labor costs are direct wage costs plus training costs, T, and the quit rate, q, is a function of the wage rate. Hence,[27]

$$F_L - (w + qT) = \frac{Lw\,q'\,T}{L'\ w}. \qquad (1.9)$$

If there are two different groups with different supply elasticities (different values of $L'w/L$), reflecting different degrees of "informational efficiency," they will receive different wages (with the presumption that the group with the lower informational efficiency will have a smaller elasticity of supply and therefore a lower wage).[28]

Notice that the greater the training costs, the more important the differential supply elasticities, and hence the greater the wage differentials. Jobs which require more training costs will in general pay a higher wage, since it is more important to such firms to discourage turnover; but the wages of the low-information group will tend to increase less with an increase in training costs, and thus there is less incentive for the low-information group to obtain more information.

The elimination of wage discrimination will tend to increase the wage of the lower information group, and reduce the wage of the other group; by increasing the return to obtaining information, it will increase the amount of resources invested in information gathering. But since much of the information involved is not "marketed" information, there is no reason to believe that information (and hence average wages) will be equalized. Affirmative action programs put the burden of providing information on the employer; quotas imply that the information of the next generation of job seekers will be equalized (if the model is correct, that is, there are no other differences between the groups). Such programs make the high-information group worse off, at least in the short run, because their very high supply elasticity must now be averaged with the low supply elasticity of the other group and because they must bear some part of the cost of providing information to the low-information group. In the long run when information is equalized, the high-information group need be no worse off, and the low-information group will be better off.

Self-Selection

In the previous discussion, the firm used information about the quit rates or other economic characteristics of different groups of individuals to set wage rates. Individuals may well have more knowledge about the likelihood of their quitting than firms have, and firms accordingly attempt to design wage structures which make the individual reveal that information.[29] This can be done in a number of different ways; for instance, the firm may confront individuals with two different wage schedules, one which starts high but does not increase with seniority, the other which starts lower, but increases more. Individuals with a higher quit rate will choose the former schedule, individuals with a lower quit rate the latter; the firm will accordingly assign the former individuals to jobs where quitting is not so important (i.e., training costs are low). In practice, the self-selection comes not in the form indicated, but in the kind of job for which individuals apply, for which the different wage structures obtain.

The difficulty arises in being able to ascertain whether the individual does not apply for the "better job" because (a) he has a higher propensity to quit or has less of the characteristic "P" required for advancement; (b) he has misperceptions about his propensities to quit or about the amount of "P" he has;[30] (c) he is being discriminated against, so that his chances for advancement are less. The effects, however, are the same: the firm claims that it has fewer individuals of the "discriminated group" in the "better jobs" not because the firm has excluded them, but because they have "screened themselves." This seems to put the "burden" for the elimination of differential incomes on the members of that group. It may be argued, however, that even if the reason for the self-screening is (a) or (b), affirmative action (quantitative guidelines) may be an effective policy instrument. It may be an effective way of changing individuals' perceptions of possibilities for advancement, propensities to quit, and so forth, and, if the reason for the members of one group having a different amount of "*P*" is related to one of the explanations provided in previous parts of this section, affirmative action may be an effective method of equalizing "*P*."

Concluding Remarks

In this chapter, we have attempted to review the various arguments explaining differences in income between groups. We have divided them into two categories: differences in wages of individuals of the same productivity and differences in productivity between groups. We have suggested that at least the standard arguments advanced for explaining differences in the wages of individuals belonging to the same group are not convincing. We have attempted to put forth some arguments why group differences in productivity might be sustained in long-run equilibrium. Whether these are themselves very convincing is a moot question. What is clear, however, is that the effect of the various policies the government may undertake to reduce these income differences depends critically on the explanation of their origin.

Notes

1. It will sometimes be convenient to think of the skilled workers as "employers" and the unskilled workers as "employees."

2. Of course, if both groups of unskilled workers prefer to work with say, skilled workers of one of the groups, factor prices will not be equalized by the opening of trade.

3. In the case where all individuals are of identical productivities, a group which constitutes x percent of the population can be completely excluded from $1 - x$ percent of the jobs without there being any wage discrimination. The group will simply find itself concentrated in the jobs from which it is not excluded, and since they have the same productivity, in equilibrium they will still receive the same wage.

4. Just as the labor forces of two countries are "segregated" yet, under the conditions under which the factor-price equalization theorem is valid, command the same factor prices. Many individuals will object to this analysis which sounds like a market justification of the old "separate but equal" doctrine, pointing out that though jobs may be separate, they do not appear to be equal. This reflects the fact that, as we have argued throughout this section, these models do not adequately explain "discrimination."

5. K.J. Arrow, "Models of Job Discrimination" and "Some Mathematical Models of Race in the Labor Markets" in A.H. Pascal, ed., *Racial Discrimination in Economic Life* (Lexington, Mass.: Lexington Books, D.C. Heath, 1972).

6. More generally, if w_i, r_i, s_i, and K_i are the ith group's wages, return to capital, savings rate, and ownership of capital, then in long-run balanced growth if all groups reproduce at the same rate,

$$ s_i \left[\frac{w_i}{K_i} + r_i \right] = \left[\frac{w_j}{K_j} + r_j \right] s_j. $$

So even if $r_i < r_j$, $w_i < w_j$ and $s_i = s_j$, $K_i/K_j > 0$. If none of the wages are saved, then the rate of growth of the ith group's capital is $s_i r_i$, so if $s_i = s_j$, but $r_i < r_j$, K_i will continue to decline relative to K_j.

7. Or assigning workers to poorer jobs than their abilities warrant; this of course, is just "disguised" wage discrimination.

8. We ignore the effects of changes in relative prices that might occur in a closed economy. In a two-sector model with given international prices, it can be shown that the elimination of discrimination increases the aggregate income of both groups, but in other cases, as Krueger has pointed out, one group may gain at the expense of the other.

9. Previous disequilibria may have an important impact on present wage differentials; if firms discriminated in the past, and firms today use past work experience to "screen" applicants, then there is "indirect" discrimination. If past work experience actually has increased productivity, then wage differentials will simply reflect these productivity differences. The differential is "passed on" to the next generation: (a) because of the apparent differential in returns to education, there will be less investment in it and (b) because of the differential information about job opportunities (as developed in later sections), children will have less "access" to the better jobs.

10. The stress on long-run equilibrium is because there may be long lags of adjustment, during which income differences persist, even though in the long run, the groups have identical incomes. Although the difference is clearly important from an analytical point of view, it is not clear how important the difference is from a policy point of view.

11. The ability (as opposed to the motivation) to supply these other factors is different in different groups, for instance, because of differences in wealth.

12. That is, an education which is appropriate for one set of students, with one set of "non-formal" inputs may not be appropriate for another set. If a teacher prepares the same lesson plan for both groups, they would each be worse off than if he prepared a lesson plan directed at each group separately; if he prepares two lesson plans, one for each group, the quality of each will necessarily be lower than if he allocated the same time to developing a single lesson plan.

13. We are not addressing ourselves to the issue of whether the externality is primarily internal to the classroom or internal to the school. The scale effect is

internal to the classroom. Thus, if the externality effect is internal to the school, efficiency would require heterogeneous schools with homogeneous classrooms. Although residentially based schools is one method of obtaining relative homogeneity, formal screening (testing) devices are an alternative way.

14. Without specifying clearly what we mean by "output" (value added) or how we measure it.

15. The arguments of this section are developed at length in J.E. Stiglitz, "Education as a Screening Device and the Distribution of Income," Yale University, 1973, mimeo. See also Chapter 7 by Chiswick in this volume.

16. This may explain at the same time why the ratio of wages for the highly educated to the less educated may well differ between the two groups.

17. This is an extension of an argument contained in Arrow, "Models of Job Discrimination," and related to G.A. Akerlof, "The Market for 'Lemmons': Qualitative Uncertainty and the Market Mechanism," *Quarterly Journal of Economics* (August 1970), pp. 488-500; M. Spence, "Job Market Signaling," ibid. (August 1973), pp. 355-74; and E.S. Phelps, "The Statistical Theory of Racism and Sexism," *American Economic Review* (September 1972), pp. 659-61.

18. There is a "fixed coefficients technology" requiring 1 laborer, firm-specific training, T, and the individual's level of P.

19. We assume that the firm can distinguish who has $\hat{P}$ after training is completed.

20. Conventional dynamic assumptions would imply that E and E'' are stable, E' and E''' unstable. If there exists only one interior equilibrium, it is unstable, as Figure 1-2 makes clear. One objection that can be raised against this model is that there would be incentives for firms to offer contracts which paid the worker w_2 if, upon training, he turns out to be successful (i.e., has "invested" $\hat{P}$), and $w_1 - T$ otherwise. Then only the workers who had "invested" $\hat{P}$ would accept the job. This argument does make an important point which we elaborate in the next section; but in this context the possibility of multiple equilibria would remain, provided only that there is not perfect screening after training or that individuals do not have perfect knowledge of their characteristic P.

21. In "Approaches to the Economics of Discrimination," I presented a slightly different model, with essentially the same results.

22. Under our assumptions, net national product per capita can be written

$$w_1 + \int \max(0, w_2 - w_1 - (1/c\hat{A})\phi) \, dF(\hat{A})$$

which clearly increases with w_2.

23. The same is true in the endogenous preference model.

24. See J.E. Stiglitz, "Alternative Theories of Wage Determination and Unemployment in L.D.C.'s," *Quarterly Journal of Economics*, forthcoming.

25. See J.E. Stiglitz, "Equilibrium Wage Distributions," Yale University, 1972, mimeo. This is an extension to a general equilibrium framework of the analyses of firm and worker behavior in markets with wage distributions (the job-search literature). See, for instance, E.S. Phelps, A.A. Alchian, C.C. Holt et al., *Microeconomic Foundations of Employment and Inflation Theory* (New York: W.W. Norton, 1970).

26. One group's quit-rate function will then lie below the other's quit-rate function, but total costs will be the same.

27. Or

$$
\frac{F_L - w}{w} = \frac{qT}{w} \left[1 - \frac{\eta_q}{\eta_L} \right] \text{ where } \eta_q = -\frac{q'w}{q}, \eta_L = \frac{L'w}{L}.
$$

The (percentage) excess of marginal product over wage is proportional to the ratio of training costs to direct wage costs, and decreases with the ratio of the quit-rate elasticity to the supply elasticity.

28. For simplicity, we have assumed here that the quit rate is a function of w alone. We could easily extend the analysis to make it a function of $\overline{w}$ as well, where $\overline{w}$ is the mean wage of the group to which the individual belongs.

29. The role of wage structures in affecting quit rates is set out in more detail in J.E. Stiglitz, "The Optimal Wage Structure," and in S. Salop, "Self-Selection and Turnover in the Labor Markets," Yale University, 1972, mimeos.

30. Individuals' expectations about the likelihood of quitting (or of not being fired, or of not advancing) are likely to be formed on the basis of the experience of other members of their group. If most of the members of the group are employed in jobs where there are not strong incentives against quitting (e.g., where possibilities of advancement are limited) then they will have a higher quit rate, and members of the group joining the labor force will take similar jobs. If they were more sophisticated, they would not take the "average" quit rate, but ask, what is the likelihood that they would quit, given that they got the better job. But even there, if individuals of one group are less certain about their abilities, or if they believe that they may be discriminated against in advancement, or if they are more risk averse, then even if their estimates of ability are unbiased, they will not apply for the job requiring foregoing present wages in anticipation of future wages with the same frequency as members of the other group.

2

Studying Black-White Differences in the Context of a Microsimulation of the Labor Market

Barbara R. Bergmann *

Whites and blacks are different in the kinds of jobs they have, in the wages they are paid, in the amount of unemployment they suffer, and in their rate of labor turnover. With ordinary theoretical and econometric methods, it is difficult to handle all of these phenomena within the context of a single model. One method which holds promise of doing so is microsimulation. The purpose of this chapter is to describe a very simple microsimulation model of the labor market which is capable of being elaborated into a model in which the actions and interactions of black workers, white workers, and employers are delineated.

The inputs to such a model are the behavioral descriptions and the values of variables which are to be considered exogenous. In the basic model we shall describe, exogenous variables are separation rates and a measure of the demand for labor based on the aggregate demand for goods and services. Separation rates and demand for labor are assumed to be independent. Outputs of the basic model are unemployment rates, distributions of the durations of unemployment, vacancy rates and distributions of the durations of vacancies. In constructing this basic model and in discussing its elaborations, we have tried to stay within formulations which would allow the use of existing data as inputs and which would allow for outputs of the model to be comparable to actual existing data. In this way, the model can, in some sense, be "validated" through tests which determine whether the output of the model tracks the analogous data series through time.

The Basic Model

Although our eventual aim is to delineate differences in behavior of black and white workers and differences in the way they are treated by employers, it is best to start very simply with a description of a labor market in which all workers are homogeneous in their behavior and in which all workers are treated identically by employers.

We shall represent the level of aggregate demand by the number of job slots which are either filled or which employers are making efforts to fill. The labor-market process is viewed as a daily one. The "scenario" of the simulation is

*Professor of economics, University of Maryland.

as follows: The day begins by the random selection of those employed persons who are to be separated and become newly unemployed (the assumption is that no one enters or leaves the labor force). Next, employers consider unemployed workers as candidates for their vacant slots. A certain number of candidates are paraded past each vacant slot, the number depending on the unemployment rate. A worker may refuse to go into an open slot because he has recently become unemployed, and therefore is in the early part of his search process. An employer may refuse to accept a worker, because the slot in question has recently been vacated, and the employer is in the early part of *his* search process. Once a month (every twenty-two work days) a count is taken at the end of a day's activity, and the unemployment rate, the vacancy rate, and the average duration of unemployment for those currently unemployed are calculated.

The separation process is carried out as follows. Each slot is considered in turn. If a slot is occupied, the occupant is separated with a probability equal to the daily separation rate. The date on which the separation occurred is recorded.

The number of unemployed persons to be paraded past a vacant slot is fixed as directly proportional to the number of persons unemployed. Vacant slots are filled (or left vacant) in order, but the starting place in the array is chosen at random. An unemployed person is chosen at random to be interviewed for a vacant slot. The probability of his wishing to accept the job depends on the number of days he has been unemployed. The relation is,

$$\text{Probability of acceptance} = 1 - A(1)^{(\text{days unemployed})} \qquad (2.1)$$

where $A(1)$, the parameter which controls the length of the probable search, is taken to the power of days unemployed.

A drawing of a random number determines whether the particular worker would in fact accept the job if it were offered to him. If the worker is interested in the job, the employer now decides whether he would like to offer the job to this particular worker. The probability of his doing so depends on how long the job has been vacant. A parameter $A(2)$ controls the rate of increase through time in the desire of an employer to fill a vacant slot, analogously to Equation (2.1). A random drawing determines whether the job offer is made. If both worker and employer are agreeable, the match is made and we move on to try to fill the next vacant slot. If the match is not made, and if the maximum number of workers who can be paraded past a slot has been reached, the slot remains vacant for that day. Otherwise, another unemployed worker is found for consideration and the attempt at a match starts again.

In this model, the exogenous variables are the separation rate, the number of slots, and the size of the labor force. The endogenous variables, which emerge as computer output, are the unemployment rate, the vacancy rate, and information on the distributions of the duration of unemployment and vacancies, on all of which there are, of course, published data.

The "slot rate," at any particular time (the ratio of the number of slots to the size of the labor force) can be deduced from the data on the unemployment rate and the vacancy rate:

$$\text{slot rate} = \frac{1 - \text{unemployment rate}}{1 - \text{vacancy rate}} \qquad (2.2)$$

$$\cong \text{employment rate} + \text{vacancy rate}.$$

The number of slots is then set equal to the slot rate times the size of the labor force.

Elaborating the Basic Model

In this section, we shall consider three ways in which the basic model needs elaboration if it is to be useful in explaining black-white differences in labor-market outcomes: the inclusion of discriminatory hiring behavior on the part of employers, differing turnover behavior on the part of blacks and whites, and differing wage behavior of employers toward blacks and whites. In what follows, we shall assume that workers have been differentiated within the computer memory as black or white.

Discrimination in Hiring. We may think of two polar descriptions of discrimination in hiring. One is complete segmentation, in which certain slots are marked as for whites only and certain slots as for blacks only. If a black worker is paraded past a white slot, he has zero probability of being hired. The second description of discriminatory hiring behavior might be called "differential employability." In this version, every black and every white are eligible for every slot, but the probability of an employer accepting a white is higher than the probability of his accepting a black, and these probabilities are uniform over all slots. Either segmentation or differential employability are, in their simplest forms, extremely easy to insert into the basic simulation.

If we are to be realistic, it is likely that the description of discrimination we adopt would lie between the two extremes just described. While some slots might be virtually reserved for whites and others for blacks, there might be some slots in the middle, so to speak, in which differential employability was the rule. How many slots are in the middle, and how slots are shifted from one category to another in the course of the business cycle is an interesting subject in which simulation can be combined with empirical research. The cyclical behavior of black unemployment rates as compared with white rates surely can be profitably studied in this context.

Differing Separation Behavior of Blacks and Whites. It is, of course, extremely easy to assume that blacks and whites have differing exogenously-given probabilities of separation from a job, and to incorporate that in the basic model. From experiments done thus far with the basic model,[1] it has become apparent that the effect on black and white unemployment rates of different separation rates depends very much on how much segmentation we believe exists in the labor market. If blacks are for the most part rigidly confined to a particular segment, then the major influence on their unemployment rate is going to be the balance within the black segment between supply of labor (the number of blacks employed or looking for slots) and the demand (the number of slots open to blacks). In the segmentation case, the influence of labor turnover is likely to be relatively unimportant. Figure 2-1 gives the results in terms of unemployment rates of simulation experiments at varying slot rates and separation rates (SEP percent) within the basic model, which in this case is adequate to handle the analysis for a single homogeneous segment. It is obvious from this experiment that within a segment, increasing the number of slots has a very large effect on reducing unemployment, while reducing turnover by quite substantial amounts has relatively little effect on unemployment.

If, on the other hand, blacks and whites are seen as competing for the same

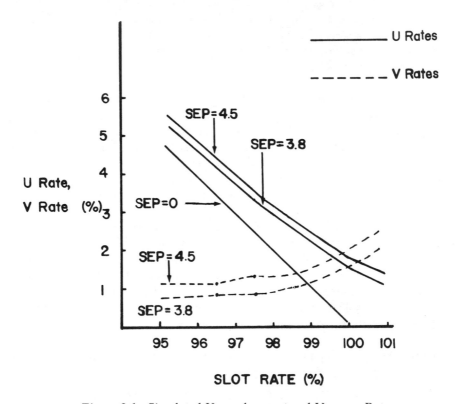

Figure 2-1. Simulated Unemployment and Vacancy Rates

slots (with blacks at a disadvantage of some particular magnitude for all slots) then the differences in turnover rates between the races are likely to be a major cause of differences in unemployment rates between the races. In the segmentation case, an extra black quit opens the way for an extra black hire, and so may not increase unemployment. In the differential employability case, an extra black quit results in an open slot for which a white may have a better chance than a black, thus most likely increasing black unemployment rates relative to white rates.

Differences in Wages. In the basic model described above, wages do not appear explicitly. In order to have them do so, we would have to specify wage-setting behavior on the part of employers, and the strategy of unemployed persons in turning down or accepting jobs with given wage rates. There is a great deal of literature on this, much of it developed in the context of the debates on the Phillips curve.[2] If the segmentation version of hiring discrimination is accepted, then these descriptions of behavior are easily adapted within each segment. In the differential employability case, specification must be made concerning differing wage offers for the same job, depending on the person hired. I have elsewhere suggested that the notion of opportunity cost may be an appropriate one to use in this context.[3]

Conclusion

We have shown how various descriptions of employer and employee behavior in hiring, job search, quitting, and wage setting can be integrated into a simulation model of the microprocesses of the labor market. Differences in behavior of black and white employees and differences in behavior with respect to them on the part of employers are easily incorporated, so as to provide a fully articulated model of labor market outcomes for blacks and for whites. The simulation model thus augmented constitutes both a theory of the labor market and an agenda for empirical research with its aid.

Notes

1. See Bergmann, "Labor Turnover, Segmentation and Rates of Unemployment."

2. See, for example, E.S. Phelps et al, *Microeconomic Foundations of Employment and Inflation Theory* (New York: Norton, 1970).

3. In "Effects on White Incomes of Discrimination in Employment," *Journal of Political Economy* (March/April 1971), pp. 294-313.

3

Alternative Theories of Labor-Market Discrimination: Individual and Collective Behavior

Richard B. Freeman*

There are two broad approaches to the problem of explaining labor-market differences between apparently similarly situated and able workers. The first is the "standard theory" of discriminatory tastes pioneered by Becker (1957), which analyzes the effect of individual prejudice on competitive market outcomes. This theory is often criticized because of the pecuniary incentive given nondiscriminators to expand in the market and possibly to eliminate the differences the theory is supposed to explain [Alexis, this volume; Freeman, 1973a; Stiglitz, 1973; Arrow, 1972]. In the standard model, nondiscriminators earn higher profits or receive greater real incomes than discriminators as a result of their willingness to employ or work with low-wage discriminated persons.

The second approach stresses collective behavior, concentrating on ways in which members of one group discriminate for their own benefit. While many analyses of discrimination for gain suffer from failure to specify the mechanism of discrimination and do not provide a plausible mode of collusion among millions of employers and workers [Thurow, 1969; Bergmann, 1971], a strong case can be made for discrimination by particular groups [Freeman, 1972, 1973a, 1973b, 1973c]. Collective actions ranging from violence to social pressures in the form of group disapproval and ostracization are, moreover, likely to produce nonmarket costs which buttress a discriminatory system.

This chapter is a detailed examination of the structure, implications, and analytic problems with the individual and collective models of discrimination. In contrast to the view prevalent in the literature, it is argued that the two approaches are best viewed as complementary rather than as competitive theories, with the individual model directing attention to collective activities that limit nondiscriminatory behavior and the collective model requiring individual prejudicial attitudes. The first two sections of this chapter recapitulate the main features of the standard model of individual discriminatory behavior in the labor market and examine the effect of nondiscrimination on the long-run persistence of discrimination in this model. Sections three and four assess the roles of governmental discrimination and of antidiscriminatory policies in determining the economic position of discriminated groups. The more complex and speculative issues pertaining to the effect of collective social pressures and nonmarket costs on market discrimination are not examined in this chapter but will be treated in future works.

---

*Associate professor of economics, Harvard University.

33

The Standard Model

The standard theory of discrimination considers the situation in which the utility functions of individuals have as arguments the characteristics of those with whom they associate in the work place. Just as pleasant or unpleasant physical work conditions generate demands for compensating differentials, so to do pleasant or unpleasant colleagues. Formally, the individual can be assumed to maximize:

$$U (X, T - t, A (N_b, t)]$$ (3.1)

subject to the budget constraint $X = wt$ where

U = utility function
X = total goods purchased, with unit price
T = total time available
t = time at work
A = degree of association with disliked black, with $A (0, t) = 0$ and A_1 and $A_2 > 0$
N_b = number of blacks at place of work
w = wage rate.

Taking w and A as given, maximization yields

$$\frac{U_2}{\lambda} = A_2 \frac{U_3}{\lambda} + w,$$ (3.2)

where U_2 is the marginal utility of leisure; $U_3 < 0$ the marginal disutility of association and λ the marginal utility of income. Given a choice between two jobs—one without association ($A = 0$) and one with—the individual will desire compensation of $A_2 U_3/\lambda$, the income value of the disutility of association. This desire for compensation can be viewed as the individual's demand for discrimination analogous to his demand for other goods.

A wide variety of testable implications can be derived from the standard theory by tracing out the way in which discriminatory demands are filtered through the market [Becker, 1957] and the way in which nondiscriminatory behavior influences market outcomes [Freeman, 1973b]. For discrimination by employers and by employees the implications of the standard theory are restated by Alexis later in this volume so that a brief review of its premises and outcomes will suffice to lead into the discussion of governmental discrimination.

Market Equilibrium, Nondiscriminatory
Behavior, and Demand for Black Workers

The equilibrium black/white wage differential that results from discrimination at a moment in time is set by the intersection of the supply of black workers with a market demand curve obtained by summing employer and employee discriminatory demands appropriately weighted by the relevant factor shares. Under certain circumstances—a reasonably large number of employers or complementary workers with no discriminatory demands in the range of black supply—the equilibrium differential will be zero. Blacks will associate solely with nondiscriminators and obtain wages equaling those of comparable whites. Despite a group "norm" for discrimination, adhered to by, say, 85 percent of the population, prejudice need not have economic consequences.[1] A relatively small number of nondiscriminators *may* suffice to eliminate discriminatory differences. Under other circumstances, with relatively many discriminators in the market, there will be an "equilibrium" black/white wage differential below unit.

The major criticism of the standard theory relates to the long-run persistence of such a discriminatory equilibrium. With wages differing as a result of discrimination, there is a substantial economic advantage to nondiscriminators in the competitive market and consequent profit incentives favoring nondiscriminatory behavior. These advantages are an incentive to expand in the market and to substitute low-cost black labor for other factors. Hence, they provide a potentially powerful market force against discrimination.

How effective will nondiscriminating employers and employees be in eliminating market discrimination? Does the existence of nondiscriminators mean the end of discrimination, turning the model "upside down," as some critics allege, by predicting the absence of the phenomenon to be explained?

The answer to these questions hinges critically on the shape of cost curves and on the supply of nondiscriminating employers and skilled workers.

Cost curves are important because they set limits on the expansion of nondiscriminators in the market. A nondiscriminatory employer will expand production until his marginal cost, which lies below that of discriminators due to the lower cost of labor, equals the market price. If the cost curve is horizontal or downward sloping (constant or increasing returns to scale), the nondiscriminator will be able to parlay his advantage into complete dominance of the market and singlehandedly eliminate discrimination. However, if cost curves are U-shaped, the advantage of the nondiscriminator is limited by the increase in cost as output expands. Figure 3-1 represents this situation: C_0 is the average cost curve of the discriminator; the cost curve of the nondiscriminator lies below it; at price p, the nondiscriminator produces output Q_1 and obtains extra profit $(P - \overline{C_1})Q_1$ —or

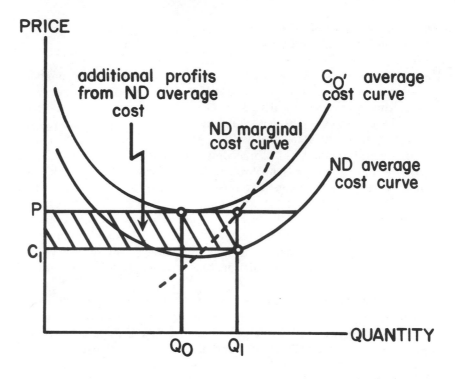

ND = nondiscriminator

Figure 3-1. Declines in Cost and Gains in Profits Due to Nondiscrimination

what may be called economic rent to the rare ability of nondiscrimination. The more elastic the cost schedule, the greater is the advantage of the nondiscriminator, the bigger his share of the market, and the smaller the black/white wage differential. Empirically, this suggests greater black employment in industries with relatively elastic cost curves.

The possibility of eliminating employer discrimination by capital market transfers of ownership, thereby sidestepping the cost-curve-expansion "barrier," also deserves attention. Is it not reasonable to expect the discriminatory capitalist to sell his enterprise to the nondiscriminator who can earn greater profits, removing the cause of discrimination? This line of reasoning faces two problems. First, and most importantly, it confuses discrimination by owners who have no direct relation to operating an enterprise (stockholders) with employer discrimination by managers, who may or may not have ownership. The latter mode of discrimination is surely more important in the market, and it cannot be eliminated by transfer of ownership. The terminology of the discrimination literature—which often refers to discriminating capitalists rather than managers—confuses the issue. Second, it is not certain that capital market transfers will eliminate the effects of discriminatory capitalists: If, as Stiglitz noted earlier in this volume, many discriminators *are* willing to accept a lower return on their money to remain as owners, they may continue to constitute a large share of the market. In the long run, however, they would have to invest relatively more than nondiscriminators to maintain this market share.

Assuming that the nondiscriminatory behavior of current market participants does not eliminate discrimination, there will continue to be a return to this "talent." The higher profits or income paid to nondiscriminating employees and workers provide an incentive for persons with this characteristic to supply skills complementing those of discriminated blacks. If the population has a reasonably large number of nondiscriminators and if their supply decisions respond to economic stimuli, nondiscriminating employers and workers will increase over time, until market discrimination is eliminated. From this perspective the supply behavior of nondiscriminators is a critical factor in the persistence or collapse of a discriminatory economic system.

An obvious potentially elastic supply of nondiscriminating complementary inputs is the black population itself, which will, in fact, tend to have greater incentive to obtain the relevant skills than nondiscriminating whites. This is because on the cost side foregone incomes are lower due to lower wages, while on the benefit side incomes will equal those of white nondiscriminators and exceed those of discriminators. Thus black investment in skills complementing those of their discriminated fellows will earn an exceptionally high return, inducing increases in supply, a convergence in black and white skill structures, and eventual elimination of discriminating differences. There is, from this perspective, considerable truth in the "black capitalism" answer to the discrimination problem.

If the arguments given above are correct, the problem of explaining economic discrimination over the long run translates into the problem of explaining limitations on the supply of nondiscriminating (black) employers and of skilled workers. The standard theory thus directs attention to restrictions on competitive market nondiscriminatory behavior and factor supplies—restrictions which presumably involve collective behavior by the discriminating group. By itself, the theory predicts the long-run demise of discriminatory differences, though the period required may be very lengthy, depending on the speed with which the supply of (black) nondiscriminators increases. In conjunction with an analysis of factors restricting nondiscriminators, however, the theory provides the appropriate price theoretic framework for investigating labor-market discrimination, with numerous interesting implications.

Collective Behavior: Governmental
Discriminatory and Antidiscriminatory
Activity

There are three basic ways in which governmental discrimination and policies can influence the relative position of blacks in the labor market:

1. By affecting black human-capital formation through discrimination in public education.
2. By discrimination for or against blacks in public employment and, less directly, in employment by public contractors.
3. By legal regulations of discriminatory practices in the market and application of laws pertaining to employment and income.

Whether governments will, in fact, discriminate in these areas of public policy or attempt to penalize discriminators, depends on the political strength of those desiring discrimination and those opposing it. When both groups have the same political rights (i.e., votes), the analysis of governmental activity is quite complicated. While one may argue that the discrimination demands of the median voter will determine matters, the existence of other political issues raises the possibility of complex coalition formation and logrolling behavior. The net result of such activities is neither theoretically nor empirically clear.

Consider, instead, two extreme but simpler situations. In the first case, political power is vested solely with one distinct group in the society while a second group has no direct political influence. This corresponds to the historical situation in the American South following disfranchisement of blacks in the 1890s, to the position of blacks in South Africa, of Jews in Russia or Poland in years past, and so forth.

In the second situation, a discriminated group and its nondiscriminatory allies have political power and are able to influence governmental policy. This corresponds to the post-World War II conditions in the northern United States and those in the South following effective refranchisement in the 1960s.

Political Discrimination and
Governmental Behavior

When a particular group has no direct say in political affairs, it seems plausible to assume that governments will ignore the interests of the disfranchised group in policy and seek to maximize the income of the "voting" population, or some function of its income. This assumption does not, of course, completely resolve the problem of coalition formation since specific policies are likely to benefit some voters at the expense of others while redistributing income from the disfranchised to the enfranchised community. In a first approximation, however, it can be postulated further that individuals share equally in community income or, more realistically, make the appropriate side payment to permit maximization of the enfranchised group's income. Relatively simple models of governmental discrimination can then be developed to address some interesting questions. In a world in which governments act to maximize the income of the franchised, what will be the pattern of spending on education and on the provision of public goods? How will the labor market be regulated? What will governmental employment practices be?

Taking the educational expenditure issue first, one may wonder why the government should spend anything on black education at all if it is solely concerned with white incomes. There are two general reasons for such expenditures. First, if black workers are complementary to white workers or to capital, the increase in white marginal productivities provides an economic rationale for investments in black education; second, if black workers desire education for themselves or their children, their supply price (or work efficiency) will be influenced by provision of this nonpecuniary communal good. In either situation, white income maximization will entail some spending on black schooling (or other public services). The optimal expenditure equates the marginal increase in white incomes to the marginal cost of black schooling and depends on complementary relations between black and white resources, the elasticity of the cost of education, and the relative number of blacks.

Taking an extreme case, assume that the number of black and white workers is fixed and that production is governed by a linear homogeneous function dependent on the complementary resources, human capital, and pure labor. The white-dominated government is assumed to maximize

$$Z = F_1 E_w L_w + F_2 L_w - C_w L_w - C_b L_b \qquad (3.3)$$

where

E_w	= education per white worker
E_b	= education per black worker
L_w	= number of white workers
L_b	= number of black workers
C_w	= $C(E_w)$, cost of education per white
C_b	= $C(E_b)$, cost of education per black.

$C' > 0$, $C'' > 0$, and F_1 and F_2 are the partial derivatives of the production function $F(E_w L_w + E_b L_b, L_w + L_b)$. Maximization of (3.3) yields the equilibrium conditions (3.4).

$$L_w(F_1 + E_w L_w F_{11} + F_{21} L_w) = C'_w L_w \qquad (3.4a)$$

$$L_b(E_wL_wF_{11} + F_{21}L_w) = C_b'L_b \tag{3.4b}$$

so that

$$F_1 = C_w' - C_b'. \tag{3.5}$$

Because the marginal gain in the income of educated white labor is taken account of in the maximand, the public demand for white education exceeds that for blacks by F_1. Maximization of white incomes dictates less spending on black than white pupils ($C_w' > C_b'$ implies $C_w > C_b$) and thus discriminatory allocation of resources used for schooling.

The simple government discrimination model can be expanded in several ways (Freeman, 1973c). Addition of nonlabor resources (capital) to the production function provides further rationale for spending on blacks by adding new complementary white-owned inputs. Disaggregation of the labor input into several types of education highlights the complementary relations between different levels and forms of education and points out the incentive to provide blacks with "different" schooling oriented toward producing complementary rather than substitute skills. In the context of decision-making by open jurisdictions (states, cities, countries), the possibilities of losing or gaining labor by migration and the effects of various tax systems can be investigated. Bowles' (1973) analysis of the amount of education which capitalists want to provide for maximizing their income represents yet another extension of the general approach, assuming capitalists control the government. In all these situations, maximization of the income of the enfranchised subset of the community produces discrimination in the provision of educational and other public resources and offers a "discrimination-for-gain" rationale for policies like those, say, of southern states in years past.

Governmental discrimination or antidiscrimination policy via regulation of the labor market or via differential application of laws is also a likely consequence of differences in political strength. The tools available for such activities would include: occupational licensing laws which require passage of examinations to work in a desirable job; legal penalization of either discriminators or of nondiscriminators—for example, by requiring segregated work facilities or by fair employment practice laws; unequal protection of life and property, permitting groups (the Ku Klux Klan, for instance) to raise the cost of "deviant behavior"; vagrancy and related laws designed to restrict the mobility and to increase the work time of the discriminated; legal restrictions on normal competitive labor-market practices, which might produce monopsonistic conditions. While governments cannot, to be sure, legislate attitudes, they can alter behavior through legal activity by changing the costs facing individuals in the market.

The conditions for governmental discrimination in employment are more complex, for discriminatory demands will conflict with the goal of income maximization via provision of the greatest public service per dollar. Even so, however, governmental discrimination can be expected to be exceptionally strong due to the absence of competitive pressures on the government. In jobs that pay above the market rate, whites will be employed exclusively; in occupations with on-the-job training whites will be favored just as they are in school training; in areas where the government serves the black community and is the sole employer of specialized labor—teaching in the segregated school system—discriminatory differences between blacks and whites should be extreme. Finally, from the perspective of the standard model, the discriminatory demands of the government as employer will be set by the median enfranchised citizen while market discrimination will depend on the marginal enfranchised or disfranchised employer or complementary worker. As a result, governments dominated by one group can be expected to have especially discriminatory employment policies, hiring few blacks, paying low wages, and so on.

Evidence

There is considerable evidence that governmental discrimination of the type described above has been significant in the United States and in other discriminatory systems. First, with regard to the allocation of school resources, data on expenditures for black and white children in the South reveal extraordinary differences for the period 1890 to 1954. At the onset of the 1890s, when blacks retained the right to vote, expenditures were, as Table 3-1 indicates, not grossly different between the races in most of the South.[2] Following the disfranchisement of blacks around the turn of the Century, the ratio of current educational expenditures rose dramatically to as high as nine or ten to one in favor of whites. The differentials remained large through the 1930s and then began to narrow. By 1954, the differentials were more or less similar to those in the early 1890s, in part because of federal court decisions requiring equal pay for teachers of both races and in part because of the fear of Southern whites that extreme inequality, violating the 'separate but equal' doctrine, would lead the Supreme Court to disallow segregated schooling.

The data on governmental employment in the South in this period also points to remarkable discriminatory practices. State by state governmental employment of blacks outside of the segregated school system was far below the black proportion of the population; the few blacks employed were in exceptionally low positions. In Alabama, for example, 5.8 percent of the male nonteaching public work force in 1940 was black compared to 24.7 percent of the total state work force. The relative occupational position of black public employees (weighted with 1939 incomes) was 0.64 compared to a statewide index of 0.83. While state governments may not have been the most discriminating employer, they were clearly far worse than average.

Table 3-1
Black-White Current Educational Spending Differentials per Child, 1880-1954

	About 1890s[a]	1915	1930	1945	1954
Alabama					
White	1.09	9.50	37.50	85.46	111.99
Black	0.92	1.47	7.16	37.59	105.02
Ratio	1.18	6.46	5.24	2.27	1.07
Florida					
White	0.58	15.10	78.25	134.76	175.92
Black	0.25	2.37	10.57	61.75	160.61
Ratio	2.32	6.37	7.40	2.18	1.10
Georgia					
White	0.64	10.09	31.52	82.57	190.15
Black	0.36	2.08	6.98	31.14	115.39
Ratio	1.50	4.85	4.52	2.65	1.65
Louisiana					
White	0.71	16.44	40.64	136.12	165.08
Black	0.44	1.81	7.84	43.81	122.07
Ratio	1.60	9.08	5.18	3.11	1.35
Mississippi					
White	0.41	8.20	31.33	75.19	98.15
Black	0.27	1.53	5.94	14.74	43.17
Ratio	1.49	5.36	5.27	5.10	2.27
North Carolina					
White	0.99	7.38	44.48	86.05	132.46
Black	0.87	2.66	14.80	70.36	124.85
Ratio	1.13	2.77	2.30	1.22	1.06
South Carolina					
White	2.75	10.70	52.89	80.30	195.52
Black	2.50	1.09	5.20	55.74	98.14
Ratio	1.10	9.82	10.17	1.44	1.90
Virginia					
White	0.42	11.47	47.46	95.68	–
Black	0.23	3.20	13.30	77.20	–
Ratio	1.80	3.58	3.57	1.24	–

[a]The figures for the 1890s are approximations based on teacher salary differentials and provide order-of-magnitude estimates only.
Source: Freeman (1972).

Examination of the legal codes of southern states reveals several attempts to regulate the labor market in favor of whites. In the period of slavery, free blacks were at times forbidden from working in particular occupations. The Black Codes tried to limit the mobility of the freedmen. In the 1890-1910 period, many states passed "enticement laws" directed against employers who tried to hire black workers away from others. Section 125 of the Georgia Code of 1910, for example, made "offering higher wages or ... any other ... attempt to entice, persuade or decoy any servant, cropper, or farm laborer, whether under a written or oral contract ... to leave his employer during the term of service" a misdemeanor. These laws, if effective in limiting competition among employers, would surely lower the income of blacks more than those of whites, even if they had been administered impartially, given the predominance of blacks in servant, cropper, and laborer jobs. When northern employers began to recruit black workers for factory jobs, the states responded by requiring substantial license fees for "persons engaged in hiring laborers to go beyond the limits of the state." Mississippi, for example, charged a $500 fee and threatened punishment of $500 to $5000 or one to six months in prison for breaking the "emigrant agent" law. [U.S. Department of Labor, 1925.] Again, laws like this were designed to benefit white employers at the expense of black workers. Finally, instances in which state occupational licensure was used to keep blacks out of skilled crafts are reported in Spero and Harris (1968).

The effects of these discriminatory patterns on the relative position of blacks are, of course, more difficult to analyze. In the case of school expenditures, several types of evidence suggest a substantial effect. First there is the evidence, due primarily to Welch (1967), regarding the effect of resources on the economic value of a year of schooling. Second, the time-series data show that in the 1900-1940 period when the spending ratios were wide, blacks made little progress in catching up with the educational attainment of whites. They advanced little in occupational position as well. Third, cross-sectional analysis by Freeman (1972) of the relative position of blacks in southern states suggests that the greater the school expenditure differential, the lower the relative black position in the labor market.

South Africa provides an even more striking example of governmental discrimination in favor of the politically dominant group. In that country a wide variety of laws designed to protect white labor at the expense of other groups have been passed over the years. Under amendments to the Industrial Concil-iation Acts of 1956 and 1959, the Minister of Labour has the power to protect workers from interracial competition by "reserving" certain jobs for certain races. In practice, this means that skilled jobs are solely in the province of whites and that the forces of competition are prevented from reducing or eliminating discriminatory differences in the labor market. Black entrepreneurship has also been discouraged by the South African government, who have forbidden the opening of new black-owned or black-directed businesses in urban areas [Hutt, 1964].

Political Power and
Antidiscriminatory Policy

When discriminated groups have substantial political power such as exercisable voting rights or the power of protest via marches, demonstrations, and the like, they may be able to translate their strength into antidiscriminatory governmental policies. If the group focuses on such policies as its principal goal and discriminators have more diffuse goals or if, for whatever reason, the discriminated align in a winning political coalition or are supported by a sizeable number of nondiscriminatory members of the dominant group, it is reasonable to expect governmental penalization of labor-market discriminations. The 1964 Civil Rights Act is the principal such attempt to reduce labor-market discrimination in the United States. Title VII of the act makes it illegal "to fail or refuse to hire or to discharge any individual, or otherwise discriminate against any individual with respect to his compensation, terms, conditions or privileges of employment because of race, color, religion, sex, or national origin." Under the same title, the Equal Employment Opportunity Commission (EEOC) was established to administer this law. Executive Order 11246, requiring federal contractors (who employ much of the work force) to take "affirmative action" in minority employment, and several voluntary programs—Plan for Progress, National Alliance of Businessmen—were initiated in the late 1960s by the federal government.

While the precise reasons for the passage of this law or of the Fair Employment Practice Laws of Northern States in preceding years have not been analyzed rigorously, the hypothesis seems plausible that these policies reflect the growing political power of blacks who migrated North and became a critical component of the Democratic Party coalition. The March on Washington which preceded the 1964 law and the extensive political pressures by organized civil rights groups are consistent with such an interpretation. The antidiscriminatory goals of northern whites opposed to labor-market discrimination for moral and related reasons should not, however, be discounted.

Statistical Estimates

How effective has the federal and the related lower-level government and private antidiscriminatory activity been in altering the market for black labor? Regression calculations of the wage and salary income of blacks relative to whites, using federal EEOC expenditures per nonwhite worker as the measure of antidiscriminatory effort, suggest a significant impact for the period 1948 ($t = 0$) to 1971 ($t = 23$). DGNP is defined as the percentage deviation of real GNP from its trend level; it is a measure of cyclical factors. The estimating equation is of the form, $M-F$ Relative Income $= a_0 e^{a_1 t} e^{a_2 DGNP} e^{a_3 EEOC}$. Thus the dependent variable is in natural log form after transformation. The standard error of estimate is given in parentheses below the regression coefficients.

$$\text{Male Relative Income} = -0.58 + 0.0032t + 0.91\ DGNP \qquad (3.6)$$
$$(0.0012)\ (0.22)$$

$$+ 0.075\ \text{EEOC} \qquad R^2 = 0.76, \text{D.W.} = 2.60.$$
$$(0.02)$$

$$\text{Female Relative Income} = -1.01 + 0.029t + 0.76\ DGNP \qquad (3.7)$$
$$(0.002)\ (0.39)$$

$$+ 0.116\ \text{EEOC} \qquad R^2 = 0.95, \text{D.W.} = 1.79.$$
$$(0.028)$$

The EEOC variable obtains a significant positive coefficient, indicating that black incomes rose following the initiation of federal activity in 1965. The extent of the effect over the period 1964-1972 was substantial, producing a 15 percent (0.09) increase in the black-white male income ratio and a 22 percent (0.16) increase in the female ratio, from levels of 0.60 and 0.73 prevailing in the early sixties. More detailed calculations in Freeman (1973d) show a similar pattern of gain in other measures of economic position such as total median income, mean income, and year-round full-time earnings. Vroman's computations (this volume), which use a trend-dummy variable for the post-1964 period, also reveal improvement in the black economic status following passage of the federal law. As a wide variety of changes in policy and in enforcement occurred in the late 1960s, Equations (3.6) and (3.7) and Vroman's results should not be interpreted as indicating the effectiveness of any particular agency or expenditure. In conjunction with direct information on changes in personnel policy in response to federally and privately initiated court actions cited in Freeman (1973d), the data do suggest that governmental antidiscriminatory policy was important in reducing discrimination against blacks.

Additional evidence on the apparent effect of post-1964 governmental and related civil rights activity is given in Table 3-2, which focuses on the relative occupational distribution of nonwhite and white workers from 1955 to 1972. The table records the results of regressing (1) an income-weighted index of the black relative to the white distribution over eleven major one-digit occupations weighted by 1959 total incomes from the census, and (2) the "penetration ratio" (percentage of workers who are nonwhite in these occupations), on three

Table 3-2

Effect of Post-1964 Civil Rights Act Activity on the Nonwhite Percentage of Occupational Employment, 1955-1972

Occupation	Male					Female				
	Const	DGNP	Time	EEOC	R^2	Const	DGNP	Time	EEOC	R^2
Income-Weighted Index	-0.31	0.35 (0.066)	0.005 (0.0005)	0.012 (0.0037)	0.96	-0.61	0.75 (0.13)	0.013 (0.001)	0.048 (0.007)	0.98
Professionals	0.26	1.80 (1.59)	0.20 (0.01)	-0.01 (0.09)	0.97	2.37	6.57 (4.12)	0.26 (0.03)	-0.09 (0.23)	0.90
Managers	0.93	0.13 (1.34)	0.07 (0.01)	0.26 (0.07)	0.93	4.44	10.73 (3.58)	-0.10 (0.03)	0.90 (0.20)	0.64
Clerical	3.44	3.48 (4.91)	0.24 (0.04)	0.43 (0.27)	0.88	0.50	4.21 (1.85)	0.27 (0.01)	0.73 (0.10)	0.99
Sales	0.44	-1.03 (1.79)	0.11 (0.01)	-0.21 (0.10)	0.86	0.41	1.67 (1.46)	0.14 (0.01)	0.24 (0.08)	0.97
Crafts	1.87	3.76 (1.44)	0.18 (0.01)	-0.01 (0.08)	0.97	5.14	9.17 (7.86)	0.14 (0.06)	0.21 (0.44)	0.52
Operatives	9.08	7.17 (4.01)	0.16 (0.03)	-0.03 (0.22)	0.81	8.22	0.87 (4.17)	0.21 (0.03)	0.48 (0.23)	0.90
Service	23.10	1.29 (4.09)	-0.10 (0.03)	-1.07 (0.23)	0.87	19.46	14.33 (4.39)	0.002 (0.04)	-0.30 (0.35)	0.50
Farmers	11.42	-2.21 (2.70)	-0.26 (0.02)	-0.25 (0.15)	0.96	19.77	-12.82 (16.35)	-0.38 (0.13)	-2.87 (0.92)	0.81
Private Household	56.80	33.39 (33.10)	-1.41 (0.27)	1.51 (1.85)	0.76	48.18	35.51 (7.48)	-0.09 (0.06)	-2.05 (0.42)	0.86
Laborers	29.73	2.65 (5.26)	-0.18 (0.04)	-1.40 (0.29)	0.90	24.90	-33.91 (19.80)	-0.19 (0.16)	-2.08 (1.11)	0.59
Farm Laborers	21.01	-19.6 (8.11)	0.09 (0.07)	-2.84 (0.45)	0.81	30.66	-75.48 (12.02)	-0.41 (0.10)	-4.94 (0.67)	0.95

The dependent variable is the percentage of workers in an occupation who are nonwhite in the occupation equations. It is the income value of the total distribution of blacks to whites in the income-weighted index regression.

The standard error of the estimated coefficient is recorded in parentheses below the coefficients.

variables. These are time (t) to pick up overall trends in the black position, the cyclical deviation of GNP from its trend level, DGNP, and EEOC spending per nonwhite worker.

The major finding of the table is that, with cyclical and trend changes in the job structure held fixed, post-1964 governmental and related civil rights activity appears to have led to an improvement in the relative occupational position of black workers. In line 1, the EEOC variable obtains a positive significant coefficient in accounting for the pattern of change in the measure of overall occupational status, the income-weighted index. The estimated effect of governmental and related activity is greater in the female than in the male job structure, possibly because the flat age-earnings profile in female jobs makes relative gains easier to attain [Freeman, 1973d].

The regressions for individual occupations show a general pattern of positive significant effects for the EEOC variable on black penetration into high-level jobs and negative effects on their relative number in low-level jobs. Among men, employment in managerial and clerical work was greatly improved in the post-1964 Civil Rights Act period, with the percentages of black managers jumping from 2.3 (1964) to 3.5 (1972) and the percentage of clericals from 7.0 (1964) to 10.0 (1972). Contrarily, there was a significant and EEOC-correlated decline in black overrepresentation in laborer, farm laborer, and service jobs.

Not all of the calculations are consistent with this picture. While the nonwhite proportion of male professional, craft, and sales jobs trends upward, the EEOC variable has virtually no effect in the first two cases and a negative impact in the third. The absence of post-1964 improvement in the black proportion of professional jobs beyond past trend and cyclical patterns, which is observed for women as well as men, probably reflects the dependence of professional employment on education. Analysis of the allocation of college-trained blacks among more detailed professional subclasses reveals a sizeable post-1964 shift into higher-paying professional fields [Freeman, 1973e]. Employment gains may have been made within the broad craftsmen category also, while the negative impact of the EEOC variable on relative sales employment might reflect shifts from sales to other white-collar jobs. Further analysis is needed to examine these and other possibilities.

The impact of the EEOC variable on the relative number of black women in particular occupations presents a clearer picture of improvement—the percentage of nonwhite females increases in clerical, sales, factory operative, and managerial jobs in the period of governmental and related civil rights activity and declines in farm, private household, and laborer work.

While not the focus of this chapter, the regression coefficients on time and on the cyclical DGNP variable are also of some import. The time coefficients reveal a steady upward trend in the number of black men and women in the better jobs and a corresponding downward trend of their number in low-paying occupations. A plausible explanation of the trend advance is the increased educational attainment of blacks, due in part to the decline in discrimination in public educational resources. [Freeman, 1972.] The positive coefficient on the cyclical variable (DGNP) in line 1 suggest that a tight labor market improves the quality as well as the number of jobs of blacks relative to those of whites. Finally, the generally positive, though statistically weak, coefficients in the regressions for individual occupations hint that black employment is cyclically more sensitive than white employment within occupations, possibly for reasons of market discrimination.

While the post-1964 improvement in the black economic position could be due to other (unmeasured) forces operating in that period, the evidence examined here supports the hypothesis of a significant governmental policy effect, in line with the general theme of this section. Still, the *mechanism* by which policy effectuated the black advancement requires more detailed investigation. Legal sanctions, required affirmative action programs, and the like raised the cost of discrimination in the market, to be sure, and thus reduced its purchase. That this is the entire story seems, however, implausible. More subtle changes in individual behavior not considered here and interactions involving social pressures and related nonmarket phenomena are also bound to be at work.

Notes

1. This statement must be modified to the extent that search costs make it difficult for the discriminated to find "good employers." Even if there were "enough" nondiscriminators to eliminate the economic consequences of discriminating tastes, some residual effect is likely.

2. More detailed analyses of spending data in Freeman (1972) show a striking change in school spending before and after legal disfranchisement.

References

Arrow, K.J. "Some Mathematical Models of Race in the Labor Market." In Anthony H. Pascal, ed., *Racial Discrimination in Economic Life*. Lexington, Mass.: Lexington Books, D.C. Heath, 1972.

Becker, G.S. *Economics of Discrimination*. Chicago: University of Chicago Press, 1st ed., 1957.

Bergmann, B.R. "The Effect on White Incomes of Discrimination in Employment." *Journal of Political Economy* (March/April 1971), pp. 294-313.

Bowles, S. "Class Power and Mass Education," mimeo. Harvard University, 1972.

Freeman, R.B. "Black-White Economic Differences: Why Did They Last So Long?" Delivered at Ciometrics Conference, University of Wisconsin, Madison, Wisconsin, 1972.

_____. (1973a) "Decline of Labor Market Discrimination and Economic Analysis." *American Economic Review, Proceedings* (May 1973), pp. 280-86.

_____. (1973b) "Labor Market Discrimination: Analysis, Findings and Problems." In M. Intriligator, ed., *Frontiers of Quantitative Economics*. Amsterdam: North-Holland, forthcoming.

_____. (1973c) "A Theory of the Discriminatory State," mimeo. Harvard University, 1973.

_____. (1973d) "Secular and Cyclical Changes in the Labor Market for Black America, 1946-1972." *Brookings Papers on Economic Activity* (1973-1), pp. 67-120.

_____. (1973e) "Implications of the Changing Labor Market for Minority Workers." In M. Gordon, ed., *Higher Education and the Labor Market*. New York: McGraw Hill, 1973.

Hutt, W.H. *The Economics of the Colour Bar*. London: Merritt & Hatcher, 1964.

Spero, S.D., and Harris, A.L. *Black Worker*. New York: Atheneum Publishers, 1968.

Stiglitz, J.E. "Approaches to the Economics of Discrimination." *American Economic Review, Proceedings* (May 1973), pp. 287-95.

Thurow, L.C. *Poverty and Discrimination*. Washington, D.C.: The Brookings Institution, 1969.

U.S. Department of Labor, Bureau of Labor Statistics. Bulletin 370 *Labor Laws of the U.S.* Washington, D.C., 1925.

Welch, F. "Labor-Market Discrimination: An Interpretation of Income Differences in the Rural South." *Journal of Political Economy* (June 1967), pp. 225-241.

4

Federal Civil Rights Enforcement Policy for the Seventies

*Jerolyn R. Lyle**

The decade of the seventies marks a change in the public attitude toward civil rights as a domestic issue in the United States. Makers of public policy in all three branches of government and academicians are rethinking some of the old issues. New issues are evolving which relate primarily to operational decisions of public bodies responsible for enforcing civil rights laws and regulations. Even civil rights advocates find themselves caught in dilemmas regarding some of these operational decisions because they require a definition of priorities among numerous civil rights concerns. This chapter discusses chronic problems in the enforcement of civil rights laws and recommends that a government-wide plan for enforcement be developed. It suggests some components of such a plan and indicates the need for high quality racial and ethnic data collection as a prerequisite to more effective enforcement.

The legislative victory of the civil rights movement of the sixties was the passage of the Civil Rights Act of 1964. What had been a highly unified coalition of civil rights interest groups became a more fragmented collection of organizations during the late sixties. Not only were black separatists questioning the value of an integrated society, other minority groups were challenging black dominance in the civil rights community. Chicanos in the Southwest and Puerto Rican groups such as the Independistas in New York City were taking issue with the growing number of black interest groups in the movement. American Indians, especially the American Indian Youth Organization, were announcing their need for support by other minorities and white liberals. The Civil Rights Leadership Conference, the major umbrella lobby organization for the movement, struggled to retain a fragmenting coalition as the women's rights movement gained momentum.

The enforcement machinery in the executive branch of the federal government reflects this fragmentation of civil rights interests. As late as 1973, nine years after the passage of the 1964 act, there is no government-wide plan for civil rights enforcement. There is no unified approach to the collection of racial and ethnic data with which to study the impact of federal assistance programs. It is therefore hard to tell whether minorities are receiving their fair share of the benefits of these programs. Thirdly, there is a great deal of ambiguity about the meaning of affirmative action as applied by federal officials to employment,

---

*Assistant professor of economics, The American University.

housing, and education. Federal outlays for civil rights programs remain scanty.

The lack of a government-wide plan for civil rights enforcement has meant that many components of the law have not been enforced. The Department of the Interior has no compliance program to assure minority group members equal access to state and local parks and recreational facilities, as guaranteed to them by Title VI of the 1964 act. Federal financial regulatory agencies have not incorporated a civil rights compliance component in their examinations of lending practices of banks and financial intermediaries. Neither the Federal Power Commission nor the Interstate Commerce Commission assume jurisdiction over their regulatees' employment practices. This passivity persists despite the fact that in 1970 the Justice Department rendered an opinion that they had such jurisdiction.[1] The tax-exempt status of private schools which deny entrance to minority students has been maintained by the Internal Revenue Service in many instances. The U.S. Civil Service Commission itself has refused to subject its own Federal Service Entrance Examination to the test validation procedures recommended by testing experts and by the U.S. Equal Employment Opportunity Commission, the Department of Justice, the Labor Department's Office of Federal Contract Compliance, and the U.S. Supreme Court.[2]

In housing, education, and private employment the lack of an overall federal enforcement plan has left much social and economic change made possible by legislation unrealized. Rules and regulations are issued but not implemented until much later, if at all. Civil rights staffs in agencies administering federal programs in these fields are often under pressure to produce favorable compliance reviews, if reviews take place. Although there are many reasons for this pressure, two are critical. One is the widespread belief among federal program managers that their particular program's purpose is not essentially a civil rights one. Income transfer and income maintenance programs might suffer a congressional backlash if administered with a civil rights purpose. In the Department of Defense, for example, compliance personnel typically are civilians reporting to military supervisors. Procurement officers are conditioned to evaluate themselves in terms of their ability to deliver military supplies on time. Since nearly one-half of military procurement comes from sole source suppliers,[3] compliance officers are encouraged to find reasons for favorable reviews if national defense objectives require it. A second reason for this pressure is the low priority which civil rights concerns often have at the presidential, cabinet, and subcabinet levels. The suggestion that a separate Department of Civil Rights be established to remove the enforcement machinery from these kinds of pressures has met strong resistance in both major political parties.[4]

Enforcement in the housing field couples steps forward with steps back. The Department of Housing and Urban Development (HUD) has issued regulations conditioning assistance to builders and developers on demonstrated efforts to sell or rent to minorities. However, issuing regulations without providing for vigorous enforcement may accomplish little. No method for determining which agencies funded by HUD should receive compliance reviews has been established. The probability of a funded agency's being subjected to a review during fiscal year 1972 was only 2 percent.[5]

The excellent compliance machinery of the Department of Health, Education, and Welfare has remained plagued by understaffing. In higher education alone, the number of compliance reviews has declined every fiscal year since 1969. Between 1969 and 1972, field reviews fell from 212 to 99 among the 2600 institutions receiving federal assistance. Sanctions have never been used by the Department's Office of Civil Rights other than for failure to submit the required compliance forms. No administrative hearing has found an institution out of compliance. Furthermore, no official notice of opportunity for a hearing on alleged violations of Title VI of the 1964 Civil Rights Act has ever been sent to an institution. In 1972, President Nixon declared that numerical goals and timetables in affirmative action plans must not be applied so as to result in the imposition of quotas. This pronouncement was his response to a letter from the American Jewish Committee expressing concern over the implicit quotas in education and employment. It is also true that no federal court has conditioned a remedy for discrimination in employment on the displacement of whites from present positions. Relief systems have focused on halting illegal employment practices and on changing those practices for the future. No policy has been developed for disestablishing dual state systems of higher education. No special attention has been paid to minorities other than blacks protected by Title VI. No particular compliance policies exist for Spanish-surnamed students or American Indian students. Even less attention has been paid to higher-education problems of white ethnic minorities.

In enforcing Title VI as applied to elementary and secondary schools, HEW has been more willing to use sanctions, though it continues to rely primarily on voluntary compliance. Technical and procedural delays have characterized enforcement proceedings brought under Title VI against school districts. Three good examples occurred in fiscal year 1972 involving Prince Georges and Wicomico Counties, Maryland, and Tift County, Georgia. The Prince Georges County case may be settled in court before the administrative process can resolve it. The administrative proceedings have been continuing since September 1971. Two interesting law suits are now in process against HEW for alleged administrative failures to enforce Title VI. In *Adams* v. *Richardson*, Adams is arguing that HEW is violating the fifth and fourteenth Amendments to the U.S. Constitution as well as Title VI of the Civil Rights Act of 1964 in failing to terminate federal funds to elementary and secondary schools and to colleges and universities which discriminate. The even more fundamental issue of public access to information about enforcement practices is being raised in another case. In *Center for National Policy Review on Race and Urban Issues* v. *Richardson*, the court is being asked to force HEW to make public detailed information on enforcement proceedings. In 1971 only two orders for fund termination were forthcoming from HEW. In 1972 no such order was given. One of the more constructive patterns emerging from HEW is the development of compliance reviews for national origin minorities in elementary and secondary education. Reviews of the treatment of Mexican-American youths have been conducted in school district in Tuscon, Arizona, in Bakersfield, California, and elsewhere.

Enforcement of Title VII of the 1964 Civil Rights Act and of Executive Order 11246, both of which deal with employment, has met with some interesting successes as well as some disillusioning setbacks. Expanded protection for minorities against employment discrimination comes from the Equal Employment Opportunity Act of 1972. Not only does this act give the Equal Employment Opportunity Commission power to enforce its decisions in courts, it extends legal protection to a greater share of the American work force. State and local government employees, employees of public and private educational institutions, and members of very small unions are covered. As revenue-sharing becomes operational, state and local public employment will continue to expand. The 1972 legislation can have significant impact on the economic well-being of minority citizens.

These potentially useful new powers and jurisdictions are to be coordinated with efforts of the Office of Federal Contract Compliance and the Civil Service Commission by the newly created Equal Employment Opportunity Coordinating Council. The EEOC's pattern regulation approach to enforcing Title VII has involved industry-wide negotiations with canneries in California and with electric, gas, telephone and telegraph utilities nationwide. The now famous intervention by EEOC before the Federal Communications Commission conditioned a rate increase requested by the American Telephone and Telegraph Company on the payment of several million dollars in back pay to blacks and women. This type of interagency cooperation in civil rights enforcement has been all too infrequent.

The overwhelming backlog of uninvestigated complaints of employment discrimination continues to grow, thwarting efforts of minorities to secure legal redress speedily. The backlog of charges exceeds 70,000 as of the close of fiscal year 1972.[6] The major step backward in the employment field, however, occurred when the Office of Federal Contract Compliance in the Labor Department was downgraded within the departmental hierarchy.

An analysis of federal expenditures for civil rights programs helps to explain these steps backward in major areas of enforcement. In the 1972, 1973, and 1974 budgets, civil rights expenditures were less than 0.5 percent of federal outlays for selected social programs. Selected social programs included outlays for education, manpower, health, income security, housing, civil rights, and crime reduction.[7] Civil rights is a low priority item, even among existing social programs. Expenditures for civil rights enforcement were about $100 million in fiscal year 1969, $190 million in 1971, and $521 million is estimated to be spent in fiscal year 1974.[8]

These examples from education, housing, and employment present a compelling argument for the development of a government-wide plan for civil rights enforcement. At a minimum, such a plan should include a uniform set of general criteria to be followed by all compliance units in determining which institutions should be reviewed and how often reviews will occur. A second essential feature of such a plan would be an explicit policy for imposing sanctions in each area of legal jurisdiction. A third component of a minimally adequate enforcement plan would be a unified scheme for determining whether minorities receive their proportionate share of the many federal assistance programs whose benefits should reach them.

Even if there were serious commitment to enforce civil rights laws in any particular administration, this particular aspect of enforcement would suffer from real data-collection problems. Title VI of the 1964 Civil Rights Act prohibits discrimination on the basis of race, national origin, or color in any program or activity receiving federal financial assistance. As delineated in Section 601 of this title, these minorities cannot be "excluded from participation in, be denied the benefits of, or be subjected to discrimination" in such activities.[9] The race, color, and national origin of beneficiaries of federally assisted programs must be known in order to determine whether benefits are distributed in a nondiscriminatory fashion.

The collection of racial and ethnic data is a prerequisite to any serious attempt to enforce this provision of the law. Uniform definitions of racial and ethnic minorities throughout the federal government would be a first step toward developing a data-collection system of reliable quality. Assessing the extent of equitable distribution of federal benefits in any federal assistance program requires data on the race and ethnic origin of persons eligible for, applying for, or receiving federal assistance. A number of federal agencies now collect racial and ethnic data, but no uniform procedure exists. The incidence of special problems varies immensely among racial and ethnic minorities, so that designing a uniform federal data collection system is not easy.

A good example comes from the health field. To reflect the spirit of Title VI, planning for hospital construction should include consideration of locating facilities in or near minority group communities. Failure to collect adequate racial and ethnic data can result in plans for health services which severely limit the opportunity for federal control of genetic diseases affecting primarily members of certain minority groups. Sickle cell anemia, a hereditary blood disease primarily affecting black children is an example of such a disease. Tay-Sachs is another. A fatal condition of mental and visual impairment, Tay-Sachs is found among children of Eastern European Jewish extraction. Trachoma, quite common among American Indians of the Southwest, is a parasitic disease which causes blindness if uncontrolled.

Three questions have shaped the dialogue between civil rights advocates and federal officials about data collection: (1) What are the racial and ethnic minorities about whom data should be collected? (2) How shall members of these groups be identified when data are collected? (3) To what use should the data be put to protect the privacy of citizens while also making it possible to determine the distribution of benefits by race and ethnic group? What follows is a discussion of the current dialogue about these questions and a general recommendation for public action during this decade.

Most federal statisticians follow the lead of the Bureau of the Census in developing statistical standards and categories. Since the first census of population in 1790, the bureau's designation of racial and ethnic categories has varied considerably. In 1790, the racial designations were for whites, other free males, and slaves. By 1970, finer differentiation was made. Persons were counted according to whether they were white, Negro or black, American Indian, Japanese, Chinese, Filipino and Hawaiian, and Korean. A 5 percent sample of households counted Mexicans, Puerto Ricans, Cubans, Central or South Americans, and other Spanish.[10] Lobby groups representing many of these racial and ethnic minorities claim that the Census Bureau undercounts their constituency. They care about undercounts, of course, because they believe that undercounts weaken their efforts to get their share of federally assisted program benefits. A recent study by the U.S. Commission on Civil Rights notes that the Bureau of the Census has been far more concerned about developing reliable racial and ethnic data than other general purpose data-collection agencies.[11] Racial designations in series collected by the National Center for Health Statistics, the National Center for Educational Statistics, and the Bureau of Labor Statistics are much less specific. Some agencies, like the Department of Transportation and the Veterans Administration, have no policy at all requiring agency-wide collection of racial or ethnic data for program beneficiaries. Others have widely varying racial and ethnic designations, along with varying methods for identifying persons as members of each designated group.

The U.S. Commission on Civil Rights, whose recommendations are not always accepted by other federal agencies, endorses the reporting of minority group membership only in the form of primary group identification as perceived by the respondent to survey questionnaires. This method of identification of one's racial or ethnic group status is warranted, the commission argues, because "it is the essence of prejudice to expect that all members of a group bonded together by ancestry and common experience will share any single characteristic."[12]

Problems of identifying American Indians buttress the commission's argument for self-perception as the basis for identifying members of minority groups rather than visual observation by someone taking a survey. Census Bureau policy has been to count persons as American Indians only if they are full-blooded American natives.[13] Identifying about a hundred tribes, the bureau overlooks language groups composed of several smaller tribes. Moreover, organizations like the United Native Americans and the Native American Legal Rights Fund argue that census instructions confuse American Indians by designating them as a racial group. Many of today's native Americans consider themselves to be members of a social grouping because of their heritage, but do not consider themselves to be a distinct race.

Even if consensus existed within government about the number of minorities to be distinguished in statistical series, consensus would still be lacking about the collection and use of the data. The Office of Management and Budget, as well as the Subcommittee for Civil Rights of the Domestic Council, have paid official attention to this issue. For the first time, OMB published a *Special Analysis of Federal Civil Rights Activities* in the *1973 Budget*.[14] While valuable for giving this special recognition to civil rights, the analysis hides as much as it reveals. It presents the level of funding for minority higher-education assistance but no estimate of the need for assistance. It presents data on the number of contract compliance reviews which took place and of the number of complaints against private employers which were investigated. Yet it includes no material on the number of government contracts held or the volume of complaints filed. Moreover, it gives no information on the findings of compliance reviews or on complaint processing.

The official federal policy on collection of racial and ethnic data for Title VI enforcement purposes is contained in OMB Circular A-11. This circular delineates procedures for all executive branch agencies to follow in submitting their budget requests to OMB. In December of 1971, OMB requested through the A-11 mechanism that agency budget requests include indicators of achievement under Title VI and beneficiary data by race and ethnic group. Two examples of acceptable indicators were given to agencies administering federal assistance programs: (1) outreach facilities established in areas with concentrations of minorities and (2) change in beneficiary composition. Race-specific beneficiary data were made optional at that time because OMB statisticians doubted that data of reliable quality could be collected. They also believed that budget examiners would have inadequate time to evaluate the reliability of data in the pressured review process. Examiners themselves vary with respect to their interest in and support for the idea of evaluating agency performance for Title VI purposes.

The OMB policy at present is to request through A-11 only data which will be used in the *Special Analysis*. Agency program plans do not have to include information on the expected racial and ethnic composition of program participants.

Narrative justifications for budget requests are not required to include material on programs as they affect minorities. The decision to leave program impact analyses as related to minorities to agency discretion is unfortunate. Whatever data is submitted to OMB comes *after* the budget hearings at present. Moreover, minority beneficiary data is required by A-11 only for civil rights enforcement and minority assistance programs.

This default by OMB reflects the judgment that consensus is unattainable among federal agencies now accustomed to using a diverse array of racial and ethnic categories. Nowhere has OMB publicly supported the use of goals and timetables to promote nondiscriminatory distribution of federal program benefits. George Shultz took the initial step in March of 1971 by suggesting that civil rights objectives be treated as an integral part of the responsibilities of program managers. He introduced a Performance Management System which included the framework for imposing impact review on all federal assistance programs. The costs of standardizing existing data-collection systems throughout the executive branch, coupled with the genuine lack of consensus among statisticians, program managers, and civil rights advocates, discouraged sympathetic officials within OMB. The current intent is to apply the system to some fifteen programs in which minorities are deeply involved.

Whether Title VI enforcement will ever become an integral part of the budgetary review process remains unclear. The rest of this decade should provide plenty of time. Public policy goals for 1980 should include, in my view: (1) the realization of uniform federal standards for the collection of racial and ethnic data; (2) the allocation of sufficient resources to collect and analyze these data for all federal assistance programs as well as for programs related to other components of civil rights statutes; (3) the development of a government-wide plan for civil rights enforcement which utilizes these materials. Enough laws, executive orders, and regulations are already on the books to eliminate discrimination against racial and ethnic minorities. The time has come to regularize and make real their enforcement.

Notes

1. *The Federal Civil Rights Enforcement Effort—A Reassessment* (Washington, D.C.: The United States Commission on Civil Rights, January 1973), p. 7.

2. See Jean J. Couturier, "Court Attacks on Testing: Death Knell or Salvation for Civil Service Systems?" *Good Government* 88, no. 4, 1971; and J. James McCarthy, "The Meaning of the Griggs Case in the Federal Service," *Good Government*, same issue.

3. For a detailed study of defense procurement, see Joint Economic Committee, U.S. Congress, *The Economics of Military Procurement*, Washington, D.C.: Government Printing Office, 1970.

4. Richard Nathan (U.S. Commission on Civil Rights), *Jobs and Civil Rights*, Washington D.C.: Brookings Institution, 1970.

5. More detailed data on this topic are in *The Federal Civil Rights Enforcement Effort*, pp. 98-186.

6. Ibid., pp. 78-97.

7. Office of Management and Budget, *Special Analyses of the United States*

Government, Fiscal Year 1973, p. 116; Office of Management and Budget, *Special Analyses: Budget of the United States Government*, Fiscal Year 1974, p. 102; and U.S. Bureau of the Budget, *Special Analyses: Budget of the United States Government*, Fiscal Year 1972, p. 116.

8. Office of Management and Budget, *Special Analyses of the United States Government*, Fiscal Year 1973, p. 209; Office of Management and Budget. *Special Analyses: Budget of the United States Government*, Fiscal Year 1974, p. 180.

9. Title VI, Section 601, Civil Rights Act, 1964; 78, Stat. 252 (1964; 42 U.S.C. 2000d (1965)).

10. *1970 Census Users Guide*, Part I, Bureau of the Census, U.S. Department of Commerce, October 1970.

11. *To Know Or Not To Know*, Washington, D.C.: U.S. Commission on Civil Rights, February 1973.

12. Ibid., p. 38.

13. *1970 Census Users Guide.*

14. Office of Management and Budget, *Special Analyses of the United States Government*, Fiscal Year 1973.

Introduction to Part 1B:
Extensions of the Formal
Theories

The competitive theory of discrimination cannot explain why discrimination has lasted so long. In particular, it does not permit of intrafactor discrimination, or discrimination between perfect technological substitutes, leading to significant wage differentials. However, all the writers in Part 1A felt that reality does not end where the conventional theory leaves off. Impressed by this deficiency and by the urgency to make the theory speak to the facts, Marcus Alexis tests a number of frontiers in Chapter 5 and then ventures beyond. For instance, he demonstrates for the case of employee discrimination with changeover (training) costs that it is possible to have total segregation and discrimination simultaneously, even when black and white workers are perfect substitutes.

Alexis develops a number of other unorthodox possibilities of conceivable relevancy. Envy-malice relationships may fuse the discriminatory intent of white workers and white capitalists and give the inferior job status of blacks a positive marginal utility in their preference functions. Hence, it may not just be that whites dislike associating with blacks and by their dislike trigger market mechanisms which leave blacks worse off, for instance by crowding them into low-paying occupations. Rather, the inferior status of blacks may be the outcome intended by discriminators in the first place who have no particular aversion to associating with blacks at all.

In Chapter 6, Saul Pleeter finds other reasons why wage differentials between whites and blacks may persist. Even if blacks and whites are perfect technological substitutes in the certainty case, with uncertainty about customer or fellow worker reactions to integration, nondiscriminating employers who are risk-averse cannot afford to hire blacks except at a lower wage. The racialist attitudes of customers and workers cannot simply be ignored in a pure profit calculus.

Barry Chiswick and Duran Bell, in Chapters 7 and 8, concentrate on employee discrimination exclusively. The notion that employees—who are not known to be less discriminatory than employers, as Bell puts it—are able to effect both segregation and wage discrimination within the labor market has been slow to take hold in the economics profession. No matter what happened at the construction sites, in the steel plants, or in any number of other trades and industries, employers and capitalists usually seemed to be more convenient targets for theorizing even though such theories have produced nothing but a "troublesome inconsistency between the persistence of employer discrimination and competitive equilibrium" (Bell).

Chiswick extends the investigation of employee discrimination by making the inequality of earnings prevailing among white and black workers a function of interracial contact and other factors. This function is then tested against

61

alternative hypotheses. Chiswick concludes that his data are consistent with the white employee discrimination hypothesis, but not with the nonwhite employee discrimination or job rationing hypotheses. Comments by Bradley Schiller are included at the end of this part. Although he focuses on the Chiswick and Bell papers, his discussion pertains to the methodology of empirical research and hypothesis testing in general.

The Political Economy of Labor-Market Discrimination: Synthesis and Exploration

Marcus Alexis*

> *It is characteristic of the age in which we live to think too much in terms of economics, to see things too predominantly in their economic aspect; and this is especially true of the American people. There is no more important prerequisite to clear thinking in regard to economics itself than is recognition of its limited place among human interests at large.*
>
> Frank H. Knight
The Economic Organization

The subject of this work is economic discrimination in employment against blacks. In a sense, this is a narrow concern because there are other groups who are discriminated against, notably women and youths. Discrimination is also present in the markets for residential housing and educational opportunities, to name but two. The models explored in analyzing employment discrimination against blacks should, however, be useful tools to investigate other forms of discrimination.

Discrimination against blacks differs from some other forms of discrimination, say, against women, in that blacks occupy a different social position and the potential power of blacks, in a numerical sense, is less than that of women. Attempts to treat discrimination against women as a mere variant of discrimination against blacks are ill-focused. To begin with, women are in a political position, should they choose to exercise their franchise, to end discrimination against them through the electoral process. Being a political as well as an economic minority, blacks do not have this option. Further, even in economic terms, some women are potentially beneficiaries of discrimination against other women. To the extent that entry restrictions based on sex are effective, some men's incomes are larger than they would otherwise be. In the case of married women, this gain in their husband's income might well be greater than the loss in their own income due to sex discrimination. If it is joint income which is important, these couples gain. Discrimination against women differs from race discrimination in another important way. Discrimination against blacks extends to opportunities to reside in particular neighborhoods, attend certain schools, and enjoy freedoms of movement and association. Women are not excluded from residential areas, and certainly public schools admit both male and female

*Professor of economics and urban affairs, Northwestern University.

children. What exclusions affect women are to be found in "male only" activities which center around private clubs, men's bars and the like. These are almost certain to exclude blacks too.

Discrimination against youths is different from race discrimination in that (1) it is temporary and (2) the exclusions are limited, i.e., some of the "surplus" received by discriminating adults is shared with the discriminated against youngsters.

It is clear from the above that this writer views discrimination against blacks as having unique elements. Indeed, we shall argue later in this work that discrimination in the marketplace is simply the working out of a much larger social process and that the emphasis on the purely economic aspects of discrimination is greatly misplaced.

There is, nonetheless, a growing body of formal analysis of racial discrimination in labor markets which is helpful in understanding the *functioning* of discriminatory processes; it does not, however, help us understand why discrimination of this sort exists, nor does it tell us anything about the noneconomic consequences of discrimination. For example, what, if anything, is the relation between labor-market discrimination and the distribution of political power? Is there any connection between labor-market opportunities and investment in education and training? Does employment discrimination affect the social structure and/or the personality and motivation of discriminated against people? We shall not be able to answer these questions in any detail, but we shall suggest possible effects of discrimination on these other relationships. To the extent that we are successful, we shall have made a contribution toward a recognition of the limited place among human interests which economics holds.

Definitions

It is common in everyday usage to use the terms *discrimination* and *segregation* as if they were synonymous. In a general way the two words can be differentiated by noting that discrimination refers to differential treatment of those in like situations. For example, discrimination between two workers of equal productivity exists if one is treated as if he were more productive than the other. This could result in the worker(s) discriminated against receiving lower wages, having higher unemployment rates, or both. In the case of segregation, on the other hand, one has reference to the separation of individuals or groups. If workers who perform the same task are separated from each other on some basis, say race, such a work force is segregated.

More formal definitions of discrimination and segregation are:

If an individual has a 'taste for discrimination' he must act as if he were willing to pay something, either directly or in the form of a reduced income to be associated with some persons instead of others. When actual discrimination occurs, he must in fact, either pay or forfeit income for this privilege. This simple way of looking at the matter gets at the essence of prejudice and discrimination.[1]

Segregation is defined as follows:

In general, if various members of different factors (such as laborers and foremen) are combined into one group by a criterion such as color or religion, one can say that market segregation of this group exists if its members are employed with each other to a significantly greater extent than would result from a random distribution of members of such a factor.[2]

Both definitions contain subtleties. First discrimination. The notion that the discriminator must pay something for discriminating comes down to meaning that by discriminating the discriminator forfeits an opportunity to make his income or profit larger than it would be if he did not discriminate. If presented with two equally productive employee candidates, one of whom is black and the other white, an employer who discriminates against blacks will hire the white candidate. If the black candidate is willing to work for something less than the white candidate and the employer still hires the white, he will forfeit the additional income (profit) he could have earned by employing the less expensive person. We shall see in the formal theory of employer discrimination that under specified conditions white employers will choose to hire the more expensive white employee. Clearly, such employers forfeit profits by so doing. Economic theory is not helpful in establishing a reason for such a decision. One of the purposes of this work is to extend the scope of considerations beyond the purely economic ones.

The definition of segregation refers to "being employed with each other to a significantly greater extent than would result from a random distribution. . . . " According to this, separation of groups need not be complete for segregation to exist. All that is required is that the "mixture" of groups of employees (factors of production, or, if you will, inputs into the production process) be more distinct than would occur if random mixing were allowed to take place. This can be tested by statistical methods. Therefore, the definition is operational as it stands.

We can have discrimination without segregation and the reverse. If equally productive workers receive the same wages but are separated into groups based on color, we have segregation without discrimination. If, on the other hand, there is no separation of workers by color but one group receives less than the other (and is equally productive), there is discrimination without segregation. We can, of course, have both discrimination and segregation. Further, both discrimination and segregation can be achieved in not-so-obvious ways. One way to both discriminate and segregate is to regularly assign one group to a lower job classification even though it does the same work. A plumber's helper might be required to do all that a journeyman plumber does (and do it quite as well) but receive lower wages. If in addition, racial groups are separated into one or the other classification more than could be explained by chance, then we have both discrimination and segregation.

In cases such as this, it is possible for a discriminating employer to enhance his income (profits) rather than have them lowered. It is true that such an employer can earn even larger profits by hiring all blacks and have them perform all the plumbers' tasks. If this were done, it would not matter whether they are then called plumbers' helpers. In a free market such choices are open to employers. In constrained markets, such as when there are union contracts, or when white workers, by collective action, can prevent employers from taking such actions, both the incomes of black workers and of white employers are reduced.

An Elementary Model of Employer Discrimination[3]

Assumptions

1. All firms have
    a) identical utility functions
    b) identical production functions.
2. Only one commodity is produced.
3. Black and white labor are perfect substitutes (in production).
4. Supplies of black and white labor are perfectly inelastic.
5. The supply of capital to each firm is given so that output is a function of the labor employed.
6. B and W are the amounts of black and white labor employed by a representative firm, output is $f(B + W)$ where f is strictly concave and increasing.
7. Employers (entrepreneurs) are assumed to maximize a utility function which depends on (a) profits π, (b) the number of black workers—B—and (c) the number of white workers—W.

Profits

The profit function is

$$\pi = f(B + W) - w_b B - w_w W, \qquad (5.1)$$

where w_b and w_w are the wages of black and white workers respectively. Nondiscriminating firms are strict profit maximizers; their level of satisfaction is independent of B and W.

Discriminating firms maximize a utility function

$$U = U(\pi, B, W). \tag{5.2}$$

We are interested in discriminating firms only. For such firms,

$$\partial U / \partial \pi = U_\pi > 0 \tag{5.2a}$$

$$\partial U / \partial B = U_b \leqslant 0 \tag{5.2b}$$

$$\partial U / \partial W = U_w \geqslant 0. \tag{5.2c}$$

For discrimination to exist either (5.2b) or (5.2c) must be a strict inequality, that is, either $U_b < 0$ or $U_w > 0$.

The previous model is a generalization of the pioneering work by Gary S. Becker (1957). Assumptions 1 through 6 are the same as his. In Becker's model, employers are assumed to act as if the net cost of employing blacks consists of a *nominal* wage rate w_b plus a term which represents a nonpecuniary cost. If w_b is the wage rate paid blacks, the net cost is

$$w_b(1 + d) = w_w, \tag{5.3}$$

in which d is a percentage of the black wage rate w_b.

From (5.3) it can be shown that

$$(w_w - w_b) / w_b = d \tag{5.4}$$

where d is Becker's *discrimination* coefficient which measures the employer's "taste for discrimination."

We obtain d directly by maximizing (5.2) with respect to B and W. First (5.1) is made explicit in Equation (5.2), so that

$$U = U\left\{[f(B+W) - w_b B - w_w W], B, W\right\}.$$

Next one derives

$$\partial U / \partial B = U_\pi(f' - w_b) + U_b = 0, \tag{5.5}$$

$$\partial U / \partial W = U_\pi(f' - w_w) + U_w = 0. \tag{5.6}$$

Since

$$\partial U / \partial B = \partial U / \partial W, \tag{5.7}$$

$$U_\pi(f' - w_b) + U_b = U_\pi(f' - w_w) + U_w, \tag{5.8}$$

and

$$f' = w_b - U_b / U_\pi = w_w - U_w / U_\pi. \tag{5.9}$$

From the definition of discrimination, $U_b/U_\pi < 0$ and $U_w/U_\pi \geq 0$. The *marginal rate of substitution* of profits for black workers, U_b/U_π, tells us the amount of profits an employer would be willing to forego to hire one *less* black worker. Employers do not react in the same way to hiring whites. If employers are neutral in terms of hiring whites, $U_w/U_\pi = 0$; only if employers are willing to forego profits (nepotism) will U_w/U_π be > 0. This latter case assumes that employers derive some (positive) satisfaction from hiring whites. Except in some uncommon cases we can expect U_w/U_π to equal 0. Thus discrimination is not symmetric.

Letting $-U_b/U_\pi = d_b$ and $-U_w/U_\pi = d_w$, (5.9) can be rewritten as

$$f' = w_b + d_b = w_w + d_w, \text{where} \tag{5.10}$$

$$d_b > 0, d_w \leq 0.$$

From (5.10) it follows directly that

$$w_w \geq f' \geq w_b. \tag{5.11}$$

In economic terms (5.11) means that: (1) at equilibrium white workers are paid a higher wage than black workers with whom they are perfect substitutes; (2) white workers receive at least the value of their marginal product while black workers receive no more than their marginal product. If discrimination against blacks exists and if white nepotism is absent

$$w_w = f' > w_b, \tag{5.12}$$

in which case white workers receive their marginal product and black workers receive less.

In the case where (5.12) holds, "exploitation" against blacks takes place in the sense that the equilibrium wage rate is less than the value of product produced (at the margin). Stated another way, the *money* value of output is greater than the money cost of black-labor input, whereas nondiscriminatory equilibrium would require equality of the two. This is explained by Becker by noting that, from the white employer's standpoint, black labor produces both a marketable output (its marginal physical product) and a nonmarketable output. The latter, call it the negative value of the presence of blacks in the work force, has to be subtracted from the value of the physical output. Thus blacks always receive less than the value of their marketable physical output because white employers subtract from it the value of their (negative) nonmarketable output which is "consumed" by them. The discrimination coefficient is then the tradeoff between money profit and the presence of an additional black (or the profits the employer is willing to forego if he can reduce his black employment by one) which leaves the employer indifferent to the hiring (firing) of an additional black worker. The theory is silent on *why* white employers have this "taste for discrimination." It is concerned solely with the effects. In that respect it is not a complete theory of discrimination but rather a theory of the market mechanisms through which it acts and the consequences of that action. An attempt to provide a rationale for the observed market behavior of whites (employers and employees) is presented later.

Gains from Discrimination

Who benefits, that is, gains, in pecuniary terms from discrimination against black workers? How is the discount from black wages divided between white employers and employees? The answers to these questions depend on (1) the difference in profits of discriminating and nondiscriminating firms; (2) the distribution of any difference in profits. Differences in profits are divided between white employees and employers (also white). Profits of discriminating firms are

$$\pi = f(B + W) - f'(B + W)(B + W) + d_b B + d_w W, \qquad (5.13)$$

where

$f(B + W) = $ output,

$f'(B + W)(B + W) = $ the nondiscriminatory payments to black and white workers, the wage rate being equal to the marginal product of labor,

$d_b B = $ the reduced payment to black workers, and

$d_w W = $ the additional payment to white workers.

Profits of nondiscriminating firms are

$$\pi_0 = f(B + W) - f'(B + W)(B + W). \qquad (5.14)$$

The difference in profits of discriminating and nondiscriminating firms is

$$\pi - \pi_0 = d_b B + d_w W. \qquad (5.15)$$

Divided by $(B + W)$, the right-hand side of (5.15) represents the additional profit to compensate the employer for an increase in the scale of operations which preserves the racial proportions in the work force.

If employers care only about the proportion of their work force which is black, then the derivative of (5.15) with respect to the scale of the labor force equals zero and the entire effect of discrimination is to raise the earnings of white workers. If, however, employers' satisfaction is related (negatively) to the number of black employees and this is little offset by the increase in white workers, then (5.15) is positive and white employers (and possibly white workers too) gain. It is an open question empirically whether employers' satisfactions are a function of the proportion of blacks in the work force or of the absolute number of blacks.

Even if one assumes that it is the proportion of blacks in the work force which is governing, it does not follow that such a utility function is neutral regarding black employment opportunities. Rather, it is clear that increasing proportions of black employees will require larger compensations for white employers. If blacks have higher unemployment rates than whites, it means that black workers will have to accept more depressed wage rates. This need not be a consequence if market intervention is permitted.[4]

The question of gains from discrimination is sufficiently important that the assumptions made earlier are relaxed somewhat to permit more generality. Up to now we have assumed that all capital is owned by whites and that blacks own only one productive resource, labor. Let us now assume that assumptions 1, 2, 3, 4, 6, and 7 are as before but substitute for the previous assumption 5, the following:

5'. There are two sectors, a black (B) and a white (W); the black sector has a smaller capital to labor ratio than the white sector. Further, there is the possibility of trade of labor and capital between the two sectors.

In this revised model, a "taste for discrimination" is interpreted as meaning "whites prefer to use their capital with white labor and can be induced to export capital only at a higher return than they can get at home."[5] By "home" is meant the white sector. It will be shown that under plausible conditions, white owners do earn a premium (in money terms) on the capital they export to the black sector.

In the absence of discrimination, white owners of capital (capitalists) would export capital (or import labor) to the point where the capital/labor ratio (and hence the marginal products of capital and labor) are equal. With discrimination, white capitalists prefer to use their capital with white labor and can be induced to export capital only by receiving a higher price (return) from the black sector.

Krueger discusses possible ways in which discrimination against exporting capital to blacks might occur even if white capitalists have no personal taste for discrimination.[6] She argues that if, for example, white owners of capital are interested in maximizing the income of the whole white community, as opposed to the income of white capitalists, the resulting welfare function would be quite similar to Becker's except that discrimination would be directed at maximizing white real income rather than avoiding the distastefulness of working with black workers.

While the inference that wage rates of black workers would be less than the wages of perfectly substitutable whites is correct, the point to be made is that the emphasis on employer discrimination is probably excessive.[7] Even granted that white capital owners have an aversion to blacks in terms of being in their presence it does not follow that discriminatory wages are a consequence. Much capital is employed where the owners are not present; take the case of large publicly-owned corporations. In such instances the aversion effect is zero but the wage differential is adverse to blacks. Two ways in which this can happen are that managers have an aversion to black workers and/or white workers have such an aversion. In either case the observed wage differential would exist, as is shown in subsequent sections of this chapter. A third possibility is that white managers believe that white capital owners prefer not to hire black workers in their firms. But even here the motivation is unclear: it is not aversion. One possible explanation is malice regarding black workers by white owners of capital. The subtle distinction between aversion and malice is the economic essence of the difference between discrimination and racism.

Imperfect Substitutes—Complementary Inputs

In the previous section it was assumed that black and white labor are perfect substitutes, that is, $MP_{b1} = MP_{w1}$. What if there is more than one labor input such as unskilled and semiskilled or production workers and foremen? Suppose that the black labor is all of one type, call it type 1 labor, and that there are two distinguishable white labor inputs—type 1 and type 2. Further assume that for type 2 labor (white) the following is true,

$$w_2 = w_2 (L_{1w}/L_1), \tag{5.16}$$

where L_{1w}, L_1 are respectively the amounts of type 1 white workers and all type 1 workers, and w_2 is the wage rate of type 2 workers. We assume that w_2 is a monotonic decreasing function of L_{1w}/L_1. For L_{1w}/L_1 equal to zero, w_2 is at its maximum, and for L_{1w}/L_1 equal to 1, w_2 is at its minimum.

There are also L_{1b} black type 1 workers and L_2 type 2 workers (all white). The total labor force L equals $L_1 + L_2$.

For a representative firm, profits are given by

$$\pi = f(L_1, L_2) - w_{1b}L_{1b} - w_{1w}L_{1w} - w_2L_2. \tag{5.17}$$

Maximization of (5.17) with respect to L_{1b}, L_{1w}, and L_2 yields

$$f_1 = w_{1b} + (\partial w_2/\partial L_{1b})L_2, \tag{5.18a}$$

$$f_1 = w_{1w} + (\partial w_2/\partial L_{1w})L_2, \text{ and} \tag{5.18b}$$

$$f_2 = w_2. \tag{5.18c}$$

Since $\partial w_2/\partial L_{1b} > 0$ and $\partial w_2/\partial L_{1w} < 0$, it immediately follows from (5.18a-b) that $w_{1b} < w_{1w}$. Further, w_2 is homogeneous of degree zero in L_{1b} and L_{1w}. Therefore

$$(\partial w_2/\partial L_{1b})L_{1b} + (\partial w_2/\partial L_{1w})L_{1w} = 0. \tag{5.19}$$

Multiplying (5.18a) by L_{1b} and (5.18b) by L_{1w} and adding, we obtain

$$f_1(L_{1b} + L_{1w}) = w_{1b}L_{1b} + w_{1w}L_{1w}. \tag{5.20}$$

Multiplying (5.18c) by L_2 and taking into account (5.20) yields

$$f_1(L_{1b} + L_{1w}) + f_2(L_2) = w_{1b}L_{1b} + w_{1w}L_{1w} + w_2 L_2. \tag{5.21}$$

Thus the profits of the firm are exactly what they would be in the absence of discrimination if the firm has the same quantities of the two types of labor in the two situations.

Since f_2 (the marginal product of type 2 labor) equals w_2 (its wage rate) and since w_{1b} is less than w_{1w}, the effect of discrimination against L_{1b} by L_2 is a transfer of income from black to white (type 1) workers. The same result was obtained when (5.15) was assumed equal to zero.

We obtain some additional information about the determination of wage differentials for type 1 white and black workers if we proceed as follows. Subtract (5.18a) from (5.18b). The result is

$$w_{1w} - w_{1b} = [(\partial w_2/\partial L_{1b}) - (\partial w_2/\partial L_{1w})] L_2. \tag{5.22}$$

Setting $L_1 = L_{1b} + L_{1w}$ in (5.16) and taking partial derivatives with respect to L_{1b} and L_{1w} it appears from

$$w_2 = w_2 [L_{1w}(L_{1b} + L_{1w})^{-1}], \text{ that}$$

$$\partial w_2/\partial L_{1b} = w_2'[-L_{1w}(L_{1b} + L_{1w})^{-2}].$$

Proceeding in the same manner it is found that

$$\frac{\partial w_2}{\partial L_{1w}} = w_2'[-L_{1w}(L_{1b} + L_{1w})^{-2} + (L_{1b} + L_{1w})^{-1}]. \text{ Thus,}$$

$$(\partial w_2/\partial L_{1b}) - (\partial w_2/\partial L_{1w}) = -(w_2'/L_1). \tag{5.23}$$

Combining (5.22) and (5.23),

$$w_{1w} - w_{1b} = -w_2' L_2/L_1. \tag{5.24}$$

In the absence of discrimination, f_1, the marginal product of type 1 labor, is the wage. The discriminatory wage differential is

$$(w_{1w} - w_{1b})/f_1 = -(w_2' w_2 L_2/w_2 f_1 L_1) = -(w_2' S_2/w_2 S_1), \qquad (5.25)$$

where S_1 and S_2 are total payments to type 1 and type 2 labor, respectively. Clearly, the more important is type 2 labor as an input the greater the discrimination to type 1 labor. Stated another way, the more important are complementary inputs who discriminate against blacks (in the absence of discrimination by the perfectly substitutable type 1 labor), the greater the wage differential of black and white type 1 labor.

Employee Discrimination

So far we have assumed that discriminatory wage differentials arise because of the aversion of either employers or complementary inputs. What about discrimination by perfect substitutes? The traditional view is that it is difficult to demonstrate that employee discrimination can lead to market discrimination though it might quite easily result in segregation. For example, if white workers demand a higher wage when they work with black workers, then it will pay for (nondiscriminating) employers to hire all blacks or all whites. Under some conditions discriminating employers might have an integrated work force; all that is required is that the (discriminating) employer has a preference for hiring whites as an offset to the presence of disliked blacks.

Suppose that white workers have the convex indifference map between w_w and the proportion W/L familiar from the analysis of consumer choice between two "goods." Then, for a given level of satisfaction, w_w is a decreasing function of the proportion of the labor force which is white.

The cost to any firm of hiring B black and W white workers is

$$C(B, W) = w_b B + w_w (W/L) W, \text{ where } L = B + W. \qquad (5.26)$$

For an all-white labor force the cost is $C(0,W) = w_w(1) L$ and for an all black labor force it is $C(B,0) = w_b L$. Since $w_w(1) < w_w(W/L)$ for $W < L$, it follows that an all-white labor force is less costly than an integrated one.

If blacks and whites are perfect substitutes, as we have been assuming, and if employers do not discriminate, then w_b equals w_w. All firms will be segregated but there will be no wage discrimination. Therefore, employee segregation but not discrimination is the consequence when there is employee discrimination which is expressed in terms of a required wage rate which is decreasing as the percentage of white employees grows.

Currently accepted theory argues, therefore, that employee discrimination does not produce wage discrimination. However, if white employees use nonmarket devices such as the ballot box, they can force employers to discriminate (in wage payments) against black workers.

Suppose that white workers organize and are successful in enacting legislation which requires government licensing or certification in terms favorable to whites but unfavorable to blacks, such as culturally biased tests or completion of courses given only in segregated white schools. Then, blacks who are in reality perfect substitutes will find themselves "unqualified" for certain jobs. They might have to work in a lower job category and be paid less. Union organization can produce the same effect. In fact, a creditable threat by white workers properly signalled and interpreted is sufficient to translate discriminatory tastes of white workers into wage discrimination. It is not always easy to discern discrimination of this form because workers in the same job category might receive the same wages or persons doing the same job might receive the same wages. A well-designed licensing or certification scheme would reserve the higher wage jobs for the political majority. The traditional view, by focusing on discrimination through ordinary market channels, misses the variety of opportunities for a white majority to induce market discrimination by the use of nonmarket devices.[8]

Employee Discrimination with Changeover Costs

In the previous section it was argued that minimum cost to the firm occurred where $B = 0$, $W = L$ or $B = L$, $W = 0$. Suppose that there exists a situation in which initially there are no blacks in the labor force. Now some blacks enter and additional whites also enter the labor force. Keeping the assumption that firms have identical production functions and adding the assumptions that (1) new firms enter owing to the labor-force increase, (2) there are costs associated with changing over to an all-black labor force, for example, hiring, firing, training, and reorganization, and (3) a return r must be earned on each additional new worker—we observe that, in equilibrium, firms can be either segregated black (SB), integrated (I), or segregated white (SW).

If a firm hires B black workers it incurs a cost of rB. There is no offset to the firm by firing white workers.

A different cost function is also assumed.

$$C(B,W) \text{ is a concave function of } W \text{ for fixed } L = B + W. \qquad (5.27)$$

By concavity of (5.27) is meant that if a linear function of B and W, say $aB + bW$ is added to $C(B,W)$ then as B and W change, L remaining constant, the total, $C(B + aB, W + bW)$ is either monotone increasing, monotone decreasing, or it rises to a maximum and then decreases. This assumption is stronger than the previously observed property that minimum cost is always to be found at one or the other of two segregated extremes.

Prior to the entrance of blacks into the labor market each firm is assumed to have the same number, L_0, of white workers. We consider the case of a firm that after the change in labor-market conditions decides to have B black workers and W white workers. For $W > L_0$, $B + (W - L_0)$ workers are added and the firm incurs a training cost of $r[B + (W - L_0)]$. For $W < L_0$, only B workers are added at a training cost of rB, there being no offsetting gain for the $L_0 - W$ white workers fired. Total costs in the two situations are therefore

$$C(B,W) + r(L - L_0) \quad \text{if } W \geqslant L_0 \qquad (5.28)$$

$$C(B,W) + rB \qquad \text{if } W < L_0.$$

Costs are minimized for $W \geqslant L_0$ when either $W = L_0$ (and therefore $B = L - L_0$) or $W = L$ (and $B = 0$). For $W < L_0$, costs are minimized for $L = B$ ($W = 0$) if and only if $w_b(B = L) + rB < w_w(W = L)$. In the latter case, w_b must be less than w_w by more than r. Consequently, firms will be in one of the following three situations

$$(SB) \quad W = 0, \quad B = L \qquad (5.29a)$$

$$(I) \quad W = L_0, \; B = L - L_0 \qquad (5.29b)$$

$$(SW) \quad W = L, \quad B = 0, \qquad (5.29c)$$

where (SB) means segregated black (I) is integrated and (SW) stands for segregated white.

Let $v(W/L)$ be the difference between black and white wages when the proportion of whites in the labor force is W/L so that $v(W/L) = w_w(W/L) - w_b$. Then the costs of (5.29a, b, c) can be written (recalling that $C(B,W) = w_b B + w_w(W/L)W$ and (5.28)):

$$(SB) \quad (w_b + r)L \qquad (5.30a)$$

$$(I) \quad (w_b + r)(L - L_0) + w_w(L_0/L)L_0 \qquad (5.30b)$$

$$= (w_b + r)L + [v(L_0/L) - r]L_0$$

$$(SW) \quad w_w(1)L + r(L - L_0) = [w_w(1) + r]L - rL_0. \qquad (5.30c)$$

The profits for a given total labor force in each situation are

$$(SB) \quad \pi_{sb}(L) = f(L) - (w_b + r)L \qquad (5.31a)$$

$$(I) \quad \pi_i(L) = f(L) - (w_b + r)L - [v(L_0/L) - r]L_0 \qquad (5.31b)$$

$$(SW) \quad \pi_{sw}(L) = f(L) \quad - [w_w(1) + r] L + rL_0. \tag{5.31c}$$

A firm in situation (SB) will choose L so as to maximize π_{sb}; call this value L_{sb}. From π_i and π_{sw} corresponding values of L_i and L_{sw} are found.

$$\pi'_{sb}(L) = f'(L) - (w_b + r) \tag{5.32a}$$

$$\pi'_i(L) = f'(L) - (w_b + r) - L_0 \, \partial v(L_0/L)/\partial L \tag{5.32b}$$

$$\pi'_{sw}(L) = f'(L) - [w_w(1) + r]. \tag{5.32c}$$

The values of L_{sb}, L_i, and L_{sw} are found by setting π_{sb}, π_i and π_{sw} equal to zero. Subtracting,

$$f'(L_i) - f'(L_{sb}) = L_0 \, \partial v(L_0/L)/\partial L \tag{5.33}$$

$$f'(L_{sw}) - f'(L_{sb}) = v(1).$$

From the viewpoint of the firm, $v(L_0/L)$ differs from $w_w(L_0/L)$ by a constant, w_b, and $w_w(L_0/L)$ is a decreasing function of L_0/L and therefore an increasing function of L. It therefore follows that

$$\partial v(L_0/L)/\partial L > 0 \text{ and } f'(L_i) - f'(L_{sb}) > 0. \tag{5.34}$$

By definition, f' is decreasing. Thus

$$L_i < L_{sb} \tag{5.35}$$

and

$$L_{sw} < L_{sb} \text{ if } v(1) > 0. \tag{5.36}$$

General equilibrium of the labor force requires that more whites be hired than before and also that blacks be hired. Under the conditions specified above, only firms in the SW position are hiring more whites; firms in the SB and I positions are hiring more blacks. For more whites to be hired, firms in the SW position must be at least as profitable as SB or I firms. This opens two possibilities: SB and SW firms are equally profitable and I firms are no more profitable than SB firms (SB and SW); SW and I firms are equally profitable and SB firms are no more profitable than I firms (SW and I).

Assume that in the final equilibrium there are SB and SW firms. For any firm for which $L = L_{sb}$, it then follows that an integrated firm ($L = L_i$) must have costs at least as great as the SB firm. This condition can be written as

$$v(L_0/L_{sb}) \geqslant r, \text{ since } \pi_i(L) - \pi_{sb}(L) = - [v(L_0/L) - r] L_0 \leqslant 0, \tag{5.37}$$

$$\text{for } L = L_{sb}.$$

And since $\pi_{sw}(L_{sw}) = \pi_{sb}(L_{sb})$, we have from (5.31a) and (5.31c)

$$f(L_{sb}) - (w_b + r)L_{sb} = \pi_{sw}(l_{sw}).\tag{5.38}$$

But from (5.31c), evaluated at L_{sb},

$$f(L_{sb}) - [w_w(1) + r]L_{sb} = \pi_{sw}(L_{sb}) - rL_0.\tag{5.39}$$

Subtracting (5.39) from (5.38) yields

$$v(1)L_{sb} = \pi_{sw}(L_{sw}) - \pi_{sw}(L_{sb}) + rL_0.\tag{5.40}$$

Since L_{sw} was the value of L that maximized $\pi_{sw}(L)$, we know that $\pi_{sw}(L_{sw})$ $\geqslant \pi_{sw}(L_{sb})$. Hence, $v(1)L_{sb} \geqslant rL_0 > 0$, so that $v(1) > 0$. This means that $w_w > w_b$ since by definition $v(1) = w_w(1) - w_b$. This result demonstrates that *it is possible to have total segregation and discrimination* simultaneously.

To get some idea of the general equilibrium conditions under which there are both *SB* and *SW* firms, recall first that $v(W/L)$ can be written as $v(L_0/L_{sb}) = w_w(L_0/L_{sb}) - w_b$, or $v(1) = w_w(1) - w_b$. Combining these results and (5.37) and (5.40) we get

$$w_w(L_0/L_{sb}) - r \geqslant w_b = w_w(1) - r(L_0/L_{sb})$$

$$- [\pi_{sw}(L_{sw}) - \pi_{sw}(L_{sb})]/L_{sb}.\tag{5.41}$$

Adding $r - w_w(1)$ to both sides and dividing the result by $1 - (L_0/L_{sb})$, we obtain

$$\frac{w_w(L_0/L_{sb}) - w_w(1)}{1 - (L_0/L_{sb})} \geqslant r - \frac{\pi_{sw}(L_{sw}) - \pi_{sw}(L_{sb})}{L_{sb} - L_0}.\tag{5.42}$$

The left side is a measure of employee discrimination; it measures the rate of change in wage rates demanded by white workers with respect to the proportion of whites in the labor force. Completely segregated firms *SB* and *SW* will arise when employee discrimination (the changes in wages demanded) exceeds the adjusted version of the capital (i.e., replacement) cost per worker shown on the right of (5.42).

Turning to the case in which the general equilibrium yields *SW* and *I* firms only, we argue as before that an *SB* firm cannot have lower costs than an *I*-type firm. From (5.31 a-b), and requiring that $\pi_{sb} - \pi_i \leqslant 0$,

$$v(L_0/L_i) \leqslant r.\tag{5.43}$$

We know that $\pi_i(L_i)$ must equal $\pi_{sw}(L_{sw})$, so that

$$f(L_i) = (w_b + r)L_i + [v(L_0/L_i) - r]L_0 + \pi_{sw}(L_{sw}). \qquad (5.44)$$

By definition,

$$f(L_i) - [w_w(1) + r]L_i + rL_0 = \pi_{sw}(L_i). \qquad (5.45)$$

Subtracting (5.45) from (5.44) and adding $v(L_0/L_i)L_0$ to both sides yields

$$v(1)L_i = v(L_0/L_i)L_0 + [\pi_{sw}(L_{sw}) - \pi_{sw}(L_i)]. \qquad (5.46)$$

Since L_{sw} maximizes π_{sw}, the expression in brackets is nonnegative and

$$v(1)L_i \geqslant v(L_0/L_i)L_0. \qquad (5.47)$$

We know that all the blacks are being hired by the I firms. Thus these firms are increasing their labor force and $L_i > L_0$. Since $w_w(W/L)$ is a decreasing function of L, $w_w(1) < w_w(L_0/L_i)$ and therefore $v(1) < v(L_0/L_i)$. If (5.47) holds, it follows that

$$v(L_0/L_i)L_i > v(L_0/L_i)L_0. \qquad (5.48)$$

Furthermore, $L_i > L_0$ assures that $v(L_0/L_i) > 0$ and hence, from (5.47), $v(1) > 0$.

Since $v(1) < v(L_0/L_i)$ means that $w_w(1) < w_w(L_0/L_i)$, wages of white workers are higher in integrated firms than in segregated ones. The result $v(1) > 0$ also means that white workers in segregated firms (SW) receive higher wages than black workers (in integrated firms). Thus all white workers receive higher wages than black workers.

As before, we can gain some insight into the conditions under which SW and I firms will exist. From Equation (5.43) we can obtain a lower bound on black wages. Equation (5.46) can be solved for w_b

$$\frac{w_w(1)L_i - w_w(L_0/L_i)L_0 - [\pi_{sw}(L_{sw}) - \pi_{sw}(L_i)]}{L_i - L_0}$$

$$= w_b \geqslant w_w(L_0/L_i) - r. \qquad (5.49)$$

By adding $r - \dfrac{w_w(1)L_i - w_w(L_0/L_i)L_0}{L_i - L_0}$

to the first and third expressions and simplifying the latter, we obtain

$$r - \frac{\pi_{sw}(L_{sw}) - \pi_{sw}(L_i)}{L_i - L_0} \geqslant \frac{w_w(L_0/L_i) - w_w(1)}{1 - (L_0/L_i)}, \tag{5.50}$$

or

$$\frac{w_w(L_0/L_i) - w_w(1)}{1 - (L_0/L_i)} \leqslant r - \frac{\pi_{sw}(L_{sw}) - \pi_{sw}(L_i)}{L_i - L_0}. \tag{5.51}$$

As before, the expression on the left is a measure of employee discrimination measuring the rate of change in wage rates demanded by white workers with respect to the proportion of whites in the labor force. Blacks are hired by integrated firms when the rate of employee discrimination does not exceed an adjusted version of the capital (replacement) cost per worker.

These changeover cost models do not pretend to mirror reality. They do not, for instance, take into account normal turnover, which would reduce the cost of hiring black workers; nor do they treat situations in which wage rates are fixed by contract as in many collective bargaining arrangements. But they do demonstrate that employee discrimination can lead to both segregation and discrimination.

Human Capital and Uncertainty

In a previous section we discussed labor markets in which there are two types of labor—unskilled labor (type 1) and a complementary factor (type 2). In this section we again discuss two types of labor. As before, type 1 labor is unskilled, but type 2 is endowed with some quality which makes it more productive, say education or training. Type 2 labor is created only if both the employer and the employee invest some human capital. This latter statement may be interpreted to mean that the employee invests in his education or training and the employer in supervision and/or monitoring the employee's work to make sure that it is up to the standard of the occupation. An employer cannot know a priori whether a worker is qualified, but he may hold subjective beliefs about the respective probabilities that a black or white worker is qualified. Denote these probabilities by p_b and p_w.

As before, assume that the return per worker the employer must earn on his human-capital investment is r. Further assume that the employer is an expected-value maximizer. The equilibrium condition for hiring both black and white workers is

$$r = (f_2 - w_{2b})p_b = (f_2 - w_{2w})p_w, \tag{5.52}$$

where w_{2b} and w_{2w} are respectively the wages of black and white workers of type 2. Define $q = p_b/p_w$ and substitute in (5.52). The result is

$$w_{2w} = q w_{2b} + (1 - q)f_2 . \tag{5.53}$$

If employers hold subjective probabilities that the probability of a black applicant (p_b) being qualified is less than the same probability for a white worker (p_w), then w_{2b} is less than w_{2w}. Assuming the objective value of q is, in fact, unity, we find discrimination in wages for black and white labor of type 2.

If for any reason—legal prohibition or union contract for example—wage discrimination is not possible, blacks will be excluded. This is a result consistent with Demsetz's argument that market arrangements which prohibit blacks from working at lower wages reduce their chances of being employed. It is also consistent with Landes' finding that state fair employment laws increase unemployment among blacks previously discriminated against.[9] Given these results, one is led to the conclusion that in the absence of some specified quota requirement, laws requiring equal wages for (skilled) black and white workers will produce greater unemployment for black workers. The options are then to permit wage differentials, to accept the higher unemployment, or to impose both equal wage (fair employment) legislation and enforceable quotas.[10] This writer opts for the combination of enforceable fair employment *and* quota legislation.

If employers do not subjectively believe that p_b and p_w are the probabilities that black and white workers are qualified, an employer cannot accurately predict the qualifications of any given worker. In such a case, the relevant population is the totality of all workers. If it is further assumed that the acquisition of human capital is costly (as in the case of a college degree) and that workers face imperfect capital markets to finance the acquisition of human capital, then p_b will be an increasing function of $w_{2b} - w_1$ and p_w of $w_{2w} - w_1$ since they are the periodic returns to the human-capital investment. Finally, assume no difference in the determinants of motivations of blacks and whites; then the functional relations determining the investment in human capital will be the same.

Let L_1 and L_2 be the number of type 1 and type 2 workers respectively. In the absence of erroneous judgments about p_b and p_w

$$L_1 = (1 - p_b)B + (1 - p_w)W, \tag{5.54}$$

$$L_2 = p_b B + p_w W,$$

where B and W are the total supplies of blacks and whites. From (5.54), L_1 and L_2 are functions of p_b and p_w. Also, w_{2b} and w_{2w} are functions of p_b and p_w. Therefore (5.52) represents a pair of equations in p_b and p_w for a given w_1.

Under the assumption stated, the equations are symmetric in p_b and p_w and thus have a solution for which $p_b = p_w$. For an initial position in which p_b is correctly perceived equal to p_w, there is an absence of discrimination in the long run.

However, the long-run nondiscriminatory equilibrium need not be stable. For instance, if p_b is initially less than p_w, even slightly, then from (5.53), $w_{2\,b}$ will be less than $w_{2\,w}$ and $w_{2\,b} - w_1$ will be less than $w_{2\,w} - w_1$. There will be an incentive for p_w to rise relative to p_b. This rise in p_w will in turn have a negative effect on $w_{2\,b}$ because there will be increased competition from whites which depresses the overall wages of type 2 workers and further discourages black attempts to acquire human capital.

New Directions

We have used neoclassical, partial static, full-employment equilibrium analysis to study racial discrimination in labor markets. Two important limiting assumptions in this analysis are that (1) capital markets are perfect and (2) wage rates are perfectly flexible. Our analysis of behavior at the margins and the derivation of partial static equilibrium conditions have been useful in the context of a two sector, single commodity model. Such a context is not, however, productive in providing answers to policy-related questions, the essence of which involves dealing with unemployment, wage rigidities, and imperfections in capital markets. To do justice to the study of such phenomena, we require a general equilibrium model with employee and employer search. (For one such attempt, see Bergmann's study in this volume.) A model of such richness presents a great many analytical difficulties but is certainly a direction that policy-oriented research will have to pursue.

In an attempt to cast racial discrimination in a less restricted mold, we have presented elsewhere an alternative model of discriminating behavior.[11] Our purpose was to determine the plausibility of the proposition that aversion to blacks, which lies at the core of much economic discussion of racial discrimination in employment, is less important than heretofore suggested.

No satisfactory answer to the question of why absentee owners should care about the skin color of their workers, consistent with the aversion doctrine, was found. The possibility that another measurable economic quantity not so dependent on physical association, and the possibility that a mechanism we call "envy-malice" might be useful to studying discrimination, led to the construction of a set of models involving interpersonal comparisons of relative incomes of black and white workers. It was found that wage differentials ($w_b < w_w$) can be generated by a model which assumes that white employers are willing to sacrifice some profit to increase the relative wages going to white workers and that white complementary labor (type 2 labor) is willing to accept lower wages if the relative wage income going to white type 1 labor ($w_{1\,w}W/w_{1\,b}B$) increases.

The decision to focus on relative wages going to white labor is not arbitrary. Ceteris paribus, white capitalists can reasonably be expected to prefer giving income to "their own kind" and might even be willing to sacrifice some profit to improve the relative income position of laboring whites. There are several reasons why this might appear sensible to white employers. First, economic resources are of importance not only in traditional economic activity such as exchange, but they are also surrogates for standing in the social order and in power relationships. What common benefit there is in being white is likely enhanced by some intraracial "benevolence." First results suggest that further research of this type is likely to be productive, and out of it will hopefully grow sufficient knowledge about discrimination as a phenomenon to end, or at least greatly reduce it.

Notes

1. Gary S. Becker, *The Economics of Discrimination* (Chicago: University of Chicago Press, 1st ed., 1957), p. 6.

2. Ibid., p. 49.

3. Except where noted, the models in these sections are to be found in two works by Kenneth J. Arrow, "Some Models of Racial Discrimination in the Labor Force," RM 6253-RC Santa Monica, The Rand Corporation, 1971 and "Some Mathematical Models of Race in the Labor Market," in Anthony Pascal, ed., *Racial Discrimination in Economic Life* (Lexington, Mass.: Lexington Books, D.C. Heath, 1972), pp. 187-203.

4. See Duran Bell, "Bonus Schemes and Racism," *The Review of Black Political Economy* 1 (Summer 1971), pp. 110-20; and "Bonuses, Quotas and the Employment of Blacks," *Journal of Human Resources* 6 (Summer 1971), pp. 309-20.

5. Ann O. Krueger, "The Economics of Discrimination," *Journal of Political Economy* 71 (October 1963), p. 481.

6. Ibid., pp. 481-86.

7. One writer who appreciates the limited place of discrimination by owners of white capital is Duran Bell. See his "Bonus Schemes and Racism," *The Review of Black Political Economy* 1 (Summer 1971), pp. 110-20; "Bonuses, Quotas and the Employment of Black Workers," *Journal of Human Resources* 6 (Summer 1971), pp. 309-20; "Occupational Discrimination as a Source of Income Differences: Lessons of the 1960's," *American Economic Review* 62 (May 1972), pp. 363-72. The section on incentives for discriminating against black workers by white capitalists has benefitted from discussion with Bell.

8. For a discussion of how the political mechanism can be put to the economic advantage of political majorities, see Harold Demsetz, "Minorities in the Marketplace," *North Carolina Law Review* 43 (February 1965), pp. 271-97.

9. Demsetz, "Minorities in the Marketplace"; W. Landes, "The Economics of Fair Employment Laws," *Journal of Political Economy* 76, pt. 1 (July-August 1968), pp. 507-52; and "The Effect of State Fair Employment Laws on the Economic Position of Nonwhites," *American Economic Review, Proceedings*, 57 (May 1967), pp. 578-90.

10. The reader is again referred to the articles by Duran Bell in the *Review of Black Political Economy* and in the *Journal of Human Resources*.

11. See Marcus Alexis, "A Theory of Labor Market Discrimination with Interdependent Utilities," *American Economic Review, Proceedings* 73 (May 1973), pp. 296-302.

6 Uncertainty and Discrimination

Saul Pleeter*

There have been a number of attempts by economists to analyze the determinants and consequences of racial discrimination. This chapter will consider uncertainty in the decision-making process as it relates to discrimination. Entrepreneurial policies have uncertain outcomes. We can think of the entrepreneur as assigning a set of probabilities to the possible outcomes of each policy and reaching decisions according to his expected gains or losses and his risk preference.

The application of this type of analysis to the problem of discrimination becomes clear if the firm is uncertain as to the costs and contributions of whites and blacks. For instance, if there is a possibility that hiring blacks will create turmoil between black and white employees with a concomitant loss in productivity, or that white skilled workers will demand higher wages since working conditions are less satisfactory than previously, there is an additional cost associated with the hiring of blacks. If the wage rate for blacks is greater than the marginal product plus the decreased productivity of whites, this may lead to a systematic preference for whites. This preference is different from the motivations typically ascribed to racial discrimination; it is not based on employer tastes for color per se.

Community or social pressures can also have an important influence on the firm's employment decisions. If hiring a black leads to fluctuations in the price received, or a withdrawal of white consumers at the given price, the employer cannot be expected to be color blind. Although, the reaction of consumers to a given racial employment mix is uncertain, still they cannot be ignored.

The reactions of employers to both production and demand uncertainties are the primary focus of this chapter. The first section reviews other studies of racial discrimination. The second section analyzes the behavior of employers given uncertainty in the demand for output, while in Section Three, uncertainty in production is examined. The conclusions of this analysis are presented in the fourth section.

Review of Discrimination Literature

One would argue on the basis of traditional economic theory, that the existence

---

*Assistant professor of economics, Indiana University.

of a wage differential between black and white workers that are perfect technological substitutes would be eroded over time by the functioning of the profit motive in a perfectly competitive world. However, the persistence of this differential has required modifications of the traditional theory.

The traditional theory can be illustrated by the following: Consider an entrepreneur who purchases his inputs and sells his output in perfectly competitive markets. Only one type of labor and one type of capital exists (although labor is available in either of two colors) and both inputs are in perfectly elastic supply. The entrepreneur's objective is to maximize his utility, where utility is a function of profits.

$$U = U(\pi) \text{ with utility assumed to be a monotonically} \tag{6.1}$$
$$\text{increasing function of profits } (\pi).$$

Profits, in turn, are the difference between revenues and costs. The relevant functions are

$$Q = f(L,K) \text{ the production function, with } L \text{ the total labor} \tag{6.2}$$
$$\text{input and } K \text{ the capital input.}[1]$$

The total labor input is the sum of the white labor and black labor hired, or[2]

$$L = B + W. \tag{6.3}$$

With given input prices, the total cost function is

$$C = p_W w + p_B b + rK \text{ where } p_B \text{ and } p_W \text{ are the wage rates} \tag{6.4}$$
$$\text{for blacks and whites respectively and } r \text{ is the rental}$$
$$\text{price per unit of capital.}$$

Letting $\frac{B}{W} = \alpha$, we can rewrite (6.4) as

$$C = \frac{\alpha}{\alpha + 1} p_B L + \frac{1}{\alpha + 1} p_W L + rK. \tag{6.4a}$$

Given the assumption of perfect competition in the product market, the demand function facing the firm is given as

$$P = P^*. \tag{6.5}$$

With costs simply a function of output, $C = C(Q)$, and assuming all functions are nonstochastic, the first-order condition necessary for a maximization of utility is[3]

$$U'_Q = U'_\pi (P - C'_Q) = 0. \tag{6.6}$$

Equation (6.6) will determine Q^* and in order to maximize profits the entrepreneur must minimize the cost of producing Q^*.

Min: $\quad p_B B + p_W W + rK$ $\hfill$ (6.7)

Subject to $Q^* = f(B + W, K)$

$B, W, K \geqslant 0.$

The optimal combination of inputs is found by first forming the Lagrangean function

$$Z = p_B B + p_W W + rK + \lambda [Q^* - f(B + W, K)] \tag{6.8}$$

and taking the partial derivatives of Z with respect to B, W, K and λ.

$$Z'_B = p_B - \lambda f'_B \leqslant 0 \tag{6.9}$$

$$Z'_W = p_W - \lambda f'_W \leqslant 0 \tag{6.10}$$

$$Z'_K = r - \lambda f'_K \leqslant 0 \tag{6.11}$$

$$Z' = Q^* - f(B + W, K) \leqslant 0. \tag{6.12}$$

Rewriting (6.9) and (6.10) we have

$$p_B \leqslant \lambda f'_B \tag{6.13}$$

$$p_W \leqslant \lambda f'_W.$$

Since λ is a constant and since the marginal products of blacks and whites are equal under perfect technological substitutability, $f'_B = f'_W$. Only if $p_B = p_W$ will the racial composition of the work force be indeterminate. If p_B is less than (greater than) p_W only blacks (whites) will be hired. If a wage differential exists, it must necessarily be temporary because firms employing the lower cost input will have higher profits and hence, invite imitation. The increased demand for the lower cost input and decreased demand for the higher priced input will eliminate the initial wage differential.

Since we observe both wage differentials and integrated work forces, modifications of this traditional theory have taken two routes. The first suggests that entrepreneurs are not necessarily solely interested in maximizing profits while the second questions the assumption of either perfect competition or of perfect substitutability of blacks and whites in production.

The initial modification of the perfectly competitive model was Gary Becker's *The Economics of Discrimination*. Becker's agents have "tastes for discrimination" in that they are "willing to pay something, either directly or in the form of reduced income to be associated with some persons instead of others" ([4], p. 6). In terms of the above model, as demonstrated by Kenneth Arrow, the utility function of entrepreneurs contains as arguments not only profits, but also the number of blacks and the number of whites. The employment of blacks produces negative utility while the hiring of whites yields positive utility for employers. The net effect, then, of introducing preferences for color is that white capitalists and black laborers lose (in terms of money) while white laborers gain but total incomes and output are lower.[4] Assuming now that firms have different intensities of distaste for blacks, it is the algebraically minimal distaste for blacks that will determine the long-run wage differential. If some employers have no such "tastes for discrimination," the long-run implications of the Becker model are that discrimination will disappear as nondiscriminatory employers capitalize on the profits attained by hiring a lower-cost work force.

An extension of Arrow's specification of the model has been made by Marcus Alexis [1]. The employer's utility function now contains not only the number of blacks and whites but also the relative share of total income going to whites. Although based on additional factors, the results of this analysis are similar to the Becker case.

Another approach to the discrimination problem rejects the perfectly competitive model as an appropriate premise. Lester Thurow [16] has indicated that monopsony and monopoly power can account for a portion of the observed wage differentials between whites and blacks. For certain instances such as restrictive labor unions or for local monopsony power in an urban area, Thurow's analysis seems valid; however, for monopoly and monopsony power to have broad explanatory power, a large degree of organized collusion will be necessary. With overt agreements frowned upon by various legal bodies, general collusion is not likely to be enforceable without the assist of government.

Still another avenue to explaining racial discrimination has been to emphasize the importance of employee racial preferences in new hiring. This approach was included in the Becker analysis and expanded upon by Finis Welch [17], George von Furstenberg [10], Kenneth Arrow [2], and others. Essentially, the argument recognizes the unequal distribution of skills between blacks and whites and allows that white skilled workers have preferences for the color of their coworkers. As von Furstenberg states, "the racial composition of the workforce within an establishment may be an important working condition. The supply function of senior labor shifts upwards if hiring more minority workers worsens human and social relations in the judgment of the older workers belonging to the racial majority" ([10], p. 72). Hiring blacks in this instance may generate higher costs as whites—through greater absenteeism and lower productivity—resist the attempts by employers to increase the racial mix. Clearly, white human capital and white workers gain from employee racial preferences, while black workers and white capitalists lose. An empirical test of the employee discrimination model by Duran Bell [6] did find a strong positive relationship between the percentage of blacks in a given industry and occupation and the wages of white workers, lending some support to this argument.

It is not the intent of this chapter to argue either for or against the hypotheses of previous studies; rather our sole purpose is to explicitly introduce elements of risk in the decision-making process and study the subsequent behavior of firms. Not all of the ramifications of the model will be discussed. Instead, the fundamental differences of the behavior of the firms under uncertainty will be indicated.

Uncertainty as to the Demand for the Output of the Firm

John Kain and others have pointed to the importance of community racial preferences to the sales of a firm. As Kain reports, "employers located outside the ghetto may discriminate against Negroes out of real or imagined fears of retaliation from white customers" ([12], p. 180). Since the anticipated damage is not known with certainty, a stochastic element is introduced in the demand function facing the firm.

Let us start by assuming we have a perfectly competitive industry comprised of firms whose owners are white and whose sales are primarily to the white community. Firms have identical utility and production functions, and initially they employ no blacks. If firms in the industry were to hire blacks, there is a probability of consumers shifting to other still segregated industries and hence the price received by each firm would fall. Let the function $\mu(\alpha)$ represent the firm's judgment as to the price that will appear if the ratio of black to white workers increases to α. Price is thus a random variable whose distribution is dependent upon the racial composition of the work force. In particular, let us assume that the expected price is a decreasing function of α. Our assumptions can be written as:

$$E(P) = \mu(\alpha) \quad \text{with} \quad \mu'_\alpha \leqslant 0. \tag{6.14}$$

The optimal ratio of black to white workers then follows from the expected utility-maximizing conditions,

$$\frac{\partial E\,[U]}{\partial \alpha} = E\,[U'_\pi \pi'_\alpha] = 0 \qquad (6.15)$$

and

$$\frac{\partial^2 E\,[U]}{\partial \alpha^2} = E\,[U'_{\pi\pi}(\pi'_\alpha)^2 + \pi'_{\alpha\alpha}U'_\pi] < 0. \qquad (6.16)$$

Using the well-known statistical definition $E\,[xy] = E\,[x]\,E\,[y] + \sigma_{xy}$, where x and y are random variables, and σ_{xy} is their covariance, the first order condition can be rewritten as

$$E\,[U'_\pi \pi'_\alpha] = E\,[U'_\pi]\,E\,[\pi'_\alpha] + \sigma = 0 \qquad (6.17)$$

or

$$E\,[\pi'_\alpha] = \frac{-\sigma}{E\,[U'_\pi]}\,. \qquad (6.17a)$$

Since $E\,[\pi'_\alpha] = \dfrac{\partial E\,[PQ - C(Q)]}{\partial \alpha} = \mu'_\alpha Q + \mu Q'_\alpha - C'_\alpha$,

and noting that $L = \alpha W + W$, we have

$$\mu'_\alpha Q + \mu f'_L W - W p_B = \frac{-\sigma}{E\,[U'_\pi]}\,. \qquad (6.18)$$

Substituting $W = \dfrac{B}{\alpha}$ and solving for α the optimal racial composition of the work force is given by

$$\alpha^* = \frac{B(p_B - \mu f'_L)}{\dfrac{\sigma}{E\,[U'_\pi]} + \mu'_\alpha Q}\,. \qquad (6.19)$$

If the entrepreneur is indifferent to risk, then U'_π is a constant and $\sigma = 0$ (the covariance between a constant and a random variable is zero). Equation (6.19) reduces to[5]

$$\alpha^* = \frac{B(p_B - \mu f'_L)}{\mu'_\alpha Q} = \frac{L(p_B - \mu f'_L) - \mu'_\alpha Q}{\mu'_\alpha Q} \qquad (6.19a)$$

In order for an integrated work force to be employed, the savings in labor costs that result from hiring blacks must be greater than the expected loss in total revenue. With $\mu'_\alpha \leqslant 0$, in order for α^* to be positive, at the very least the wage rate of blacks must be less than the marginal revenue product of labor. If $p_B = \mu f'_L$ or if the absolute value of $\mu'_\alpha Q$ exceeds that of $L\,(p_B - \mu f'_L)$, α^* will be zero.

What the risk-averse and risk-taking firm will do depends upon the sign and magnitude of the covariance term, σ. With $E\,[\,U'_\pi\,]$ positive, if σ is negative clearly α^* will be smaller, while a positive σ will increase α^*. The sign of σ is determined by observing how U'_π and π'_α are affected by changes in the random variable P. If the changes are in the same direction, that is, if $U'_{\pi P}$ and $\pi'_{\alpha P}$ are both positive or negative, then $\sigma > 0$, while if they change in opposite directions, $\sigma < 0$. Since the first term $U'_{\pi P}$ equals $U'_{\pi\pi}\pi'_P$ and since $U'_{\pi\pi} > 0\;(<0)$ for the risk taker (risk averse firm) with $\pi'_P > 0$, the sign of $U'_{\pi P}$ will differ between risk-taker and risk-averse firms. The result for the second term on which the sign of the covariance depends can be ascertained by noting that $\pi'_{\alpha P} = \pi'_{P\alpha}$ and $\pi'_P = Q$, so that $\pi'_{\alpha P} = Q'_\alpha = f'_L W$. Since $f'_L \geqslant 0$ and $W \geqslant 0$, if blacks are hired at all, we would expect risk-taking firms to hire a greater percentage of blacks since $\sigma > 0$ than risk-neutral firms who, in turn, have a higher value of α than do risk-averse firms. In the case of risk takers, the unconstrained optimum α^* can be very large so that all-black employment may be approached.

If we now consider a more realistic case of a price-setting firm that is uncertain of the *quantity* that will be sold at the stated price because of the racial composition of the firm's work force, the results given above are essentially the same. In particular, we assume that

$$Q = D(P, \mu) \tag{6.20}$$

is the firm's demand curve where μ is a random disturbance term whose expected value is an increasing function of α. As the expected value of μ increases, expected sales will decrease.

The optimum racial composition of the work force is derived from the first-order condition for expected utility maximization which requires that

$$E\,[\,U'_\pi\,]\,E\,[\,\pi'_\alpha\,] + \sigma = 0.$$

Letting bars denote expected values, we can substitute for $E\,[\,\pi'_\alpha\,]$ the following expression

$$E\,[\,\pi'_\alpha\,] = P\bar{D}'_\mu\,\mu'_\alpha - \left(\frac{\alpha p_B + p_W}{\alpha + 1}\frac{1}{f'_L} + \frac{r}{f'_K}\right)\bar{D}'_\mu\,\mu'_\alpha = \frac{-\sigma}{E\,[\,U'_\pi\,]} \tag{6.21}$$

Multiplying by $(\alpha + 1)$ and rearranging terms we have,

$$E[U'_\pi]\overline{D}'_\mu \mu'_\alpha \left\{P(\alpha+1) - \frac{\alpha p_B}{f'_L} - \frac{p_W}{f'_L} - \frac{(\alpha+1)r}{f'_K}\right\} = -\sigma(\alpha+1). \qquad (6.22)$$

Solving this expression for α^* yields,

$$\alpha^* = \frac{-E[U'_\pi]\overline{D}'_\mu \mu'_\alpha (P - \frac{p_W}{f'_L} - \frac{r}{f'_K}) - \sigma}{E[U'_\pi]\overline{D}'_\mu \mu'_\alpha (P - \frac{p_B}{f'_L} - \frac{r}{f'_K}) + \sigma}. \qquad (6.23)$$

Note that in this expression, α^* depends upon the difference in wage rates for B and W, the expected loss in sales, and the optimal price.

For the risk-neutral firm, $\sigma = 0$ and the optimal racial composition of the work force can be given as

$$\alpha^* = \frac{-(Pf'_L - p_W - \frac{rf'_L}{f'_K})}{Pf'_L - p_B - \frac{rf'_L}{f'_K}}. \qquad (6.23a)$$

Since we constrain the lower bound of α^* to be zero, if $p_W = p_B$, α^* will be zero. In order for α^* to be equal to unity, the relationship between black and white wages must be

$$p_W = 2(Pf'_L - \frac{rf'_L}{f'_K}) - p_B. \qquad (6.24)$$

If $Pf'_L = p_W$, then p_B has to be less than p_W by an amount equal to $2rf'_L/f'_K$.

For the risk-taker and the risk-averse firm, α^* will again depend upon the sign and magnitude of the covariance, σ. To fix the sign of σ we need to know how U'_π and π'_α are affected by changes in the random variable Q. Since $U'_{\pi Q} = U'_{\pi\pi} \pi'_Q$ is negative for the risk-averse firm and positive for the risk-taker, and since $\pi'_{Q\alpha}$ is also negative,[6] σ will be positive for the risk-averse firm and negative for the risk taker. Examining Equation (6.23) we see that α^* will be smaller (larger) for the risk-averse (risk-taking) firm in comparison with the risk-neutral case.

The optimal price, in turn, is derived by setting the partial derivative of the expected utility maximization condition with respect to P equal to zero, so that

$$P^* = (\frac{\alpha p_B + p_W}{\alpha+1} \frac{1}{f'_L} + \frac{r}{f'_K}) - \overline{Q}P'_Q - \frac{\sigma}{E[U'_\pi]}. \qquad (6.25)$$

Assuming the marginal cost curve to be strictly convex and increasing, the impact of uncertainty on the optimal price that the firm sets is a positive one. This is so because once price is fixed, only output variations will affect total cost. Noting that for a convex function $E[MC] > MC_{\bar{Q}}$, or that expected marginal cost is greater than the marginal cost of the certain mean output, equating marginal revenue to expected marginal cost will result in a higher price.

The determination of the sign of σ is essentially the same as the above, except here $\pi'_{PQ} > 0$ so that $\sigma < 0$ for the risk averter (RA) and $\sigma > 0$ for the risk taker (RT). Thus the optimal prices can be given as $P^*_{RA} \geq P^*_{RN} \geq P^*_{RT}$. Although the risk-neutral firm's price will be higher than the certainty price, the risk taker may in fact charge a lower price.

Two modifications of this model can be made. First, we have implicitly assumed that the random disturbance term is a monotonically increasing function of α. In reality, the community may have established a quota on the acceptable percentage of blacks. Uncertainty in the demand for output arising from the unknown racial preferences of the community will only appear if the quota has been surpassed. In this instance, the establishment of mandatory quotas for all firms will actually increase profits given the assumptions of perfect technological substitutability and unequal wages.[7]

The second modification would incorporate the fact that blacks can be employed in certain occupations without fear of consumer boycotts. There are certain jobs that the community will accept as appropriate "black" jobs while others belong exclusively to "whites." The existence of "white" jobs and "black" jobs has been referred to frequently in the literature.[8] Where the racial prejudices of the community are strong, the employer will choose a percentage of blacks that will be less than in the absence of these pressures, even if he has no preferences for color. One would expect also that the magnitude of the pressure imposed by the community would be different depending upon whether the firm was principally an exporter or a producer for local consumption.

This second modification essentially produces the market "crowding" or "job rationing" hypotheses of Barbara Bergmann [7] and others. Although Barry Chiswick [8] could find no empirical support for the "crowding" or "rationing" hypotheses, the level of aggregation and consequent failure to take account of urban-rural differences as well as the export versus local sales orientation of the firm may partly invalidate the interpretation of his results.

Uncertainty in Production

Another factor to be considered in the determination of the racial composition of the work force is the attitudes of the workers toward integrated work forces and the working habits of blacks as presumed by the management. Many arguments against mixed labor forces have been put forward. For instance, blacks have been thought to be unreliable or unstable factors of production. Further, some employers believe that the hiring of blacks introduces frictional costs in that white workers become less productive if they have to associate with blacks. Reporting on a survey of 247 major companies' attitudes toward hiring disadvantaged workers (the term as used in the study considered those subject to racial discrimination as being disadvantaged), Jules Cohn found that many refused to participate in hiring the disadvantaged because of fears of "new people in the company, new ways of training them, new attitudes in hearing grievances, and new rules of behavior for employees" ([9], p. 128).

To analyze the influence of these factors on the employment decision of the firm, let us first draw a distinction between the amount of each input desired and the amount of services yielded by each input. Obviously firms do not desire the physical input but instead the services rendered by that input. We can therefore write:

$$\widetilde{B} = \beta(B, \mu).\tag{6.26}$$

$\widetilde{B}$ indicates the level of factor services yielded by blacks and $\widetilde{B}$ is assumed to be a monotone increasing concave function of B, the number of blacks hired. The term μ is a random disturbance factor whose expected value is a function of α, the ratio of black to white workers. This is given as:

$$E[\mu] = \mu(\alpha) \quad \text{and} \quad \widetilde{B}'_\mu < 0, \quad \mu'_\alpha > 0.\tag{6.27}$$

White labor services and capital services are also assumed to be monotone increasing concave functions of the number of units employed, and are given by the following:

$$\widetilde{W} = \gamma(W)\tag{6.28}$$

$$\widetilde{K} = \delta(K).\tag{6.29}$$

With these relationships we can write the firm's production function as:

$$Q = f(\widetilde{B}, \widetilde{W}, \widetilde{K}) \text{ where again the tildes denote levels of factor services.}\tag{6.30}$$

The first order conditions for expected utility maximization can be given as

$$E[U'_\pi] E[\pi'_D] + \sigma = 0\tag{6.31}$$

or

$$E[P(f'_\beta \beta'_B + f'_\beta \beta'_\mu \mu'_\alpha \frac{1}{W}) - p_B] = \frac{-\sigma}{E[U'_\pi]},\tag{6.31a}$$

$$E[U'_\pi] E[\pi'_W] + \sigma = 0 \tag{6.32}$$

or

$$E[P(f'_\gamma \gamma'_W - f'_\beta \beta'_\mu \mu'_\alpha \frac{B}{W^2}) - p_W] = \frac{-\sigma}{E[U'_\pi]}, \tag{6.32a}$$

and

$$E[U'_\pi] E[\pi'_K] + \sigma = 0 \tag{6.33}$$

or

$$E[P(f'_\delta \delta'_K) - r] = \frac{-\sigma}{E[U'_\pi]}. \tag{6.33a}$$

Rewriting these first-order conditions, we have for the two types of labor i,

$$P \cdot MEP_i - p_i = \frac{-\sigma}{E[U'_\pi]}. \tag{6.34}$$

To maximize expected utility, therefore, the firm will hire inputs until the difference between the marginal expected revenue product and the marginal cost of the input is equal to the expression on the right-hand side of (6.34)—the covariance divided by the expected marginal utility of profits. For the risk-neutral firm, $\sigma = 0$ so that Equation (6.34) reduces to

$$P \cdot MEP_i = p_i. \tag{6.34a}$$

The behavior of risk-averse and risk-taker firms in relation to the risk-neutral firm will again be determined by the sign of o. With output the random variable $U'_{\pi Q}$ is negative for the risk-averse firm and positive for the risk-taker, as before. The other term, π'_{iQ} is equal to $-C'_{iQ}$, with C'_{iQ} denoting the change in the marginal cost of output effected by a change in input i. With C'_{iQ} positive, σ is positive for a risk-averse firm and negative for a risk-taker. The optimal quantities of all of the inputs will thus be greatest for the risk-taker and smallest for the risk-averse firm.

Comparing these results with the certainty case, we find that with a given level of inputs the presence of uncertainty results in a lower expected output since, by Jensen's inequality, the expected value of a concave function is less than the function evaluated at the expected value.

Another interesting point is that uncertainty changes the technological conditions of production. Whereas in the certainty case, blacks and whites are perfect technological substitutes and only blacks are hired if $p_B < p_W$, with uncertainty present, integrated work forces can appear. We must now consider B

and W to be rivals in the sense that their services are substitutable at a diminishing rate. Since $f'_{\widetilde{W}}$ is a monotonically decreasing convex function of B, more of W will be hired than under certainty. Interestingly, if white capital, including human capital, is complementary with B, less capital will be demanded than in the certainty case. Finis Welch [17] has analyzed the certainty case of blacks and whites being complementary factors of production and whites possessing greater amounts of human capital. His conclusion, however, differs from ours in that blacks bear the entire burden of white employee discrimination while with uncertainty less capital will be demanded.

Finally, if $f'_{\widetilde{B}}$ is a strictly decreasing concave function of $\widetilde{B}$, the marginal expected product of $\widetilde{B}$ is less than the marginal physical product of $\widetilde{B}$ so that the demand for black labor services will be reduced. According to these results then, white capitalists and black workers lose while white workers gain from uncertainty related to the productivity of blacks. These outcomes are even more pronounced when we assume the firm to be selling in an imperfectly competitive market.

Conclusions

This chapter has shown that the presence of uncertainty can reduce the level of black employment and explain integrated work forces. We have shown this in terms of both market and production uncertainties related to the hiring of blacks. These results were seen to be independent of employer preferences for color; instead they depended on his preferences for risk. For both risk-averse and risk-neutral firms, the level of black employment is lower than in the certainty case, with white workers the beneficiaries and black workers and white capitalists the losers. The actions of a risk-taker cannot readily be compared with the outcomes under certainty. However, a risk-taker's employment of blacks will be greater than that of a risk-averse or risk-neutral employer.

Uncertainty is surely not the only explanation for the observed wage differences between whites and blacks. To deny the existence of bigotry, discrimination in education, and other factors would be extremely naive; still, the implications of this theoretical analysis should lead to testable hypotheses as to whether uncertainty is an important element in determining the racial composition of particular work forces.

Notes

1. We assume the production functions to be concave in the inputs and homogeneous of some degree $\leqslant 1$.

2. Black and white workers are assumed to be perfect technological substitutes in production.

3. In this chapter primes will be used to designate partial derivatives while the subscripts will indicate the differentiating variable.

4. Arrow's formulation of the Becker model concludes that the net effect of discrimination is a transfer of income from blacks to whites neglecting the reduction in total output and income. This result follows from Arrow's assumptions of optimal allocation of capital and full employment of resources. See [2].

5. We restrict the domain of α to be positive, so that $0 \leqslant \alpha \leqslant \infty$. The identity $B = \alpha L /(1 + \alpha)$ is used in the last part of (6.19a).

6. π'_Q does not have a unique sign for the price setter. A firm *forced* to sell beyond the point where price is equal to marginal cost will lose money on each subsequent unit sold so that $\pi'_Q < 0$ whereas up to that point $\pi'_Q \geqslant 0$. It seems reasonable to restrict attention to the case where $\pi'_Q > 0$.

7. Bell ([15], p. 320) has also advocated a quota system as a means of increasing black employment although he did not consider the benefits accruing to entrepreneurs in the form of higher profits.

8. Baron and Hymer [3] state that, "In general, Negro workers tend to be hired by certain industries" (p. 97) and "a large segment of the Negro labor force has been frozen into positions that are regarded as traditional Negro jobs" (p. 96).

References

[1] Alexis, Marcus. "A Theory of Labor Market Discrimination with Inter-dependent Utilities." *American Economic Review, Papers and Proceedings* 63 (May 1973), pp. 296-302.

[2] Arrow, Kenneth. "Some Mathematical Models of Race Discrimination in the Labor Market." In Anthony H. Pascal, ed., *Racial Discrimination in Economic Life.* Lexington, Mass.: Lexington Books, D.C. Heath and Co., 1972, pp. 187-203.

[3] Baron, Harold M., and Hymer, Bennet. "The Dynamics of the Dual Labor Market." In David M. Gordon, ed., *Problems in Political Economy: An Urban Perspective.* Lexington, Mass.: D.C. Heath and Co., 1971, pp. 94-101.

[4] Becker, Gary S. *The Economics of Discrimination.* Chicago: University of Chicago Press, 1957.

[5] Bell, Duran, Jr. "Bonuses, Quotas, and the Employment of Black Workers." *Journal of Human Resources* 6 (Summer 1971), pp. 309-320.

[6] _____ . "The Economic Basis of Employee Discrimination," Paper prepared for IU-OEO Conference on Racial Discrimination, Indiana University, Bloomington, May 11, 1973.

[7] Bergmann, Barbara R. "The Effect on White Incomes of Discrimination in Employment." *Journal of Political Economy* 79 (March/April 1971), pp. 294-313.

[8] Chiswick, Barry R. "Racial Discrimination in the Labor Market: A Test of Alternative Hypotheses." *Journal of Political Economy* 81 (November/December 1973), reprinted in this volume.

[9] Cohn, Jules. "Private Industry and the Disadvantaged." In David M. Gordon, ed., *Problems in Political Economy: An Urban Perspective.* Lexington, Mass.: D.C. Heath and Co., 1971, pp. 127-137.

[10] von Furstenberg, George M. "A Model of Optimal Plant Integration in the Presence of Employee Discrimination." *The Review of Regional Studies* 2 (Spring 1972), pp. 72-85.

[11] Horowitz, Ira. *Decision Making and the Theory of the Firm.* New York: Holt, Rinehart and Winston, Inc., 1970, pp. 378-400.

[12] Kain, John F. "Housing Segregation, Negro Employment, and Metropolitan Decentralization." *Quarterly Journal of Economics* 82 (May 1968), pp. 175-197.

[13] Krueger, Anne O. "The Economics of Discrimination." *Journal of Political Economy* 71 (October 1963), pp. 481-486.

[14] Roodman, Gary M. "Production Uncertainty and the Theory of the Firm." Unpublished DBA dissertation, Indiana University, 1969.

[15] Sheatsley, Paul B. "White Attitudes Toward the Negro." in John F. Kain,

ed., *Race and Poverty: The Economics of Discrimination.* Englewood Cliffs, N.J.: Prentice-Hall, Inc., 1969, pp. 128-38.

[16] Thurow, Lester. *Poverty and Discrimination.* Washington, D.C.: Brookings Institution, 1969.

[17] Welch, Finis. "Labor-Market Discrimination: An Interpretation of Income Differences in the Rural South." *Journal of Political Economy* 75 (June 1967), pp. 225-240.

7

Racial Discrimination in the Labor Market: A Test of Alternative Hypotheses*

Barry R. Chiswick†

In his pioneering study of discrimination, Gary Becker presents a theoretical analysis of the labor-market implications of what he calls "tastes for discrimination." Becker writes that "money, commonly used as a measuring rod, will also serve as a measure of discrimination. If an individual has a 'taste for discrimination,' he must act as if he were willing to pay something, either directly or in the form of a reduced income, to be associated with some persons instead of others. When actual discrimination occurs, he must, in fact, either pay or forfeit income for this privilege" ([2], p. 14). Using this framework, Becker analyzes theoretically the effects of four possible kinds of discrimination: by employers, by employees, by consumers, and by the government.

The employee-discrimination hypothesis has been discussed by several authors,[1] but to my knowledge no one has tested to see whether it is, in fact, operative. This chapter is concerned with making such a test. The employee-discrimination hypothesis is presented in the first section, and, using a human-capital framework, a labor-market implication is derived from it which is not derivable from the employer, consumer, or government discrimination hypotheses. Two additional hypotheses, a labor-supply hypothesis and a job-rationing hypothesis (both of which have been referred to in the literature as "crowding hypotheses"), are also considered. The implications of these hypotheses are then tested in the second section, using data for adult males and with the coterminous states of the United States as the units of observation. It is shown that the hypothesis that white male workers act as if they have a taste for discrimination against nonwhites is substantiated for the country as a whole, the South and the non-South. The hypothesis that nonwhite male workers act as if they have a taste for discrimination against white workers is not accepted.

The Hypotheses

White Employee Discrimination

Let us assume that workers are either white or nonwhite and that the only group in the economic system with a taste for discrimination is white workers. All

*©Journal of Political Economy; reprinted by permission.
†Senior staff economist, Council of Economic Advisers, on leave from Queens College, C.U.N.Y.

white workers require a wage premium for them to be willing to work with nonwhites. If whites and nonwhites are assumed to be perfect substitutes in production, no firm would have an integrated work force. As long as there is no discrimination on the part of employers and consumers, competition in the labor market would result in equal wages per unit of skill for white and nonwhite workers.

Becker defines market discrimination in terms of differences in wages received by various groups for equal levels of skill. Market segregation is defined in terms of the distribution of employment regardless of incomes. The white-employee discrimination hypothesis when whites and nonwhites are perfect substitutes in production would result in market segregation without market discrimination ([2], pp. 55-58).[2]

However, white and nonwhite workers may not be perfect substitutes for several reasons. First, they may be performing different jobs which involve complementarity, such as foreman and laborer.[3] Second, even if white and nonwhite workers are perfect substitutes in physical output production, they may not be viewed as perfect substitutes by the firm. For example, if a union is controlled by an identifiable group, a firm may be subject to union pressure to give preference to members of that group. Also, the enforcement of fair employment laws may reduce the substitutability of workers.[4] Suppose that an employer with no taste for discrimination employs nonwhite and white workers with equal (observable) physical productivity and pays them the same wage, but his work force is 99.9 percent white. The fair employment law now requires that he hire more nonwhites or be subject to fines. The firm would no longer view white and nonwhite workers as perfect substitutes.

If white and nonwhite workers are not perfect substitutes, a firm which initially employs only whites and then adds nonwhites raises the marginal product schedule of whites. If the increased value of the marginal product of white workers is greater than the increase in their money wages (necessitated by their distaste for working with nonwhites), it is profitable for the firm to hire the nonwhites. Thus tastes for discrimination by imperfect substitutes which are not perfect complements can result in some integration of work forces.

Labor-Market Implications of
White Employee Discrimination

If it can be shown that the employee-discrimination hypothesis has a unique labor-market implication, we will have a means of testing its statistical significance.

Let Y_i^* be the weekly wage of a white worker of a given level of skill (i.e., schooling and labor-market experience) if he does not work with nonwhites. Let X_i be a dichotomous variable which takes the value of unity if he works with nonwhites and the value of zero if he does not. It is assumed that white and nonwhite workers are neither perfect substitutes nor perfect complements, so that some white workers have $X_i = 1$ and others $X_i = 0$. The mean value of this variable is the proportion of the white labor force that works in an "integrated" situation; the ratio of X to the proportion of nonwhites among males (p) can be thought of as an index of market integration.[5] Let d_i be a market discrimination coefficient, the percentage increase in wages paid to the worker if he works with nonwhites.[6] If there is only one degree of contact with nonwhites for each skill level, only one d_i would exist in the labor market for each skill level. If, however, there are degrees of "working with" nonwhites, the d_i's may vary within a skill level.

The weekly wage of a white worker of a given level of skill can now be described by Equation (7.1).

$$Y_i = Y_i^* (1 + d_i X_i).$$ (7.1)

If he does not work with nonwhites, ($X_i = 0$), his wage is Y_i^* and if he works with nonwhites ($X_i = 1$), his wage is $Y_i^* (1 + d_i)$. Taking the natural log of both sides of Equation (7.1) and assuming d_i is small,[7]

$$Ln(Y_i) = Ln(Y_i^*) + d_i X_i.$$ (7.2)

Evaluating the variance of both sides of Equation (7.2) across all white members of the labor force in the state,

$$\sigma^2 (LnY_i) = \sigma^2 (LnY_i^*) + \sigma^2 (d_i X_i) + 2\text{Cov} (LnY_i^*, d_i X_i).$$ (7.3)

The variance of the natural log of income $[\sigma^2(LnY)]$ is a commonly used measure of income inequality. Thus Equation (7.3) relates the relative inequality of labor-market income among white workers in a region to the effect on the distribution of income of:

(a) differences in skill and weeks of employment $[\sigma^2(LnY^*)]$,
(b) differences attributable to a discrimination effect $[\sigma^2(d_i X_i)]$ within productivity classes, and
(c) a covariance term $[\text{Cov}(LnY^*, d_i X_i)]$.

Let us assume that d_i and X_i are independent random variables as this assumption simplifies the analysis and is not implausible. In a competitive labor market, if a skill group experiences an increase in its taste for discrimination, the discrimination coefficient at equilibrium increases, but the proportion of whites working with nonwhites decreases. This predicts a negative correlation between d_i and X_i in a population. On the other hand, holding the distribution of tastes for discrimination constant, if a larger proportion of whites in a skill group works with nonwhites (e.g., because of greater complementarity), the discrimination coefficient at equilibrium is larger. This imparts a positive correlation. The net effect on the correlation of d_i and X_i of these opposing forces is unclear.

If d_i and X_i are independent, Goodman has shown that

$$\sigma^2 (dX) = \bar{d}^2 \sigma^2 (X) + \bar{X}^2 \sigma^2 (d) + \sigma^2 (X) \sigma^2 (d) \tag{7.4}$$

$$= (\bar{d}^2 + \sigma^2 (d)) \sigma^2 (X) + (\sigma^2 (d)) \bar{X}^2 .$$

We would like to have data on the level and inequality of d_i and X_i, but such data do not exist. Data do exist, however, on the percentage of the population of a state which is nonwhite. If k is an index of market integration such that $k = \bar{X}/p$, where p is the percentage of nonwhites in the adult male population, then $\bar{X} = kp$ and[8] $\sigma^2 (X) = (kp) - (kp)^2$.

The covariance term $\text{Cov}(LnY_i^*, d_iX_i)$ is negative if those with higher relative incomes (LnY^*) are in occupations with lower discrimination coefficients or are less likely to work with nonwhites. Whereas it is debatable whether skilled white workers have lower tastes for discrimination than unskilled whites, it is true that white workers with higher levels of schooling have fewer nonwhites at their level (or higher levels) of schooling with whom to work. The covariance term is not measurable and is replaced by a residual, U, which is assumed to vary randomly across the states.

After these adjustments Equation (7.3) can be rewritten as

$$\sigma^2 (LnY) = \sigma^2 (LnY^*) + k [\bar{d}^2 + \sigma^2 (d)] \ p + (-\bar{d}^2 k^2) p^2 + U. \tag{7.5}$$

The coefficient of p is positive and that of p^2 is negative.

Differentiating Equation (7.5) with respect to p indicates that income inequality is a rising function of p as long as less than half of the whites in a state work with nonwhites, which seems reasonable.[9] Thus it is hypothesized that, holding $\sigma^2 (LnY^*)$ constant, *white* income inequality in a state is a rising function of the percent nonwhite.

Holding tastes for discrimination constant $[\bar{d}$ and $\sigma^2 (d)]$, it seems likely that the more integration in the state (the higher k), the greater is the inequality of white income.[10] Similarly, holding integration in the state constant, the greater the taste for discrimination among whites against nonwhites, the greater the inequality of income.[11] Finally, for the same integration coefficient (k) and the same mean discrimination coefficient ($\bar{d}$), the larger the inequality in discrimination coefficients, the larger the inequality of white income.

The variable $\sigma^2 (LnY^*)$ is the inequality of income among white males abstracting from the effects of white employee discrimination. Recent work on the theory of the distribution of labor-market income provides a means of estimating $\sigma^2(LnY^*)$.[12] The variables indicated by this theory are substituted for σ^2 (LnY^*) in the empirical analysis. By running a linear regression of observed white male income inequality on the percent nonwhite (p), holding constant the effect on income inequality of the distributions of skill and employment, we can test for the presence of white employee discrimination.

Let us speculate about the difference between the two major regions of the country. Suppose tastes against nonwhites are similar in the South and non-South but there is a greater degree of integration (large k) in the non-South.[13] Then there would be a larger effect of percent nonwhite on white income inequality in the non-South. Even if there are weaker tastes for discrimination in the non-South, these weaker tastes need not offset a higher degree of integrated work and may result in the appearance of a larger effect of percent nonwhite on white income inequality.

Alternative Hypotheses and Their Labor-Market Implications

It may be asked if other hypotheses would generate the same predictions. As mentioned in the introduction, capitalists, consumers, and the government may engage in discrimination. If capitalists have a taste for discrimination and against having their capital work with nonwhites, nonwhite workers would have to take a lower wage than white workers in order to work with the discriminators' capital. This creates a wedge between white and nonwhite labor-market income, but it says nothing about the dispersion of labor-market income among whites within skill groups.

The consumer-discrimination hypothesis says that consumers prefer dealing with some workers over others. This hypothesis will predict segregated employment (e.g., nonwhite clerks in nonwhite neighborhoods and white clerks in white neighborhoods, or attractive women as receptionists and less attractive women on the assembly line). For discrimination based on race, the consumer hypothesis does not lead to a prediction of the effect of the presence of nonwhites on the inequality of income among whites. Given competition, wages for a given level of skill will tend to be equal for all whites and unrelated to the proportion of the population that is nonwhite. Also, discrimination by the government offers no prediction as to the correlation between the proportion of the population (or labor force) which is nonwhite and the inequality of labor-market income of whites within skill groups.

The literature on discrimination contains several versions of the effect on incomes expected from the crowding hypothesis.[14] I believe these models fall into one or both of two analytically cleaner hypotheses which I shall call the labor-supply hypothesis and the job-rationing hypothesis. The labor-supply hypothesis implies that the presence of nonwhites increases the income inequality of whites by raising the rate of return from schooling. Let us assume that whites in a state have a given distribution of schooling and nonwhites have lower levels of schooling than whites. The proportion of the labor force which is nonwhite is then highly positively correlated with the proportion of the labor force which has low levels of skill. Unskilled nonwhites and unskilled whites are likely to be closer substitutes for each other than are unskilled nonwhites and skilled whites. Thus an increase in the percentage of nonwhites increases the wages of the skilled relative to the unskilled and, consequently, the rate of return from schooling to whites. This, in turn, increases the white income inequality.[15]

Unlike the employee-discrimination hypothesis, the labor-supply hypothesis offers no prediction as to the effect of nonwhites on the inequality of white income within skill and weeks of employment cells when the rate of return is held constant. In the empirical analysis, the rate of return will be held constant.

The job-rationing hypothesis looks at the distribution of wages within skill levels. Under this hypothesis there is a distribution of wage offerings for each level of skill, and these wage offerings are rationed with whites always receiving the better-paying jobs. As can be seen in Figure 7-1, for a given distribution of wage offerings, the greater the proportion of nonwhites in a skill level, the smaller the income inequality of whites. Also, the greater the percentage of nonwhites, the greater the income inequality of nonwhites within skill levels.

Thus, only one of the alternative hypotheses, namely the job-rationing hypothesis, predicts an effect on the income inequality among white males within skill and employment levels that is related to the percentage of the labor

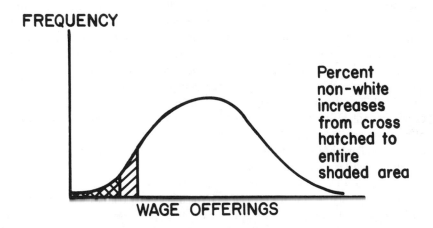

Figure 7-1. Job-Rationing Hypothesis

force that is nonwhite. But this hypothesis predicts lower white income inequality as the percentage of nonwhite increases, rather than greater inequality as predicted by the white-employee discrimination hypothesis.

Nonwhite Employee Discrimination and Labor-Market Implications

We can also develop a test for the hypothesis that nonwhite male workers have a distaste for working with whites. If we use primes to designate variables for nonwhites, a nonwhite's earnings could be described by

$$Y_i' = Y_i^{*'}(1 + d_i'X_i'), \tag{7.6}$$

where d_i' is the wage premium a nonwhite would receive if he works with whites. By taking the logarithm, and then the variance of both sides of Equation (7.6), the variance of the natural log of income of nonwhite adult males, $\sigma^2(LnY')$, is a function of $\sigma^2(d'X')$. As with whites, it is assumed that d' and X' are independent random variables.

Data by state on the distribution of nonwhites working with whites do not exist. It shall, however, be assumed that the percentage of nonwhites in a state working with whites is proportional to the percentage of the population which is white. If the state were entirely nonwhite, no nonwhites would work with whites. Thus it is assumed $\bar{X}' = k'q$, where k' is the nonwhite integration coefficient and q is the percentage of the adult male population which is white ($q = 1 - p$).

Then the nonwhite equivalent of Equation (7.5) is

$$\sigma^2(LnY') = \sigma^2(LnY^{*'}) + k'[(\bar{d}')^2 + \sigma^2(d')]q \tag{7.7}$$
$$- (\bar{d}'k')^2q^2 + U',$$

where the coefficient of q is positive and that of q^2 is negative. Differentiating Equation (7.7) with respect to q indicates that nonwhite income inequality is a declining function of q as long as $\bar{X}' = qk' > (1/2)[1 + CV(d')^2]$, where $CV(d')$ is the coefficient of variation of d'. If $k' = 1$, when a given percentage (e.g., 90 percent) of the population are white, the same percentage (e.g., 90 percent) of nonwhites work with whites. For $k' = 1$, $(\partial\sigma^2(LnY')/\partial q) < 0$ for the states as long as $CV(d')$ is small. Thus income inequality for nonwhites is a declining function of q or a rising function of the proportion of the population nonwhite (p).

By differentiating Equation (7.7) with respect to the nonwhite integration coefficient k' and using arguments similar to those above, one finds that nonwhite income inequality is a declining function of k'.[16] That is, holding tastes for discrimination constant, the inequality of income among nonwhites is smaller, the greater the extent of integration.

The white-employee discrimination hypothesis offers no prediction as to the sign of the slope of percent nonwhite in the function for nonwhite inequality. Similarly, the nonwhite-employee discrimination hypothesis offers no prediction as to the sign of the slope of percent nonwhite in the white income inequality equation.

Summary

Table 7-1 presents a summary of the implications for the partial effect of the variable "percent nonwhite" on the income inequality of whites and of nonwhites. For the white equation, the white-employee discrimination hypothesis predicts a positive slope, and the job-rationing hypothesis predicts a negative slope coefficient. For the nonwhite income inequality relation, the nonwhite-employee discrimination model and the job-rationing model both predict a positive effect of percent nonwhite. Recall that since the rate of return from schooling is to be held constant, the labor-supply effect offers no prediction as to the sign of percent nonwhite.[17] These hypotheses are tested in the next section.

Empirical Analysis

The Data

In this section the white employee, nonwhite employee, and job-rationing models of racial discrimination are tested for white males and nonwhite males using data from the *1960 Census of Population* with the forty-nine coterminous states as the units of observation.[18] We wish to relate the variance of the natural logarithm of labor-market income within schooling, age, and weeks-worked cells to the race composition variable for the states.

Table 7-1
Partial Slope Coefficient of Percent Nonwhite on Income Inequality

Discrimination Hypothesis	White Income Inequality	Nonwhite Income Inequality
White Employee	Positive	Zero
Nonwhite Employee	Zero	Positive
Job Rationing	Negative	Positive

Because of the absence of data on labor-market income, it is the total money income of adult males which is used to compute the dependent variable for each race-state observation.[19] Rather than looking within schooling-age-employment cells, the empirical analysis holds constant the effects on income inequality of interstate differences in the distributions of these variables. In particular, the variables held constant are race-specific values for the rate of return from schooling, mean and variance of schooling and age, covariance of schooling and age, and variance of the natural log of weeks worked.[20]

The race composition variable is the percentage of adult males with income who are nonwhite. Equations (7.5) and (7.7) indicate that p and p^2 should be the explanatory variables for the white and the nonwhite income inequality equations. For the forty-nine states these variables are highly correlated, $R = 0.927$. Thus, p is a good proxy for p^2. Deleting p^2 biases downward the slope coefficient of p and reduces the problem of multicollinearity.[21]

For ten of the thirty-two nonsouthern states, separate data do not exist for nonwhites; thus for these states nonwhites are included in the white data. These ten states (Idaho, Maine, Montana, Nevada, New Hampshire, North Dakota, Rhode Island, Utah, Vermont, and Wyoming) have relatively small nonwhite populations. Two procedures are used to control for this defect in the data. One is the creation of a dummy variable Z which takes the value 1 for the 10 states without separate race data; otherwise, it is zero. The second is the deletion of these states from the data.

North-South differences could affect the results in two ways. If white income inequality is larger (or smaller) in the South for some reason which is not related to discrimination and which is not controlled by the other explanatory variables, this may show up as a positive (or negative) partial slope coefficient of the variable "percent nonwhite" since the proportion of the population nonwhite is larger in the South. Or, if patterns of discrimination differ in the two regions, because of either a different integration coefficient or different market-discrimination coefficients, when other variables are held constant, the slope coefficient of the percent nonwhite may be biased. For these reasons some regressions contain a region dummy variable NSD (where $NSD = 1$ in the South), and other regressions are computed separately for the South and the non-South.

Regression Results

Table 7-2 presents the partial slope coefficients of percent nonwhite when the dependent variables are the income inequality of white and nonwhite adult males.[22] For white males, percent nonwhite has a significant positive effect at the 5 percent level for the country, the non-South, and the South in six of the eight regressions.[23] For the two exceptions, percent nonwhite has a positive and significant effect at a ten percent level. For nonwhite male income inequality the variable "percent nonwhite" is never statistically significant. The regional

Table 7-2
Partial Effect of Percent Nonwhite on Income Inequality[a]

States	White Regression Slope Coefficient (t-Ratio)	Nonwhite Regression Slope Coefficient (t-Ratio)	Number of Observations	Degrees of Freedom
(1) All States	0.1330[b] (1.79)	—	49	40
(2) All States (Z and NSD Entered)	0.1848[b] (2.23)	—	49	38
(3) States with Separate Race Data	0.1061[c] (1.49)	−0.1160 (−1.30)	39	30
(4) States with Separate Race Data (NSD Entered)	0.1426[b] (1.73)	−0.1243 (−1.28)	39	29
(5) All Non-South	0.5872[b] (2.76)	—	32	23
(6) All Non-South (Z Entered)	0.6288[b] (2.54)	—	32	32
(7) Non-South with Separate Race Data	0.5105[c] (1.54)	0.0684 (0.11)	22	13
(8) All South	0.1395[b] (2.96)	−0.1009 (−0.75)	17	8

[a]For full regression results, see Appendix B, available from the author upon request. $Z = 1$ for states without separate race data, otherwise $Z = 0$. $NSD = 1$ for Southern states, otherwise $NSD = 0$.

[b]Significant at 5 percent level, one tailed test.

[c]Significant at 10 percent level, one tailed test.

Source: Appendix A. Both appendixes are available from the author upon request.

dummy variable (NSD) and the control variable Z are never statistically significant.

The white-male analysis indicates that the white-employee discrimination hypothesis can be accepted but by itself does not dismiss the job-rationing hypothesis. The nonwhite-male analysis indicates that neither the job-rationing nor the nonwhite-employee discrimination hypothesis is accepted.[24] Thus the only hypothesis which is consistent with the empirical analysis is based on white-male employee discrimination.

This conclusion is supported by regressions computed for two other formulations of the effect of race composition on income inequality. In the first formulation, p and p^2 were entered as separate variables. For the white income inequality equation the F-ratio for the pair of added variables, p and p^2 , was statistically significant, but because of multicollinearity the coefficients of the separate variables were never significant. In the nonwhite income inequality analysis for the country as a whole and for the South, the separate slope coefficients of p and p^2 were not significant and the F-ratio for the pair of added variables p and p^2 was less than unity. For the non-South nonwhite equation, both p and p^2 were statistically significant, but for the range of the variable p, the effect of race is a reduction of income inequality.[25] In the second formulation the variable $p(1 - p)$ was entered to capture the effects of discrimination.[26] This variable tends to have a positive and significant slope coefficient for white males, but is not significant for nonwhites (see Table 7-3).

Regional Differences

In the white regression equations, the slope coefficient of the variable percent nonwhite appears to be larger in the non-South than in the South.[27] This difference could be due to a lower premium for working with nonwhites ($\overline{d}$), a lower integration coefficient (k), or a larger proportion of nonwhites in the South.[28]

We can gain some insight into the cause of the observed regional difference for white males by comparing the boundaries of the confidence interval for the slope coefficient of p with hypothesized population values for the slope. The lower and upper ends of a 90 percent confidence interval for the slope of p are:[29]

	Lower Bound	Upper Bound
1) All States	0.0070	0.2190
2) Southern States	0.0519	0.2271
3) Non-Southern States	0.2233	0.9511

Hypothesized population values for the slope coefficient of p are computed by differentiating Equation (7.5) with respect to p and hypothesizing alternative

Table 7-3
Partial Effect of $p(1 - p)$ on Income Inequality

States	White Regression Slope Coefficient (t-Ratio)	Nonwhite Regression Slope Coefficient (t-Ratio)	Number of Observations	Degrees of Freedom
All Non-South	0.6462[a] (2.75)	—	32	23
All Non-South (Z Entered)[c]	0.6945[a] (2.53)	—	32	22
Non-South with Separate Race Data	0.5585[b] (1.52)	−0.0646 (−0.10)	22	13
All South	0.2444[a] (2.82)	−0.1571 (−0.51)	17	8

[a]Significant at 2.5 percent level, one tailed test.
[b]Significant at 10 percent level, one tailed test.
[c]$Z = 1$ for states without separate race data, otherwise $Z = 0$.
Source: Appendix A, available upon request.

values for the parameters k, $\bar{d}$ and $\sigma(d)$.[30] Table 7-4 contains hypothesized population values for the United States, the South and the Non-South for $\partial\sigma^2(LnY)/\partial p$, under the assumption that the coefficient of variation of d_i is one-third. The hypothesized values which are within the 90 percent confidence interval computed on the basis of the regression equation are indicated by an asterisk.

For the states as a whole, the observed regression slope is consistent with an integration coefficient of one ($k = 1.0$) and a 10 percent average wage premium paid to whites for working with nonwhites ($\bar{d} = 0.10$). In the South, an integration coefficient of one is consistent with the observed slope coefficient at

Table 7-4

Hypothesized Values for the Effect of Percent Nonwhite on White Income Inequality[a]

	$\bar{d} = 0.05$	$\bar{d} = 0.10$	$\bar{d} = 0.20$	$\bar{d} = 0.30$	$\bar{d} = 0.40$
U.S.					
$k = 0.5$	0.001	0.005	0.021^b	0.046^b	0.081^b
1.0	0.002	0.009^b	0.038^b	0.084^b	0.148^b
1.5	0.003	0.012^b	0.051^b	0.114^b	0.201^b
2.0	0.004	0.015^b	0.061^b	0.135^b	0.239
2.5	0.004	0.016^b	0.067^b	0.149^b	0.262
South					
$k = 0.5$	0.001	0.004	0.019	0.041	0.073
1.0	0.002	0.007	0.030	0.066^b	0.116^b
1.5	0.002	0.008	0.033	0.073^b	0.129^b
2.0	0.002	0.007	0.029	0.063^b	0.111^b
2.5	0.001	0.004	0.017	0.036	0.062^b
Non-South					
$k = 0.5$	0.001	0.005	0.022	0.048	0.085
1.0	0.003	0.010	0.042	0.093	0.164
1.5	0.004	0.015	0.060	0.134	0.237^b
2.0	0.005	0.019	0.077	0.171	0.303^b
2.5	0.006	0.022	0.092	0.205	0.362^b

[a]Hypothesized values computed from the relation $\dfrac{\partial\sigma^2(LnY)}{\partial p} = k[\bar{d}^2 + \sigma^2(d)] - 2\bar{d}^2 k^2 p$, for alternative values of k and $\bar{d}$ under the assumption that the coefficient of variation of d equals one-third. The values of p are 0.09 for all states in the U.S., 0.10 in the South, and 0.04 in the Non-South.

[b]These numbers fall in the 90 percent confidence interval for the population value of the slope coefficient of percent nonwhite (p). The confidence intervals were computed from Table 7-2, rows 1, 5, and 8.

a 30 percent, but not at a 20 percent, wage premium. For the non-Southern States, an integration coefficient of 1.5 and a wage premium of 40 percent are consistent with the observed regression slope for p. Thus it would seem that the regression slope of p obtained for the states as a whole is reasonable. When the data are examined by region, the regression slope may be large for the South, and it appears to be quite large for the non-South. It is not clear why such a large value appears for the non-South slope of percent nonwhite.

Employee Discrimination and Income Inequality

It may be asked, to what extent does the existence of white-employee discrimination increase the income inequality among white males? The data indicate that the mean white income inequality is larger by 2.3 percent in the country as a whole, 3.7 percent in the non-South and 3.1 percent in the South (see Table 7-5). Although these effects are small, they are not insignificant when compared with the stability of personal income inequality over time and with the effects on income inequality of various social policies.[31]

Summary and Conclusion

This chapter is concerned with testing alternative models of labor-market discrimination by looking at the relative inequality of income (i.e., the variance

Table 7-5
Effect of White-Employee Discrimination on White Income Inequality

Regression	Slope Coef. of p	Mean Value of p	Increment in Inequality at Mean	Observed Inequality at Mean	% Increase in Inequality
(1)	(2)	(3)	(4) = (2)x(3)	(5)	(6) = $\frac{(4)}{(5)-(4)}$ x 100
All States (Z and NSD Entered)	0.1848	0.0931	0.0172	0.7764	2.27
State with Separate Race Data (NSD Entered)	0.1426	0.1111	0.0158	0.8005	2.02
All Non-South (Z Entered)	0.6288	0.0403	0.0253	0.7206	3.65
All South	0.1395	0.1924	0.0268	0.8815	3.14

Sources: Column (2) from Table 7-2.
Columns (3) and (5)—see Appendix A (available upon request from the author) and *United States Census of Population: 1960.*

of the log of income) among adult white males and among adult nonwhite males in the coterminous states when the rate of return from schooling, and the distributions of schooling, age, and weeks worked are held constant.

The white-employee discrimination hypothesis under which white workers have a distaste for working with nonwhites is presented. It is shown that, if firms do not view white and nonwhite workers as perfect substitutes, there will be some integration of work forces. White workers of a given skill level will receive higher weekly wages if they work with nonwhites. This creates a component of income inequality within skill levels. Up to some point, the income inequality of whites is larger, the larger the proportion of whites who work with nonwhites. The white-employee discrimination hypothesis predicts a rise in white income inequality as the percentage of the nonwhite labor force increases.

It is also hypothesized that nonwhite male workers have a taste for discrimination against working with whites. This leads to the prediction for the states of a positive partial effect of percent of the labor force nonwhite on the inequality of income among nonwhites.

Several other discrimination models are considered. However, discrimination by capitalists, consumers, and the government all do not appear to lead to a prediction of the effect of the percentage of the adult labor force which is nonwhite on the inequality of income among whites or among nonwhites.

The literature on discrimination contains two versions of the crowding hypothesis. One is a labor-supply hypothesis which says that the greater the proportion of nonwhites in a state, the lower the income of unskilled relative to skilled workers, since nonwhites tend to have lower levels of skill than whites. This predicts a positive correlation of the rate of return from schooling in a state and the percent nonwhite, but does not predict a relation between percent nonwhite and income inequality within skill levels. A measure of the rate of return from schooling is held constant in the empirical analysis. The second form of the crowding hypothesis is the job-rationing hypothesis, which says there is a distribution of wage offerings within skill levels and nonwhites are always given the lowest wages. This predicts a decline in white income inequality and a rise in nonwhite income inequality as the proportion of nonwhites increases.

In the empirical analysis, for the states as a whole, within the South and within the non-South the race variable is positive and significant for white males. This is consistent with the white-employee discrimination hypothesis but does not dismiss the job-rationing hypothesis. In the analysis of nonwhite income inequality, the race variable is not significant. This means that neither the job-rationing nor the nonwhite-employee discrimination hypothesis can be accepted. Thus the data are consistent with the white-employee discrimination hypothesis, but not with the nonwhite-employee discrimination or job-rationing hypotheses.

Notes

1. Arrow, Becker, Bergmann, Edgeworth, Kuznets, Landes, Reich, Thurow (p. 121), Welch, Zellner.

2. Note, however, even if there is no discrimination, if workers are randomly selected, some firms will be racially segregated. If 10 percent of a large pool of workers are nonwhite, a random selection of workers would result in approximately 60 percent of firms with five workers being racially segregated since $(11)^5 + (0.9)^5 = 0.59$.

3. See Becker, p. 59, Arrow, pp. 7-8, and Welch.

4. For a summary of the provisions of state fair-employment laws, see Sovern. For an analysis of the wage and employment effects of fair-employment laws, see Landes.

5. If W is the number of white males in the labor force, W_0 is the number of white males working with nonwhite males, and N is the number of nonwhite males, we can write $k = \bar{X}/p = (W_0/W)/(N/(N+W)) = W_0/W + W_0/N$. The signs of the partial derivatives are $\partial k/\partial W < 0$, $\partial k/\partial W_0 > 0$ and $\partial k/\partial N < 0$. Thus, k can be viewed as an index of labor-market integration.

6. The market-discrimination coefficient is determined by the tastes of the white employee at the margin. White workers with weaker tastes for discrimination will work with nonwhites and receive economic rent. White workers with stronger than market tastes against nonwhites will work only with whites. Only if firms are wage-discriminating monopsonists will workers be paid according to their individual discrimination coefficient rather than the market-discrimination coefficient (d_i).

7. If d_i is small, $Ln(1 + d_i X_i) \cong d_i X_i$.

8. $\sigma^2(X) = E(X^2) - (E(X))^2 = \bar{X} - \bar{X}^2 = kp - (kp)^2$.

9. $\partial \sigma^2 LnY/\partial p = [(\bar{d}^2 + \sigma^2(d)]k - 2(k\bar{d})^2 p > 0$, if $\bar{X} = kp < (1/2)[1 + CV(d)^2]$ where $CV(d)$ is the coefficient of variation of d. This holds if $\bar{X} < 0.5$.

10. $\partial \sigma^2(LnY)/\partial k = [\bar{d}^2 + \sigma^2(d)]p + 2(-\bar{d}^2 p^2)k > 0$ if

$$\bar{X} = pk < 0.5[1 + CV(d)^2].$$

Again, the partial derivative is positive if less than one-half of whites work with nonwhites ($\bar{X} < 0.5$).

11. Since $\partial \sigma^2(LnY)/\partial(\bar{d}^2) = kp - k^2 p^2 = \bar{X} - \bar{X}^2 > 0$ for $\bar{X} < 1$.

12. This research is based on a human-capital framework. The model attributes the distribution of income to the effects of the rate of return from schooling, and the distributions of schooling, age and weeks worked. The model (not including the variable, percent nonwhite) has been shown to explain (R^2) 92 percent of interstate differences in white income inequality and 85 percent of

interstate differences in nonwhite income inequality. See Chiswick (1974). For a time-series application of the model, see Chiswick and Mincer.

13. A greater degree of integration in the non-South could be a consequence of the earlier passage and greater enforcement of fair-employment laws reflecting less discrimination against nonwhites in the political process, or the greater presence of white "minority" groups who would also favor such legislation. A greater degree of integration in the non-South may also be due to historical differences, the larger average size of firms, or differences in industrial structure. We lack empirical research on regional differences in labor-market integration.

14. Bergmann, Bluestone, Edgeworth, Reich, Thurow (p. 121), Zellner.

15. For analyses of the effect of the rate of return on income inequality, see Becker and Chiswick, Chiswick and Mincer, or Chiswick (1974).

16. $\partial \sigma^2 (LnY')/\partial k' < 0$ if $q > [0.5k'] [1 + CV(d)^2]$.

Since in the coterminous states $q > 1/2$, this condition holds approximately when $k' \approx 1$ and $CV(d')$ is small.

17. If the measured rate of return from schooling does not capture all of the labor supply effects, this hypothesis predicts positive partial slopes for the race composition variable in both the white and nonwhite analyses.

18. The District of Columbia is treated as a state. The variables are defined in detail and the data sources are presented in Appendix A, available from the author upon request.

19. This does not cause difficulty in interpreting the results. First, the upper open-end interval of the income variable has $10,000 as the lower bound, and the mean of the interval is estimated by the Pareto equation. The distribution of income among those with large incomes (over $10,000 in 1959) does not affect the results. Second, owners of nonhuman capital need not "live" in the same state as their capital, while owners of labor services can generally be assumed to live and work in the same state. Our model, however, related income distribution among the residents of a state to discrimination in that state. Thus the hypothesis that white capitalists discriminate against nonwhite workers does not predict a positive partial correlation between the percent nonwhite in a state and the measure used here for the inequality of white incomes in that state.

20. The explanatory variables are derived from a general theory of the distribution of labor-market income. See Chiswick and Mincer or Chiswick (1974). The functional form is presented in the tables in Appendix B, which is available from the author upon request.

21. An alternative specification is to assume $k = 1$ and $\sigma^2(d) = 0$, so that Equation (7.5) becomes $\sigma^2(LnY) = \sigma^2(LnY^*) + \overline{d}^2(p - p^2) + U$. In this specification the regression's slope ($\overline{d}^2$) is expected to be positive for the white (nonwhite) equation under the white (nonwhite) employee discrimination hypothesis. This follows for the nonwhite equation because $q - q^2 = p - p^2$. Since p is not greater than 0.5 for any observation, $p - p^2$ changes in the same direction across states as does p.

22. Appendix B, not published here but available upon request from the author, contains the complete regression equations.

23. The small number of degrees of freedom when separate regressions are computed for the regions does raise problems concerning the appropriateness of using Student's t-test, unless it is assumed that the residual is normally distributed.

24. Recall that if the measured rate of return is not capturing the effects of the labor-supply hypothesis, this hypothesis predicts a positive slope of percent nonwhite for both the white and nonwhite equations. The slope in the nonwhite equation is usually negative and never significant. Thus it is concluded that the labor-supply hypothesis is not operating on the slope coefficient of percent nonwhite in the white income inequality regression.

25. The partial equation is, $\sigma^2 (LnY) = \ldots -5.03p + 49.27p^2$.

(t-ratios in parentheses)   (2.56)   (2.68)

For the twenty-two nonsouthern states, p ranges from 0.01 to 0.09 with a mean of 0.05.

26. This assumes $k = 1$ and $\sigma^2(d) = 0$. See note 21.

27. The Student t-ratio for the difference in the slope coefficient of p between the non-South and the South for white males was for the South (seventeen states) compared with (1) all non-South (thirty-two states) 2.05, (2) all non-South (Z entered) 1.94, and (3) non-South with separate race data (twenty-two states) 1.11. See Table 7-2.

28. The slope coefficient of p is biased downward by the exclusion of p^2, and the downward bias is greater the larger is p. This problem could not be mitigated by including p^2 because of the small sample size and high correlation between p and p^2.

29. The confidence intervals were computed from the data in Table 7-2, rows 1, 5, and 8.

30. $\partial \sigma^2 (LnY)/\partial p = k [\overline{d}^2 + \sigma^2(d)] - 2\overline{d}^2 k^2 p$.

31. For example, for adult males in the country as a whole, the change from the current distribution of schooling to a uniform level of schooling of sixteen years would decrease income inequality by only 9.4 percent. For a time-series analysis of the inequality of income and alternative scenarios, see Chiswick and Mincer.

References

[1] Arrow, K. *Some Models of Racial Discrimination in the Labor Market*. Rand Corporation Memorandum, February 1971.

[2] Becker, G.S. *The Economics of Discrimination*. 2nd ed. Chicago: University of Chicago Press, 1971.

[3] Becker, G.S., and Chiswick, B.R. "Education and the Distribution of Earnings." *American Economic Review, Proceedings* (May 1966), pp. 358-69.

[4] Bergmann, B.R. "The Effects on White Incomes of Discrimination in Employment." *Journal of Political Economy* (March/April 1971), pp. 294-313.

[5] Bluestone, B. "Personal Earnings Distribution: Individual and Institutional Determinants." Paper presented at Econometric Society Meeting, December 1971.

[6] Chiswick, B.R., and Mincer, J. "Time Series Changes in Personal Income Inequality in the United States from 1939, with Projections to 1985," *Journal of Political Economy*, Supplement (May/June 1972), pp. 34-66.

[7] Chiswick, B.R. *Income Inequality: Regional Analyses within a Human Capital Framework* (New York: National Bureau of Economic Research, forthcoming 1974).

[8] Edgeworth, F.Y., "Equal Pay to Men and Women for Equal Work," *Economic Journal* (December 1922), pp. 431-57.

[9] Goodman, L. "On the Exact Variance of a Product," *Journal of the American Statistical Association* (December 1960), pp. 708-13.

[10] Kuznets, S. "Economic Structure of U.S. Jewry: Recent Trends." Mimeo, June 1971.

[11] Landes, W. "The Economics of Fair Employment Laws." *Journal of Political Economy* (July/August 1968), pp. 507-52.

[12] Reich, M. "Racial Discrimination and the White Income Distribution." Paper presented at Econometric Society Meeting, December 1971.

[13] Sovern, M.I. *Legal Restraints on Racial Discrimination in Employment*. New York: Twentieth Century Fund, 1966.

[14] Thurow, L. *Poverty and Discrimination*. Washington: Brookings, 1969.

[15] Welch, F. "Labor Market Discrimination: An Interpretation of Income Differences in the Rural South." *Journal of Political Economy* (June 1967), pp. 225-240.

[16] Zellner, H. "Discrimination against Women, Occupational Segregation, and the Relative Wage." *American Economic Review, Proceedings* (May 1972), pp. 157-60.

8

The Economic Basis of Employee Discrimination

Duran Bell, Jr.*

The relatively poor earnings and occupational position of black male workers in the American economy has proven to be rather intractable to public-policy initiatives. In part this intractability may be due to the rather limited extent to which policymakers and the society as a whole have dealt with the matter. Additionally, however, it may be the case that we do not understand the problem sufficiently well, and that policies to change the chronically second-class position of black workers have been *inefficient*, as well as inadequate.

The purpose of this chapter is to consider a model of employee discrimination which rests upon empirically relevant assumptions about labor markets and the options available to employers. The model demonstrates the implications of employee discrimination for task segregation and wage discrimination within occupations; and it shows the conditions under which an employer may profitably integrate an occupational category within his firm.

The most noteworthy findings of this chapter are that employee discrimination may imply (a) that the opportunities of black workers to enter previously proscribed occupations depend largely upon the excess demand for white workers, (b) that white workers who work with black workers will have higher money earnings than other white workers in the same occupation (although all white workers in the occupation may be absolutely worse off in terms of money income); (c) that there exists not only an optimal black-white ratio in those firms which decide to integrate, but also an equilibrium number of integrating firms; and (d) that the conclusions of the conventional model of employee discrimination are valid only under very special conditions.

It is important to understand employee discrimination and its implications. White workers are the most obvious beneficiaries of employment discrimination. Their gains from discrimination are real and need not be eroded by tendencies toward competitive market equilibrium nor by greater recognition of the "true" productive capacities of black workers. Hence, if white workers are able to effectively express their economic interests in the labor market, the second-class position of black workers may remain chronic in the absence of specific countermeasures.

The fact that certain classes of white workers have much to lose from the elimination of discrimination has been made clear by Bergmann.[1] Bergmann's

---

*Associate professor of economics, University of California at Irvine; the Rand Corporation.

121

study indicates that the effect of discrimination on white incomes is not great when all workers are considered, but becomes very significant for lesser-educated white workers whose short-run loss would be 6 to 9 percent of income if they lost their preferential job access. The magnitude of the average loss to *all* white workers is irrelevant to the reaction of individuals. In the context of actual social behavior, each group of white workers protects its work place from black entry. The threat posed by black workers is especially great since the racial barriers to most occupational positions give rise to a "crowding" of those occupations into which blacks may gain entrance.

A reading of the history of black labor in the United States makes quite clear the significant role of white workers in protecting jobs from intrusion by black workers.[2] The objective of white workers has seldom been to exclude black workers from the workplace *as such*. Indeed, amicable on-the-job interaction of black and white workers has been the norm, not the exception. Difficulties have arisen primarily when black workers have been offered jobs for which there is a sufficient, or excess, supply of white workers. Such offers tended to precipitate strikes and riots during the nineteenth century, before a racialist occupational structure was institutionalized. Hence, it may be argued that it is not an "aversion to associating" with black workers which has been operative, but an effort to maintain a racially segmented occupational structure wherein white workers possess special access to jobs with higher wages and status.[3]

Since the option of an all-black work force is seldom available to a firm of moderate size, or to one which requires a wide range of skills, the attitudes of white workers cannot be ignored easily. George von Furstenberg has shown[4] that employee-motivated discrimination poses a far more intractable problem for corrective policy than employer-motivated discrimination. For even if the employer is totally indifferent to race, the existence of racist attitudes within his work force implies that the hiring of black workers could significantly raise the costs of production. Workers can openly resist a nondiscriminatory policy; they may exhibit higher turnover rates and absenteeism; and they may openly demand the maintenance of established black-white status relationships. According to Bergmann, "the fears of white employees may in turn be the principal incentive to white employers, concerned about the morale of their present employees and the stability of their present arrangements, to stand pat or move very slowly in the matter of integration."[5]

This chapter presents a model of employee discrimination. The perspective of our model differs from that which is common in the literature in that it takes the existing distribution of workers among industries and occupations as given and focuses attention upon the factors which may induce, or limit, changes in the existing structure. Most previous studies of racial discrimination have accepted the premises of Becker's model[6] which imply that, at any time, firms can make decisions about the composition of their work force *ab initio*. While such models have interesting properties, they can hardly be used to study the dynamics of change in actual structures.

The existing structure has two very important consequences for the *evolution* of industrial and occupational positions held by blacks and whites: (a) If black workers have been systematically excluded from a particular occupation, there may be no black workers who (by specific training) immediately "qualify" for the occupation, except at the "entry level." Hence, if an employer seeks to hire blacks into a hitherto proscribed type of work, he may be forced to proceed slowly. And (b), since there are already white workers employed by the firm, the employer cannot act with total indifference to their desire to maintain the racial exclusiveness of certain occupations, unless he cannot only replace whites with blacks in the particular occupation, but in many other occupations, as well. Moreover, since an employer is likely to have made valuable investments in his present (white) workers, he will be reluctant to part with them in response to moderate or temporary wage differentials.[7]

The ability of white workers to exert pressure and to impose costs upon the employer in response to the "threat" of hiring black workers does not depend upon open collusion. The disaffection of each worker, *individually*, may have a dampening effect upon overall productivity and may give rise to higher turnover rates. Collusion among white workers to oppose entry of black workers is more likely to result in the continued exclusion of blacks from the occupation. Our model, however, permits limited black entry in a manner most likely to arise when white workers, as individuals, are made to accede to a policy of integration.

The basic result of the Becker and related models is that the existence of employee discrimination leads to market segregation without price discrimination, because if blacks and whites are perfect substitutes in production it is cheaper for a given employer to select an all-white, or an all-black, labor force rather than a mixture of the two. This conclusion was modified by Becker to allow an integrated work force, provided black and white workers are to some extent complementary in production. In this case, the extra costs associated with placing both types of workers into one work place can be absorbed by the increased marginal value productivity of white workers.[8]

Our model, however, is one in which *integrated occupations* may arise in the presence of employee discrimination. It will be shown that this result is a consequence of our assumption that the market for white labor is tight, so that as firms seek to expand their labor force during a period of rising production, it may be cheaper to hire surplus black workers even if their presence raises the cost of white workers. Hence, the assumption of a tight market for white labor is analogous to the assumption of complementarity in the Becker model in that both may produce integration. However, the assumption of tight labor markets is important to the empirical relevance of the model and is not made for the sake of analytic convenience. Considerable historical evidence indicates that it has been during periods of strong economic expansion that black workers have been able to obtain entry into new occupations.

When labor markets are not tight for white workers, our model suggests that black workers will experience little if any access to previously proscribed occupations. Moreover, the possibility of access would depend upon the existence of a significant wage differential at the *entry level*, whereas such a differential is not required when white labor markets are tight.

The Model

The model to be considered here emerges from the problem which faces an employer who seeks to hire minority workers into his firm in spite of opposition from white workers. The employer's motivation for changing his ethnic ratio is not relevant, so long as he has some discretion about the matter.

Even in the case of "affirmative action" programs which became common during the 1960s, the external pressure to hire minorities was seldom definitive. When subjected to a specific type of pressure, not all firms in a given industry adopted minority programs or pursued them with equal vigor. Hence, public or private pressure to change ethnic ratios simply introduce a new parameter into the employment process but leave considerable degrees of freedom for managerial decision.

The first basic assumption of this model is that one of the critical factors affecting the firm's decision to pursue a minority recruitment program is the extent to which such a program reduces labor costs. The second assumption is that within a given firm all white workers in a specific occupation will require "bribes," or job-status augmentation, in order to accept black workers in that same occupation.

Status augmentation may require that white workers receive a modest differential in responsibility, special access to overtime pay, and perhaps different wage rates at the same responsibility level. Let B and W denote the number of black and white workers in a given occupation, respectively, so that total labor input, L, is given by the identity, $L = B + W$. Then a bribe, or white status maintenance function, $g(W/L)$, can be defined. Assume that the bribe required for a change in the initial percentage of whites in the labor force, r, depends upon the difference $(r - W/L)$, so that

$$g(W/L) = f(W/L)(r - W/L)$$

where $f(W/L)$ is the average bribe per white worker, per unit decrease in W/L.

If the employer knows the bribe function of white workers, it should be possible for him to neutralize white opposition to the integration of an occupation, *leaving the white worker indifferent to the presence of black workers*. This bribe function defines a kind of "discrimination coefficient" in the Becker sense, but it does not depend upon "distaste for association" but upon economic (status) variables.

When there is unemployment among white workers, the required bribe may become unreasonably large, since the hiring of black workers for a task desired by unemployed whites defies a basic characteristic of the black-white job status access system.[9] However, when white labor markets are tight, the bribe function may be such that the employer can pay the bribe and *still* effect cost savings by hiring black workers. Moreover, if the occupation is a relatively lowly one, the demand by whites for those jobs may be less intense, and the bribe function will be lower. Hence, the opportunities for employers to effect cost reducing job integration will depend upon the status level of the particular job and the tightness of the relevant labor market.

A tight labor market imposes very special burdens upon the firm, for it is not possible to hire any desired number of workers at the going wage. Rather, each worker must be located and bid away from his current employment so that even at the firm level, the slope of the occupational supply curve is positive.

If there are n identical firms which hire persons of a given occupation, and if these firms are all increasing their labor forces at the same rate, then the supply curve of the occupation is directly related to that of each firm. Let (α/n) be the slope of the occupational supply function, and let nW' be the number of additional white workers hired (where each firm hires W'), then the market effect $(\alpha/n)(nW')$ must equal the increase in wage rates for each firm, $\alpha W'$. Hence, α is the slope of the firm's labor supply function, given the identical and simultaneous activity of other firms.

The critical parameters of the model are listed below:

1. The slopes of the firm's black and white labor supply functions are γ and α, respectively.
2. The bribe function, $g(W/L) = f(W/L)(r - W/L)$, is a monotonically increasing function of $(r - W/L)$.
3. There may be wage discrimination, over and above that which arises from job-status differentiation. The wage differential is called $D_\mu - \mu_w - \mu_b$, where μ_w is the initial white wage rate net of special bribes.

The task of the model is to derive an expansion path of the firm's ethnic ratio, given an initial wage rate μ_w for the initial W_0 white workers. If the white labor market is tight, the hiring of additional whites implies paying higher wages to them, and the hiring of blacks requires the bribing of those whites already hired.

The cost of white workers will be μ_w plus the wage inflation which results from the tight labor market. Hence, for each firm, the total cost of all white workers in the specific occupation will be

$$C(W) = (\mu_w + \alpha(W - W_0))W, \qquad (8.1)$$

where W_0 is the initial number of whites in the specific job category.

The cost of black workers must take into consideration the required compensation to whites; and when B exceeds B_s the black labor market becomes tight in the sense that increasing the number of black workers requires a wage rate greater than μ_b, so that

$$C(B) = \begin{cases} \mu_b B + g(W/L)W, & \text{for } B \leqslant B_s \\[2mm] (\mu_b + \gamma(B - B_s))B + g(W/L)W, & \text{for } B \geqslant B_s. \end{cases} \qquad (8.2)$$

Since the employer seeks to minimize the cost of expanding his labor force, he will hire only blacks into the job category, with whites receiving wage and status augmentation, so long as the difference between the marginal cost of promoting whites and moving up the white supply function is less than the wage differential. Starting from an all white position ($r = 1$), the first order condition is obtained by setting $C_w'(W) \geqslant C_b'(B)$:

$$D_\mu \geqslant f_b'(W/L)(1 - W/L)W + f(W/L)(W/L)^2 - 2\alpha(W - W_0/2). \qquad (8.3)$$

This gives us a general principle, but tells us little about the path of the ethnic ratio as the labor force expands. Before presenting a detailed elaboration of the process, it may be useful to obtain an overview of the labor-force expansion path implied by this model. See Figure 8-1.

For diagrammatic simplicity, assume that black and white workers have identical supply functions ($\alpha = \gamma$), and that $\mu_w > \mu_b$. Then, at the beginning of the process, there are W_0 white workers in the relevant occupation in the typical firm and no black workers. This is a disequilibrium situation if the bribe function is not too steep, and the firm begins to hire black workers. The disequilibrium arises from two factors: (a) the decision to integrate an occupation is a major policy decision, not made on the basis of simple marginal calculations; and (b) the firm will wish to delay its decision until the new labor supply situation seems to be long term in nature.

It can be shown that in the case of a linear bribe function, where $f(W/L) = \rho L/W$, it will remain optimal to hire *only* black workers until $B = B_s$. However, if the bribe function is rising at an increasing rate with L/W, it may be optimal to begin to hire *both* black and white workers after B reaches some value less than B_s. Regardless of the shape of the bribe function, the firm will suspend its recruitment of black workers when $B = B_s$ because the marginal cost of hiring black workers is suddenly greater than that of hiring additional white workers, given the bribe function. The firm then hires only white workers until some point, W_s, before beginning again to hire both black and white workers.

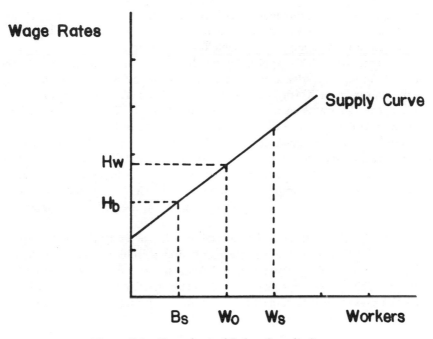

Figure 8-1. Hypothetical Labor Supply Curve

A Special Case

In this chapter we shall restrict our consideration to the case where white workers require a bribe that goes up at an increasing rate as the ethnic ratio B/W increases

$$f(W/L) - \rho L^2/W. \tag{8.4}$$

Since $L^2/W = W[1 + 2B/W + (B/W)^2]$, it is also assumed that the bribe is increasing with the number of whites per firm in a given occupation. The other nonlinear bribe function for which we have been able to obtain reasonably simple explicit results involves the strictly quadratic form, $f(W/L) = \rho(L/W)^2$, which does not contain such scale effects. The nonlinear form employed here has an important peculiarity, relative to the other specifications. This peculiarity will be indicated when "the importance of D_μ" is discussed in a later section.

Others have suggested to the author that a bribe function should be considered which allows whites to "learn to like" black workers so that at some point the price of the bribe may *fall* as a function of (L/W). However, we shall not consider any changes in attitudes or tastes in this model, since such changes can have an infinite variety of reasonable forms. Rather, it shall be assumed that the bribe function which is appropriate at the point of initial black recruitment will hold throughout. Hence, only those bribe functions which are linear or strictly convex seem worthy of serious consideration. Any exogenous factors which affect the status maintenance requirements of white workers may be presumed to affect the value of ρ, rather than the shape of the function.

It will not be assumed that all firms which hire people into a given occupation will adopt minority recruitment plans. Rather (an employment weighted) x (100) percent refuse to do so. Hence, the slope of the labor supply function facing those who are recruiting black workers will be $(1 - x)\gamma$, and the average number of black workers which each firm can hire at the initial black wage, μ_b, will be $(1/1 - x)B_s$.

Finally, it will be assumed that the labor force of every firm grows at the same rate and that whenever an integrating firm recruits a black worker, the segregated firm recruits a white worker. (We are ignoring the employment effect of the—possibly—lower wage paid to blacks.) Hence, the wages of whites will rise in all firms, even though some firms are hiring only blacks. The cost of white workers in the *integrating* firms is

$$C(W;x) = [\mu_w + \alpha(W - W_0)]W + \alpha(xB)W. \qquad (8.5)$$

The first term on the right-hand side of (8.5) is the cost of hiring whites when all firms are hiring whites. This term is still appropriate because when the integrating firm hires whites, all firms are doing so. The second element in (8.5) reflects the fact that the segregated firms hire white workers *whenever* the integrated firms hire blacks. The effect on white wages which results from the peculiar activity of segregated firms is weighted by x, the proportion of such firms.

The cost of black workers in the integrating firms depends upon the tightness of the market for black workers and reflects the bribe costs which are required to maintain the relative status of white workers:

$$\mu_b B + (\rho/W)L^2(1 - W/L)W, \qquad \text{for } B < B_s(1 - x)^{-1}$$

$$C(B; W_0) = (\mu_b + \gamma(1 - x)(B - B_s(1 - x)^{-1}))B \qquad (8.6)$$

$$+ (\rho/W)L^2(1 - W/L)W, \qquad \text{for } B \geqslant B_s(1 - x)^{-1}.$$

Initially, the market for black labor is not tight and the marginal cost of hiring will be for white workers:

$$C'(W) = \mu_w + 2\alpha(W - W_0/2) + \alpha x B. \tag{8.7}$$

and, using $W_0 + B = L$, it will be for black workers

$$C'(B) = \mu_b + \rho(L + B) = \mu_b + \rho(2L - W_0). \tag{8.8}$$

Hence, the hiring of black workers is the least cost alternative if

$$D_\mu \geqslant \rho(2L - W_0) - \alpha(W_0 + xB). \tag{8.9}$$

When the above inequality holds, the "integrating" firms hire only B until (8.9) becomes an equality. The value of B at that point is called $B(W_0)$:

$$B(W_0) = \frac{D_\mu + W_0(\alpha - \rho)}{2\rho - \alpha x}. \tag{8.10}$$

After $B(W_0)$ is reached, the firm hires B and W in such a way as to maintain the equality of $C'(W)$ and $C'(B)$, so that, substituting $L = W + B$,

$$B(W) = \frac{D_\mu + W(2\alpha - \rho) - \alpha W_0}{2\rho - \alpha x}; \tag{8.11}$$

and the ratio of blacks to whites that the integrating firm hires is $B/W = (2\alpha - \rho)/(2\rho - \alpha x)$. This ratio, or quota, continues until $B(W)$ approaches $B_s/(1 - x)$, at which point the supply of blacks who will work for μ_b per hour has been exhausted.

The integrating firms, after hiring all blacks who are available at μ_b, discover that the hiring of additional blacks requires giving them higher wages than before and that, given this fact, the best ratio of blacks to whites is given by:

$$B(\gamma, W) = \frac{D_\mu + W(2\alpha - \rho) - \alpha W_0 + \gamma B_s}{(2\rho - \alpha x) + 2\gamma(1 - x)} \tag{8.12}$$

This new value of B is less than the actual value, so that the firm must hire only W until the actual value becomes optimal. That is, *the firm suspends its black recruitment policy* until after it has hired $(W_s - W_u)$ new white workers. See Figure 8-2. The suspension of black recruitment after $B = B_s/(1 - x)$ may be interpreted as a "shortage of qualified applicants" (at the substandard wage μ_b). *Rather than pay a little more to blacks, the firm is willing to pay much more for additional white workers.* All of this is a consequence of the access-status requirements imposed upon the employer by his white employees.

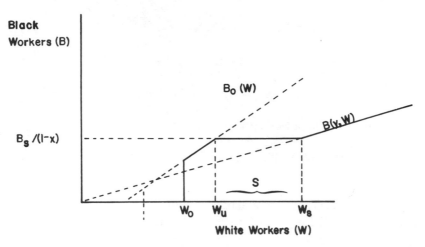

Figure 8-2. Expansion Path of Participating Firm

The Importance of D_μ

The existence of a positive wage differential, $D_\mu \geq 0$, is clearly not crucial to the above results. This differential simply exerts an upward shift on $B(W)$ and $B(\gamma, W)$.

However, if there is some unemployment among white workers, then α may go to zero and $D_\mu > 0$ may become a necessary condition for $B > 0$. Furthermore, it is interesting to note that when α approaches zero, the opportunities of black workers are severely limited, even when large wage differentials are posited and ρ is held fixed, though ρ is in fact likely to be much larger when white workers are unemployed.

For simplicity, assume that $\alpha = 0$, $x = 0$, and $D_\mu > 0$, so that

$$B(W) = \frac{D_\mu - \rho W}{2\rho}$$

$$B(\gamma, W) = \frac{D_\mu + \gamma B_s - \rho W}{2(\gamma + \rho)}. \tag{8.13}$$

Note that these functions suggest that only those occupations with few workers, where $D_\mu/\rho > W_0$, will begin a minority recruitment campaign in this case, and that very few black workers will be hired. By contrast, had the bribe function been in the linear or purely quadratic form, the percentage of black to white workers hired would have been independent of the size factor, W_0.

It can be concluded that in the absence of tight labor markets for white workers, the employment of black workers in previously proscribed occupations depends upon the existence of a significant wage differential. Moreover, as employment expands in the integrated firms, these firms either reduce, or hold fixed, the number of black workers.

Who Gains and Who Loses

It can be seen that the monetary loss of each white worker in the integrated firm is approximately $[\alpha(1 - x) - \frac{\rho L}{W}]$ for each black worker hired.[10] This loss is the difference between the increase in the wage rate which would have taken place with greater exclusion of black workers and the bribe paid to whites per black worker. Unless this loss is positive, the recruitment of black workers was not a cost-reducing strategy.

The psychic (status) loss associated with the presence of black workers in the same occupation (and firm) has presumably been compensated for via the bribe function. This is especially true if all whites have the same need for status maintenance, relative to black workers. However, if there is a set of bribe functions, described (say), by allowing ρ to take on a range of values, then some white workers may suffer an uncompensated psychic loss. Some of these white workers may quit and join segregated firms; they should have no difficulty in doing so, given the tight labor market. However, in the segregated firms, the effect of B upon the white wage rate is felt equally (by assumption) and there is no bribe to mollify this loss. Hence, each worker in the segregated firm loses $\alpha(1 - x)B$ per hour.

Finally, there are white workers who work in neither the segregated, nor the integrated firms, but would have done so had black workers not been hired. In the absence of black workers, they would have earned $\mu_w + \alpha(L - W_0)$. Instead, these workers must accept lower wages or less desirable working conditions in other occupations.

Although all white workers in the occupation lose, the loss will be inversely related to the number of black workers with whom they work. As the number of blacks recruited into the occupation increases, the average wage rate in the occupation falls, but the absolute size of the bonus increases in the integrated firm, so that the recruitment program should create a growing gap between the wages of whites in segregated and integrated firms. This gap has the value $B[\rho L/W]$.

All employers will gain from minority recruitment, including those who maintain segregated occupations. Those who recruit minorities will gain the amount lost by their white workers (and potential white workers) *minus* the wages paid to blacks. However, the owners of segregated firms also gain. Note that the firm which recruits blacks pays the same wages to white workers as do other firms *plus a bribe*, but benefits from the recruitment of blacks to a degree which depends on the number of black workers recruited. The segregated firm avoids paying ρLB to its white workers but is penalized by having to pay an additional cost, $[D_\mu + \alpha x B] B$, for hiring B more white rather than black workers. The segregated firm *gains more* than the desegregated firm if

$$B[D_\mu + \alpha x B] < (\rho LB). \tag{8.14}$$

Assume $D_\mu = 0$. Then (8.14) implies that segregated firms gain more when $(L/B) > \alpha x/\rho$. Unfortunately, this condition is easily satisfied. Only in very tight labor markets where ρ is small and α is large may we expect the greater gains from integration to accrue to the integrating firms. This follows from the fact that (L/B) is necessarily no less than unity, while αx may approach zero.

It is particularly unfortunate that the differential advantage to the segregated firm is greater when there are few of them. That is, a segregationist "hold-out" has much to gain. This is the case because if more firms integrate, the pressure on white labor markets is weakened, making whites a relatively better bargain.

These results hold for the linear and (strictly) quadratic bribe function as well. In the linear case, segregated firms gain more from integration when $1 > \alpha x/\rho$ and in the quadratic case when $(L/WB) > \alpha x/\rho$. Regardless of the shape of the bribe function, the relative position of integrating firms is lower when the number of integrating firms is larger.

The paradox implied by this result uncovers a weakness in the model, as presented: x is a parameter, not a variable which each individual firm may observe. That is, we have assumed that there are two types of firms, those that decide to integrate (as a group) and those that do not. This is not a realistic assumption.

In an atomistic context, the value of x will change gradually. When $x = 1$, the relative advantage of integration is maximal and some firms may be induced to hire black workers. As x falls, the inducement to each additional firm decreases, so that the eventual value of x should not be less than that which makes the firm indifferent between integration and segregation.

In order to consider probable values of x, assume that for each firm which integrates, B is set equal to $B(W_0)$. Then we may find the value of x which makes it *just* worthwhile to integrate. Setting $D_\mu = 0$, we have

$$B(W_0) = \frac{W_0(\alpha - \rho)}{2\rho - \alpha x}. \tag{8.15}$$

so that $(L/B) = \alpha x^*/\rho$ implies that $x^* \equiv \rho(\alpha + \rho)/\alpha^2$. If $\rho \sim \alpha$, then $x^* > 1$ and no firm integrates. If $4\rho = \alpha$, then $x^* = 5/16$ and the majority of firms may integrate. Similar boundary points may be found using the other bribe functions.

It appears, then, that in competitive equilibrium, there is no (profit) gain to the firms which integrate. This is true regardless of the distribution of black workers among the industries which hire a specific occupation.

In actual fact the entrance of black workers into a given occupation is not likely to be important to the relative profit positions of firms unless the specific job category is large relative to the firm's labor force. Hence, construction firms, which typically hire persons in only a few categories, are more likely to be sensitive to the process of occupational integration than diversified manufacturing concerns.

Implications of the Model

The most important characteristic of this model is that it demonstrates the likelihood of integrated occupations within firms in spite of employee discrimination. The demonstration was accomplished through the use of assumptions which we consider to be of greater empirical relevance than those in the Becker model. Employee discrimination is also shown to require wage discrimination (or, perhaps, special overtime privileges for white workers, or some other kinds of prerequisites), but does not necessarily require different wage rates at the entry level.

It is also true that employee discrimination can lead to occupational segregation. When white labor markets are not tight and/or the bribe functions are too steep, employers will not find it profitable to place black workers into certain occupations. This result is similar to the results of conventional models which implicitly assume that white labor markets are never tight.

These findings have special importance given the troublesome inconsistency between the persistence of employer discrimination and competitive equilibrium. While a number of models may be devised to circumvent this apparent inconsistency, the issue loses its urgency when one realizes that *employees*—who are not known to be less discriminatory than employers—are able to effect both segregation and wage discrimination within the labor market.

The model demonstrates the fact that all white workers in an occupation will suffer lower earnings as a result of black entry including those whites who are bribed to work with blacks. Finally, we have shown that there exists not only a set of optimal black/white ratios in the firms which seek to integrate, but that there is also an equilibrium fraction of firms which integrate; and this faction may lie between zero and unity.

While our model of the employment process has several novel features, it can be seen quite accurately as a refinement of Donald Dewey's "laws" of racial patterns: (1) "Negro workers seldom hold jobs which require them to give orders to White workers," and (2) "Negro and White workers do not ordinarily work side by side at the same job."[11] We are amending Dewey by suggesting that black and white workers may work side by side in the same job, but that white workers will exact a price for that relationship. The real meaning of this price is not only that white workers maintain a status differential, but that they also have prior rights to desired occupational opportunities.

Our results also relate to the crowding hypothesis, as propounded by Bergmann. The crowding hypothesis is largely a description of the structure of the labor market but fails to delineate the underlying processes and motivations. The existence of bribe functions supplies the required explication of that model.

Finally, the prominence of employee discrimination has implications for public policies to improve the relative economic position of minority workers:

1. A subsidy to induce segregated firms to integrate would be inequitable, since the reduction of x to a point less than x^* imposes costs upon all integrated firms. Only by reducing ρ relative to α can the benefits of integration be available to all integrated firms on an equitable basis. On the other hand, if $x > x^*$, then additional integration is profitable and further monetary inducement would be undesirable.
2. A full-employment economy is essential in that it lowers the bribe function and raises the effective slope of the white supply function. Both factors induce autonomous efforts by firms to hire black workers into new job categories.
3. In order to encourage the entry of blacks into "higher" occupations, efforts to reduce the bribe function should be made. A resolute attitude by government enforcement agencies will be of indispensable help by conveying to white workers that change must come immediately and that this change will be universal.
4. Detailed studies at the work-place level should be encouraged, so that the many subtle methods by which white workers exact bribes from employers and place barriers before black workers may be fully understood.

Notes

1. Barbara R. Bergmann, "The Effect on White Incomes of Discrimination in Employment," *Journal of Political Economy* (March/April 1971), 294-313.

2. See especially, Charles H. Wesley, *Negro Labor in the United States, 1850-1925* (New York: Russell and Russell, 1927, rev. ed., 1967), and Vernon L. Wharton, *The Negro in Mississippi 1865-1890* (New York: Harper and Row, 1947, reissued 1965).

3. Alexis has shown that the assumption of an "aversion to association" is not required in order to derive the results of Gary Becker's analysis. However, Alexis was primarily concerned with employer-motivated discrimination. See Marcus Alexis, "A Theory of Labor Market Discrimination with Interdependent Utilities," *American Economic Review, Proceedings* (May 1973), pp. 296-302.

4. See George M. von Furstenberg, "A Model of Optimal Plant Integration in the Presence of Employee Discrimination," *Review of Regional Studies* (Spring 1972), pp. 72-85. Furstenberg shows how assumptions about the shape of the worker's racial preference functions affect the likelihood of integration within firms and occupations.

5. Barbara R. Bergmann, ibid., p. 295.

6. Gary Becker, *The Economics of Discrimination* (Chicago: University of Chicago Press, 1957).

7. I would like to thank Barry Chiswick for suggesting this point.

8. See Barry R. Chiswick's study, "Racial Discrimination in the Labor Market: A Test of Alternative Hypotheses," in this volume. Chiswick estimated the effect of black workers on the wage rates of white workers under the assumption of (partial) complementarity.

9. M. Alexis, "A Theory of Labor," has suggested that the managers may be willing to cooperate with white workers in their desire to preserve the relative economic status of the white community. See also Alexis' study in this volume.

10. The average bribe per white worker in integrated firms is $(\rho/W) L^2 (1 - W/L) = \rho(L/W)B$. Increasing B, and hence L, by one unit raises the bribe per white worker by $\rho(L + B)/W$, which is approximated by $\rho L/W$ for small B. The psychic loss associated with the presence of black workers is presumably fully covered by the bribe price, but the net monetary loss may not be apparent to the worker.

11. Donald Dewey, "Negro Employment in Southern Industry," *Journal of Political Economy* (August 1952), p. 283.

Tinker Toys and Model-building: Some Critical Thoughts

Bradley R. Schiller*

Perhaps introductory textbooks are a poor index to the state of mind of the economics profession. Nevertheless, it seems worthy of note that virtually every principles textbook now on the market starts out with a defensive exposition on the relevancy of economics. The defenders of our profession nearly always point with assertive pride to the great concern of economists with the problems of poverty and discrimination. These important social problems, students are informed, are ones about which economists have a great deal to say.

Given the critical position which the problems of poverty and discrimination play in our profession's defenses, some may wish to view the Conference on Racial Discrimination as a litmus test of social relevancy. Assembled in Bloomington were those economists whose work and interests have reportedly demonstrated the relevancy of economics to the pressing issues of our day. What then did this avant-garde have to say?

In the interest of protecting the innocent and guilty alike, I shall try not to single out the contributions of particular conference participants, although this will be unavoidable when I discuss the two chapters (7 and 8) on which I was asked to comment. One might begin to acquire a nonparametric "taste" for the orientation of the conference, however, by reviewing the empirical content of the papers presented. There are, to be sure, more than the usual quota of empirical tables and some intensive disaggregate studies in the earlier parts of this volume, and these do suggest great concern for relevancy. Nevertheless, one may still question the significance and use to which some of these numbers have been put.

To begin with, there is a disconcerting tendency for all empirical fact-finding efforts to stop at the highest level of aggregation. There is an ample supply of data, for example, about the relative position of blacks on a *national* basis, and extended analyses of observed trends and nontrends. But does anyone really think that all of the components of such national averages move together or that their movements are conditioned on identical forces? In the one chapter that initiated the most elementary inquiry into the component parts of such averages, the author concluded that different age, sex, and regional populations within each race classification experienced markedly different relative income patterns. That suggests to me that we may be learning less, not more, from studies that

*Assistant professor of economics, University of Maryland.

consider and analyze only national trends, and that the relevancy of associated policy implications is seriously suspect.

Taking the problem of disaggregation many steps further, what significance can we make of the observation that OEO expenditures had little impact on the relative position of blacks (or that EEOC expenditures had much effect, for that matter) until we identify the groups within the black population that participated in OEO programs and gauge the change in *their* relative incomes? While I assume that all of the conference participants are capable of making this distinction, how many actually did so in their empirical work? For that matter, how many mentions can one find of *any* specific OEO, Labor, HEW, or other government effort to reduce discrimination or raise black incomes except in the chapter by Lyle? Can the claim of empirical relevancy be asserted from the depths of such an institutional void?

My own review of several of the chapters has impressed me with the notion that the alleged social relevancy of economics is too often founded more on the construction of theoretical models than on any awareness of the dimensions or dynamics of the problems to which those models are addressed. This criticism of the conference focus is not intended as a condemnation of all theoretical model-building—though it may well sound that way—but rather as an appeal for more attention to the relationship between those models and the real world, for an honest-to-Henry sense of relevancy. We cannot afford the complacency of models which are theoretically consistent and attractive but have not been developed or tested on the basis of hard data. We can even less afford to promulgate policy recommendations based on such models.

It is not sufficient to respond that the models are offered for the data explorations and testing of others. First of all, very few economists spend much time collecting data to test someone else's model. Secondly, and more importantly, the model builders have rarely exhibited a reluctance to provide policy prescriptions in the absence of empirical testing. Nearly every paper presented at this conference (and most published in the economic journals) included a section on policy implications, *as if* the models told us something about the world we live in. Maybe they do, but should we not demand a little evidence?

Just adding data to a paper does not imbue it with a sense of relevancy, of course. We must look not only for empirical substance, but also assess the nature and content of the data employed. Does the data offered relate in a meaningful way to either the specifications of the model or the realities of the marketplace? On this count, there is an evident tendency to grasp the most accessible data or, in a clutch, to make up data on the computer. Worse still, there is an all-too-pervasive feeling of *mea culpa* which leads many of us to ignore the sleight-of-hand practiced by others.

In this frame of mind let me turn to the two chapters on which I was asked to provide commentary, in particular, the chapters on employee discrimination contributed by Chiswick and Bell. Both authors have addressed important questions and attempted to build and test theoretical models: they make perfect guinea pigs for the kind of inquiry I should like to advance.

Chiswick starts out with a comparison of several different models of discrimination and attempts to determine the distinctiveness of each in terms of their empirical implications. Although Chiswick focuses only on the implications of the models and does not discuss the plausibility of their starting assumptions directly, the thrust of his inquiry is consistent with the analytical objectives I have outlined. He then turns to an examination of income inequality among whites, and asks whether such inequality is due, in part, to (1) differential skill levels as well as (2) different tastes for, or contacts with, blacks on the part of whites at each skill level. He believes that the second explanation is more valuable and sets out to demonstrate the validity of his employee-discrimination hypothesis.

In light of the social importance of his hypothesis and his evident concern for empirical relevance, the kinds of tests that Chiswick utilizes to examine his are profoundly disappointing. To begin with, he treats each *state* as a homogeneous labor market, pretending that the degree of black-white contact and the extent of white inequality is constant throughout the area encompassed by a state's boundaries. The utter foolishness of such a pretension should be obvious to anyone, especially someone from the state of New York. How can we know whether black-white contact affects income distribution when we are unable to identify where such contacts or inequalities occur? The response that "such data do not exist" is not only wrong, but misses a greater point. If the parameters of the model and the content of the data are incompatible, then a test of the hypothesis on such data tells us nothing, nothing at all. Yet Chiswick claims that his hypothesis is "substantiated for the country as a whole." Is this the kind of relevant economics that molds policy prescriptions?

The same lack of concern about the relationship between model parameters and real-world phenomena is evident in his specification of skill levels. Admittedly, the successful identification and measurement of "skills" is a feat which has evaded the efforts of a good many economists. Nevertheless, I am certain that few students of the labor market would accept educational attainment as an adequate proxy for the concept of skill level, though Chiswick also uses the rate of return from schooling and the distribution of years of postschool experience. What Chiswick really wants to demonstrate is that the presence of blacks in a particular employment setting will alter white incomes. To do so, he must utilize a more complete measure of skill, one which at least includes industry or occupational criteria, criteria which other economists have shown repeatedly to be influential in determining labor incomes. At a bare minimum we should ask to be shown whether or not the presence of blacks in a particular industry affects the wages received by whites. Here again, lack of a significant association between the data utilized and the content of the model undermine the usefulness of the empirical test. The conclusion is inescapable that research convenience, not conceptual relevance, dictated the dimensions of the empirical test.

The Bell chapter addresses a set of issues similar to those studied by Chiswick in this part of the volume. He, too, has formulated an employee-discrimination hypothesis to explain the distribution of income among whites. Because white workers desire to maintain their superior position in the income distribution, he argues, they must be paid a premium (or "bribe") for consenting to the integration of their firm or industry. Thus he shifts some of the burden of discrimination away from employers (as in the basic Becker model) to the employees of a firm or industry.

In the formulation of his model, Bell makes a much greater effort to relate his hypothesis to the dynamics of a real world labor market. Thus he demonstrates an awareness of the distinction between microeconomics and macroeconomics, and argues that individual employee behavior is conditioned on the former, not the latter. Hardly a revolutionary notion, but refreshing in comparison with most studies on this subject. He argues further that the operation of his model depends on tight labor markets, not on exogenous and largely unobservable shifts in tastes or complementarity. Finally, he endeavors to specify a set of specific and testable implications of his model.

In the paper he presented at the conference, Bell attempted to test his model on industry/occupational data for the state of Illinois. In so doing, he abandoned some of the rigor of his model, and fell prey to many of the same criticisms leveled at the Chiswick paper. Although I had planned to comment at length on that empirical test, I have been informed by the editor of this volume that Bell eliminated the empirical section of his paper prior to publication, and that such comments are no longer appropriate. I concur, and in so doing commend Bell's decision and hope that he will later provide us with a more rigorous test of his well-formulated model.

In assessing the prospects for an empirical test of the Bell model, I would like to make a couple of observations. First of all, Bell's chapter still starts with the view that the black-white income gap has been relatively stable and seeks to find an explanation for the maintenance of that status differential. There is convincing evidence available that the differential has been substantially reduced for some groups, particularly younger people, women in the North, and all groups in the South. In another chapter, in Part I of the companion volume, Bell himself showed some of the new developments. Continued model-building and testing should endeavor to take these relative status changes into account. As I understand Bell's chapter, such a reduction in the status differential could be explained only by an attitude change on the part of whites, a plausible, but largely untestable hypothesis. The issue should at least be addressed.

Some greater consideration must also be given in the literature on discrimination to the possibilities for explaining racial income differences with the help of factors other than prejudice and discrimination. Prejudice and discrimination certainly exist and have undoubtedly contributed heavily to the creation and maintenance of status differentials. But there has been an excessive tendency to explain the maintenance of racial differentials *solely* on the basis of personnel preferences. Surely, the dynamics of labor-market adjustments could help explain racial income differences, and especially changes therein, without resort to attitudinal variables. I am not suggesting that tastes for discrimination play no role, but only that other variables may have an independent impact on racial incomes.

Suppose we are concerned with a firm that is experiencing an increase in sales. In a world of uncertainty, the firm cannot be sure whether any observed increase in sales is a fleeting phenomenon or a quasi-permanent shift of demand. Hence, it will be reluctant to initiate major increases in the size of its internal labor force or in plant capacity until the trend of sales is clearer. As a short-run adjustment, it will seek to meet the increased demand by recalling laid-off workers or utilizing overtime provisions. This suggests an increase in the incomes of the firm's existing work force, but no new hires.

Once the firm becomes convinced that the higher level of sales is relatively permanent, it will seek to make more fundamental adjustments. In particular, it will seek to expand plant facilities and hire new workers. When the new workers enter the firm, a substantial differential will exist between the wages and incomes of the old and new workers. As the new workers are trained and overtime for the old workers is reduced, however, the wage/income differential will diminish. Thus an expansion of demand can help explain both an initial increase in income differentials and their later diminution. Call the old workers white, and the new workers black, and you have a plausible explanation for observed changes in racial income differences. (More discussion of this adjustment process is included in Schiller's book, *The Economics of Poverty and Discrimination*, Prentice-Hall, 1973.)

This abbreviated model of firm-specific market adjustments is not offered as a complete explanation for patterns of racial income differentials, but as evidence that relatively nonpsychic hypotheses are available to aid in that explanation. A comparison of the labor-market adjustment model to the employee-discrimination model also underscores an important point about empirical testing. In the adjustment model, white incomes increase in response to higher sales *before* new workers (blacks) are hired; the Bell model suggests a greater degree of simultaneity. Accordingly, to sort out causal influences we need to ask not only what happens in particular firms and industries but also *when* parameters change. This, of course, increases the demands put upon empirical research.

My comments on the Bell and Chiswick chapters and my more general remarks on the conference are intended to convey a greater sense of responsibility than is customary in claims of relevancy made for the subject of economics. No one would sensibly argue that model-building is a fruitless and irrelevant endeavor; theoretical formulations are an indispensable aid in organizing our thoughts and directing our attention to needed inquiries. However, the importance of model-building cannot be allowed to obscure the equally important tasks of empirical research and validation. If the models we construct are to be useful in understanding and changing the world we live in, then their parameters must be related to real world phenomena and they must be subjected to rigorous empirical testing. To content oneself with structurally glamorous models which are untested, untestable, or mistested is to risk irrelevancy.

Part 2:
The Measurement of Racial
Inequality: Analyses of
Recent Trends in the Income
and Earnings Distributions
of Blacks and Whites

In the early 1960s Batchelder wrote that "the trends of the sixties seem to remain those of the fifties" and questioned whether "exhortation could ever be as effective a means to Negro advance as is buoyant demand." The studies in Part 2 show that contrary to the outlook in the early 1960s, the trend of the sixties differed substantially from that of the previous decade. Even after allowing for the favorable effects of a tight labor market, the statistical results show significant increases in the ratio of black to white income.

As encouraging as these developments are, we cannot afford to become complacent. First, the differences between black and white incomes remain large, too large to be accounted for by differences in age distributions, in education, or in skills. Second, the post-1964 trends discovered in the relative median income data are small, an annual increase of about 0.01 for families, 0.03 to 0.04 for females, and 0.01 for all males, and the increase is not statistically different from zero for black males in the North. Even if these trends persisted in the future, the black-white income disparity would not disappear soon. Third, improvement was not uniform at all points of the income distribution, for all age groups, or for all regions. The results of these studies show that the effects of improved education and a prosperous economy benefited younger workers more than older.

Fourth, the statistical analyses cannot claim to have correctly disentangled the effects of a buoyant economy with a tight labor market from the long-term trends. Fifth, too often in the past, the statistical findings have changed substantially with an additional observation. Already the 1972 statistics, which became available after the completion of these studies, show that the ratio of black to white family income fell in 1972, the second decline in two years. Furthermore, within regions, the declines have been even more pronounced. The relative income of black males, which some consider the crucial determinant for lifting blacks out of poverty, has declined sharply within the Northeast and North Central regions from its highs of 1967-1968. Finally, we do not know why there was an upward trend net of cyclical effects between 1964 and 1971. This upward trend may have been due to the war on poverty programs or programs designed to improve the life of those in the urban ghetto, programs which have already experienced cutbacks.

The chapters in Part 2 are concerned with income differences by race. Chapter 10 is a survey by Ann Horowitz of both the changes in black-white income differentials since 1947 and of the literature that has attempted to determine the causes of these changes. The chapter summarizes the major contributions to this vast literature, and it relates the findings of the four other chapters in Part 2 to the earlier literature.

Chapter 11 is by Wayne Vroman. Vroman utilizes data from both the Current

Population Survey conducted annually by the U.S. Bureau of the Census, and from the Continuous Work History Sample of the Social Security Administration, to analyze changes between 1948 and 1971 in relative income of nonwhites by sex, age, region, and position in the distribution of income. His analysis of the CPS data shows that the relative median income of nonwhite men did not increase prior to 1964 but did increase between 1965 to 1971, net of the favorable effects of a low unemployment rate. Both sets of data show that women experienced an upward trend over the entire period, with the trend accelerating after 1965. The Social Security data, however, do not reveal an upward trend in the relative median income of nonwhite men, either prior to 1965 or between 1965 and 1969. Analyzing by region, and adjusting for changes in the age composition of the population, Vroman finds that nonwhite men in the South, but not in the North, did experience an increase in relative income after 1965. Vroman also finds that changes over time varied by income position, and that low rates of unemployment favorably affected the relative income of nonwhite men, particularly younger men.

Chapter 12, again by Horowitz, considers differences in the shape of the distributions of nonwhite and white family incomes, as well as differences in central tendency. These differences are analyzed over the 1954-1971 period for evidence of change and of cyclical effects. Nonwhite incomes displayed greater inequality than white incomes throughout this period. The difference in inequality between the two distributions was widening until 1964, but since then the inequality of both white and nonwhite incomes has declined at approximately equal rates. In contrast, the disparity between means declined over the entire period, and the disparity in medians remained constant until 1964 and then began to decline. High rates of unemployment also caused a widening in the difference between the shapes of the two distributions, but affected the medians about equally. The widening of the inequality differential occurred primarily because a high rate of unemployment was associated with a sharp increase in the proportion of nonwhites with income under $3,000.

These chapters on race differences in income over time are followed by two chapters on race differences in the return to schooling. Finis Welch finds that for urban males who entered the labor force in the 1960s, the direct return from an additional year of schooling is greater for blacks than for whites. After including the indirect return resulting from an increase in the number of weeks worked associated with increased schooling, Welch finds the greater return for blacks than whites begins with those entering the labor force between 1955-1958. Welch concludes that the greater return is due to an improvement in the quality of education received by blacks relative to whites.

Barry Chiswick is concerned with another aspect of race differences in the return to schooling. Chiswick finds that in addition to a lower average rate of return, blacks face greater uncertainty as to the rate of return than whites. Chiswick estimates the variance of the rate of return is one-third larger for blacks than for whites and the coefficient of variation is twice as large. Chiswick notes that the greater uncertainty experienced by blacks rather than any greater aversion to risk may account for the lower investment in schooling by blacks compared to whites.

The chapters in Part 2 provide a detailed picture of the disparities in black-white income and of the changes in these disparities during the last quarter of a century. Although none of them provide forecasts of the trends in the 1970s, they are helpful for understanding the past and for isolating those factors that many determine future trends as well.

10 The Pattern and Causes of Changes in White-Nonwhite Income Differences: 1947-1972

Ann R. Horowitz *

In the past decade there have been many empirical studies analyzing changes in relative and absolute income differentials between nonwhites, particularly blacks, and whites in order to detect any time trends in these differentials. The purposes of this chapter are to provide (1) a statistical review of the changes in income disparity between nonwhites and whites during the 1947-1972 period, and (2) a summary of the findings of the major empirical studies as to the causes of these changes.

Most of these studies analyze the trend in relative income after adjusting for the effects of changes in other factors that are known to affect the relative income of nonwhites. Any remaining trend is generally interpreted as being suggestive of changes in discrimination. The approach has several weaknesses. First, some of the variables included in the model are themselves representative of discrimination. For example, the existence of cyclical variation in relative nonwhite income is indicative of discrimination. Gilman (1965) has estimated that half of the differences in unemployment rates is due to differences in the occupational distribution of whites and nonwhites, which may represent discrimination in hiring, or past discrimination in providing blacks with the opportunities to acquire the necessary education and skills to enter more cyclically stable occupations. Second, multicollinearity exists among many of the variables that affect the ratio of nonwhite to white incomes, which makes it virtually impossible to correctly disentangle their separate effects. Also, data for many variables frequently are unavailable, or are available only infrequently so that it is often impossible to accurately adjust for all relevant variables. Adjustments often have to be made on the basis of surrogates, or from data from two rather distant points in time. Because the trend may include the effects of omitted variables that have varied systematically over time, or may be improperly adjusted for variation in the included variables, the trend is usually interpreted as being only suggestive of the direction of change in discrimination, and of progress or the lack of progress in eliminating discrimination, rather than as an exact measure of the change in discrimination.

The studies reviewed here consider both the income of families and the income of individuals. In comparisons concerned with the relative affluence of the different groups, the usual justification for examining family income is that

*Associate professor of economics, University of Florida.

thc family is thc basic spending unit. Most studies of poverty, for example, have concentrated on family income. The relative income of black families will not be a good surrogate for their relative welfare, however, if there are substantial differences between blacks and whites in preferences for income and leisure, in net worth, in family size, in prices paid, and in the number of wage earners per family. Little is known about whether there are differences in preferences for income and leisure. There are differences in the number of weeks worked, but these are related to differences in education and may reflect differences in opportunities. Terrell (1971) has argued that differences in the other factors cause the differential in black and white family income to understate the true economic disparity. Differences in savings and in households incomes from capital between the races have been considered by von Furstenberg (1974). Wage and salary income of individuals rather than family income is the variable of interest, however, for the purpose of measuring current labor-market discrimination. Some have also argued that income of males is the crucial variable even in studies of poverty on the grounds that male income is the principal determinant of *long-run* movements out of poverty.

This chapter is divided into four sections. The first section is a statistical review of changes in white-nonwhite income differentials for both families and individuals, by sex, since 1947. The review begins with 1947 because that is the year when data first became available annually, and because most of the detailed analyses of the causes of income differences by race use post-1947 data. Income data by race are available for 1939 but not for earlier years. Studies of earlier periods were made by Becker (1957), Rayack (1961), and Iliestand (1964) using an index of the occupational position of black males relative to white males, weighted by earnings in 1940 or 1950.

The second section is a review of the findings of studies that have estimated the changes in the income of nonwhites relative to whites since 1947 that were due to the level of economic activity and to long-run secular trends. Section three considers the findings of studies regarding the effect of age, education, and migration on white-nonwhite income differentials. Finally, the fourth section includes some concluding remarks on the findings of the various studies and the outlook for the future.

Changes in the Ratio of Nonwhite-to-White Income, 1947-1972

From 1947 to 1965 median family income of nonwhites fluctuated between 51 and 57 percent of that of whites, with the percentage falling sharply during recessions and recovering when employment picked up. In 1966 nonwhite family income experienced an upsurge to 60 percent of white family income. This was followed by slight but steady increases in the percentage to a high of 64 percent in 1970. The percentage fell slightly in 1971 and 1972, perhaps reflecting the rise in unemployment rates that began in 1970. The figures cited compare nonwhites to whites. Data are also available for black families since 1967. Since nonwhites consist primarily of blacks, the nonwhite-white figures parallel the black-white figures, except that the latter have been consistently 3 percentage points less than the nonwhite percentage since 1967. The ratio of black to white family income since 1967, and of nonwhite to white family income from 1947 through 1967, is shown in Table 10-1.

Although the ratio of nonwhite to white median income showed a decline in nonwhite-white income disparities during the last decade, absolute measures of the disparity in median incomes showed a widening gap. In 1947, for example, the difference between nonwhite and white median family incomes was $2,886 (in 1972 dollars). By 1967, when the ratio of nonwhite to white income had increased from 0.51 to 0.62, the difference had widened to $3,939 (also in 1972 dollars). By 1972 with the ratio still at 0.62, the difference had widened still further to $4,443.

Table 10-1
Relative Median Income of Black and White Families, 1947-1972[a]

	U.S.	Northeast	North Central	West	South
		Ratio of Black-to-White Family Income			
1972	0.59	0.64	0.70	0.71	0.55
1971	0.60	0.67	0.69	0.71	0.56
1970	0.61	0.71	0.73	0.77	0.57
1967	0.59	0.66	0.77	0.75	0.54
		Ratio of Nonwhite-to-White Family Income			
1967	0.62	0.68	0.79	0.84	0.54
1966	0.60	0.69	0.74	0.79	0.51
1965	0.55	0.66	0.74	0.83	0.49
1964	0.56	0.67	0.72	0.78	0.49
1963	0.53	0.65	0.73	0.76	0.45
1960	0.55	0.68	0.73	0.81	0.43
1958	0.51	0.69	0.72	0.70	0.44
1957	0.54	0.71	0.71	0.72	0.46
1953	0.56	0.72	0.76	0.82	0.49
1950	0.54	–	–	–	–
1949	0.51	–	–	–	–
1947	0.51	–	–	–	–

[a]Regional data are not available in the *Current Population Reports* prior to 1953. Data for blacks are available only since 1967.
Source: U.S. Bureau of the Census, *Current Population Reports*, Series P-60.

There are also substantial regional differences in the size of black to white family income ratios and in their rates and directions of change. The black to white family income ratio is still 0.09 to 0.16 lower in the South than elsewhere, despite the fact that the ratio began to increase in the South during the 1960s and has fallen outside the South since 1953. In fact, in every major region outside the South, the income of blacks relative to whites in 1972 was 0.07 to 0.08 below the regional peaks realized in the late 1960s.

The median income ratio for males, fourteen years of age and over, has not followed the same patterns as the ratios for families. These ratios, shown in Table 10-2, have been extensively analyzed by several researchers beginning with Batchelder (1964). Using income data from the 1950 and 1960 censuses, Batchelder observed that the relative income of black men declined during the 1950s. Despite the migration of large numbers of blacks from the low-income South to the high-income North and West, the black-to-white median income ratio for men fell slightly, from 0.525 to 0.520. Furthermore, Batchelder found that the decline continued in the early 1960s according to Current Population Survey (CPS) data which showed the income ratio for nonwhite to white men falling from an average of 0.50 in 1958-1960 to 0.49 in 1962.

Batchelder also observed that during the 1950s the ratio of black to white male income fell in every major region of the country. In a later study of these data, Raymond (1969) tabulated the ratios for 1949 and 1959 by Standard Metropolitan Statistical Areas. He found a wide variation in the amount of

Table 10-2
Ratio of Median Income of Black-to-White Males, Fourteen Years of Age and Over

	U.S.	Northeast	North Central	West	South
1972	0.602	0.698	0.789	0.842	0.561
1971	0.596	0.731	0.819	0.796	0.519
1968	0.593	0.774	0.823	0.777	0.517
1967	0.571	0.738	0.842	0.735	0.495
1965	0.520	0.693	0.746	0.741	0.468
1964	0.567	0.738	0.761	0.758	0.462
1962	0.492	0.670	0.711	0.753	0.439
1960	0.525	0.763	0.758	0.732	0.373
1959	0.520	0.719	0.766	0.711	0.466
1949	0.525	0.747	0.812	0.736	0.500

Note: Ratios for 1960-1965 are nonwhite-to-white income. Other years are black to white. In years which both sets of figures are available there is very little difference except in the West.

Sources: Data for 1949 and 1959 are from the *U.S. Census of Population*, 1950 and 1960. Data for 1960-1972 are from U.S. Bureau of the Census, *Current Population Reports*, Series P-60.

change in the ratios, with the only SMSAs showing improvement located in the West. The regional declines observed by Batchelder are not surprising, in that the migration of blacks out of the South might be expected to lower the ratio in other regions and if the more productive southern workers moved, the ratio in the South would also be expected to fall. The surprising thing is that the ratio for the nation as a whole fell during a time when blacks were moving from low- to high-income regions. Thus, without the migration, the national ratio would have fallen even more.

Fein (1966) noted that CPS data for 1963 and 1964 indicated a reversal in the downward trend for males, with the ratio rising to 0.52 in 1963 and still further to 0.57 in 1964. After falling again in 1965, the ratio for males continued to increase through 1972 when it equalled 0.602. Regionally, however, the ratios have been somewhat erratic. In the Northeast the relative income of blacks fell after 1970, and in the North Central it has fallen every year except one since 1967. The West, however, achieved a high of 0.84 in 1972.

For women, the ratios are somewhat less meaningful. While an increase in the median income ratio for men is generally interpreted as an improvement, the female ratio is affected by the larger proportion of white women who are employed part-time, and by the fluctuations in the proportion of part-time workers in the female labor force. Batchelder observed that for women, unlike men, the income of blacks relative to whites rose during the 1950s. For the nation as a whole, the ratio of black-to-white median female income increased from 0.511 to 0.600 between 1949 and 1959, with an increase occurring even in the South. Outside the South, the 1959 ratio ranged from 0.957 to 0.986, close to parity. Since 1960 the relative median income of black females has continued to make dramatic increases. In fact, for each region outside the South, this ratio has exceeded one in nearly every year since 1960. The ratios for females for the country as a whole and by region are shown in Table 10-3.

So far, we have been comparing the nonwhite and white income distributions only at their medians. Wohlstetter and Coleman (1972) have calculated the ratio of nonwhite-to-white income at various corresponding points of the income distributions for 1967 and for the late 1940s. For 1967 they found that from about the 20th to 80th percentiles of the distributions of nonwhite and white family income, the ratio of the nonwhite-to-white percentiles increases with increasing income. Within both the lowest and highest 20 percentiles, however, the ratio declines with higher income. Wohlstetter and Coleman conclude that at the lower end of the distribution, income maintenance programs tend to put a floor under both nonwhite and white incomes and raise the relative income of nonwhites compared to the ratio at other points of the distribution, while at the upper tail there are many obstacles to nonwhite advancement to high-level income positions that lower the relative income of nonwhites.

For individual persons, Wohlstetter and Coleman find the ratios at corresponding percentiles generally decrease with higher income, with particularly

Table 10-3
Ratio of Median Income of Black-to-White Females Fourteen Years of Age and Over

	U.S.	Northeast	North Central	West	South
1972	0.934	1.288	1.147	1.097	0.764
1971	0.876	1.253	1.172	1.082	0.640
1970	0.910	1.270	1.290	1.185	0.713
1969	0.843	1.236	1.179	1.120	0.618
1967	0.780	1.141	1.182	1.210	0.570
1966	0.761	1.194	1.126	1.076	0.571
1964	0.702	1.087	1.002	1.258	0.529
1961	0.670	1.003	1.095	1.256	0.520
1960	0.620	.952	1.076	1.010	0.479
1959	0.600	.986	.973	.957	0.556
1949	0.511	.828	.864	.913	0.465

Note: Ratios for 1960-1966 are nonwhite-to-white income. Other years are black to white. In years when both sets of figures are available, there is very little difference except in the West.

Sources: Same as Table 10-2.

sharp decreases occurring within the lower 40 and the upper 20 percentiles. Neither is there much tendency for nonwhite-white income ratios in the middle of the distribution to increase with increasing income. The lowest ratios occur for the upper 10 percentiles. This is not just a problem of differences between millionaires, however, because income to nonwhite individuals at the 90th percentile in 1967 was only about $6,796.

Comparing the income distributions of persons between 1949 and 1967, Wohlstetter and Coleman found there was greater improvement over time in the income of nonwhites relative to whites at the lower end of the distribution than at the upper end. In fact, the amount of improvement falls steadily over the distribution with no statistically significant improvement between 1949 and 1967 for the upper 10 percent of the distribution of income of individual persons.

For families, the difference between 1967 and the late 1940s depends partly on whether 1967 is compared with 1945 and 1949 or with 1947 and 1948. This suggests that unemployment has different effects at different points along the distribution of family income. In comparing 1967 and 1947, Wohlstetter and Coleman reported about equal improvement occurred at the lowest 10 percentiles and the 50th through 80th percentiles, while much less improvement occurred at the 20th through 40th and in the upper 10 percentiles. Thus the overall improvement was slightly greater for the upper half than for the lower half of the distribution of family income.

Wohlstetter and Coleman's findings of differences in the size of the nonwhite-white income disparity and its rate of change at various percentiles of the distribution of income, make it clear that the entire distribution should be considered in analyzing changes in income disparities between nonwhites and whites. Income disparities over the entire distribution in 1972 will be measured by looking at the proportion of whites and nonwhites in each income bracket. Without discrimination of any kind, we would expect to find the same proportion of each group within a given income bracket. In 1972, however, while only 5.9 percent of white families were below $3,000, 17.7 percent of nonwhite families were below this level. At the upper tail, 32.2 percent of white families had income in excess of $15,000 compared to only 15.6 percent of nonwhite families.

Fein (1965) suggested measuring disparities between blacks and whites by the time gap between the year that whites achieve a given level and the year that blacks achieve the same level. A dynamic measure of the disparities is obtained by considering the change in the time gap over time. Thurow (1969) found that both the mean and dispersion of the nonwhite distribution in 1965 were slightly larger than the mean (in constant dollars) of the 1929 white distribution. He concluded, therefore, that in 1965 the nonwhite income distribution lagged about thirty years behind the white. In 1971 the median income of black families was $6,714, a level that was first exceeded by the median of the white distribution in 1955, indicating that the lag at the median has been reduced to about sixteen years. The lags at the two tails differ, however, from the lag at the median. In 1971, 19.4 percent of nonwhites had income less than $3,000, while the last time over 19 percent of whites were below this level was 1950, a lag of twenty-one years. At the upper tail, 12.2 percent of black families had income in excess of $15,000 in 1971, while the first time more than 12 percent of white families exceeded $15,000 was in 1961, ten years earlier.

The comparisons of this section are based on actual data for various years unadjusted for changes in other variables. Part of the observed changes appear to be due to changes in the level of economic activity. Comparisons between two years cannot distinguish the long-run trend from the cyclical effects. The next section considers attempts to disentangle the cyclical and long-run secular effects.

Cyclical and Long-Run Secular Effects, 1947-1971

Several studies have been undertaken to estimate the trend in the nonwhite to white income ratio after allowing for cyclical effects. Rasmussen (1970) found a positive trend in the relative income of nonwhite men over the 1948-1964 period. He therefore concluded that Batchelder's results were due to cyclical effects. Ashenfelter (1970), however, using wage and salary earnings, found no statistically significant change for men over the 1950-1966 period. Vroman (1974) found that the results depend on position in the income distribution, age, and region of residence, as well as sex.

Rasmussen's study is based on the median income of nonwhite and white males over the period 1949 to 1964. Rasmussen assumed the ratio of nonwhite-to-white median income is a linear function of the percentage change in GNP, the national unemployment rate lagged one year, and a trend variable. Both cyclical variables were statistically significant at the 5 percent level of significance. The trend coefficient indicated that net of the cyclical effects the relative income of nonwhite men increased by a statistically significant 0.003 per year. Rasmussen concluded, therefore, that cyclical fluctuations were responsible for the declining income ratio noted by Batchelder for the 1950s. After estimating that 38 percent of this secular rise was due to improved education of nonwhites and changes in the age structure of the white and nonwhite populations, and after observing that technical change, changes in the relative size of the nonwhite population, and changes in residential segregation during this period all would have worked to reduce nonwhite income relative to white, Rasmussen concluded that at least 62 percent of the secular increase in the income ratio represented a decline in discrimination against nonwhite males.

Some comments are in order: (1) As Rasmussen noted in his concluding paragraph, the increase in the income ratio may reflect the migration away from the South. (2) Even with a buoyant economy in which GNP increased at an annual rate of 5 percent and the unemployment rate was reduced to 3 percent, Rasmussen's equation means that the relative income of nonwhites would decrease by 0.029 per year. With a 3 percent unemployment rate, GNP would have to increase by nearly 8 percent a year in order to keep the nonwhite-white income ratio from falling.

Ashenfelter's model is in some ways similar to Rasmussen's. Ashenfelter regressed the logarithm of the nonwhite-white wage and salary income ratio by sex against the national unemployment rate, the ratio of the nonwhite unemployment rate to the white rate by sex, and a trend variable. Income ratios both for all workers and for full-time workers, by sex, were used. The data covered the period 1950-1966 for all workers, and 1955-1966 for full-time workers.

Unlike Rasmussen, Ashenfelter found that, for both full-time and all male workers, the trend was negative although not statistically different from zero. In fact, for both regressions the standard errors exceeded the absolute value of the trend coefficient. Furthermore, the unemployment rate was significantly *positive* at the 5 percent level for full-time workers, although it was not statistically significant for all workers. Thus, for full-time workers the sign of the unemployment variable was the opposite of what would be expected. The unemployment rate of nonwhite relative to white males had the expected negative sign, but was statistically significant at the 5 percent level only for the full-time workers.

For female workers, the trend coefficient was significantly positive at the 1 percent level of statistical significance for both full-time and all workers. The relative unemployment rate of nonwhite women was also statistically significant for both sets of data, with the relative wage and salary income of nonwhite women decreasing as their relative unemployment rate increased. The national unemployment rate was not statistically significant for full-time females, but was significantly less than zero at the 1 percent level for all workers.

Although the results are not clear-cut in that (1) the overall unemployment rate was significantly negative for all female workers and significantly positive for full-time male workers, and (2) the relative unemployment rate of nonwhite males was not statistically significant for all male workers, Ashenfelter concluded that there is "substantial evidence in favor of the hypothesis that the relative extent of unemployment has a negative effect on relative nonwhite earnings, and very little evidence that aggregate labor market tightness has had any appreciable effect on relative nonwhite earnings in the postwar period."

Ashenfelter also attempted to estimate the proportion of the secular trend that was due to a change in discrimination by subtracting an estimate of the proportion due to changes in the relative educational attainment of nonwhite labor. After adjusting for an improvement in the relative quality of nonwhite female labor, Ashenfelter concluded that decreased discrimination increased the relative earnings of full-time female workers by 1.5 to 1.7 percent per year, and those of all female workers by between 2.8 to 3.0 percent per year. For males, Ashenfelter estimated that increased discrimination decreased the relative earnings of both full-time and all nonwhite male workers by from 0.1 to 0.4 percent per year after adjusting for changes in the relative quality of nonwhite male labor. Since the Civil Rights Act of 1964 and the creation of the U.S. Equal Employment Opportunity Commission were aimed at reducing discrimination, Ashenfelter also tested for an upward shift in the relative earnings of nonwhites after 1964. He found no evidence of such a shift in the 1964-1966 period for either men or women.

Vroman's Chapter 11 in this volume extends the attempt to distinguish between cyclical and secular movements in the relative income of nonwhites to data through 1971. Vroman also distinguishes between trends prior to and after 1965. Using CPS data for the period 1948-1971, Vroman finds that although the relative income of nonwhite men did not increase up to 1965, it did increase in the post-1965 period. For women, Vroman confirmed the upward trend prior to 1965 found by Ashenfelter, and also discovered that this upward movement accelerated in the post-1965 period.

Vroman also used data from the Social Security Administration's Continuous Work History Sample for the period 1957 to 1969 to analyze the cyclical and trend effects in the nonwhite-white income ratio by age and region, as well as sex. For males of all ages combined, the Social Security data did not show that nonwhite men experienced an upward trend relative to white men either prior to

1965 or between 1965 and 1969. After adjusting for changes in the age distribution of the two races, Vroman found a post-1965 trend of 0.047 per year, which was significantly different from zero at the 1 percent level of statistical significance. The analysis by age groups revealed that prior to 1965, older nonwhite men experienced a statistically significant downward trend in relative median income. After 1965 nearly all age groups experienced a rising trend.

Analyzing the ratio of median income of men by region, with the age distributions held constant, Vroman found that the post-1965 trend observed in the national ratio was caused by an upward trend in the South, and that there was no statistically significant trend in the North. The same was true for the ratio of nonwhite-to-white income at other points of the income distribution. Prior to 1965 he found a significant *downward* trend for the ratio at the first decile in the South. In addition, Vroman found that a low rate of unemployment favorably affected the nonwhite-white income ratio for all men age 16-64, but the favorable effect was greater for younger men. On a regional basis, a low rate of unemployment increased relative nonwhite income at the first through seventh deciles in the North and the third through seventh deciles in the South, but was not statistically significant at either the first decile in the South or at the ninth decile in either region.

For women, Vroman found a statistically significant positive trend both before and after 1964 for nearly all age groups. The pre-1965 upward trend in relative nonwhite income occurred in the North at all deciles except the first, but this upward trend was not experienced in the lower half of the income distribution in the South. In fact, there was a significant downward trend prior to 1965 in the South in relative nonwhite income at the first decile for women as well as men. The post-1965 upward trend was experienced, however, at all deciles except the first in both North and South. A tight labor market had the unexpected result of decreasing the nonwhite-white median income ratio, but the decrease was not statistically significant for most individual age groups or at any position of the income distribution in the North, although it significantly decreased relative nonwhite income in the middle section of the income distributions in the South.

Similar analyses have been performed using income data for families. Using data for 1947-1964 Thurow found that the long-run secular growth of nonwhite and white family incomes is affected by two cyclical variables. Relative nonwhite-white income varies directly with the percentage of the labor force employed, and inversely with the ratio of personal income to GNP. Thurow assumed that the long-run growth of income is determined by the growth of productivity. Productivity was measured by GNP per employee. He found that increases in productivity have essentially the same effect on both nonwhite and white median family incomes. Thus his model reveals no long-run trend in the nonwhite-white income ratio between 1947 and 1964.

Thurow's cyclical results indicate that both nonwhite and white median incomes fall as the percentage of the labor force employed declines, with the nonwhite falling nearly twice as much as the white. In addition, a larger part of the decline is offset for whites than for nonwhites by the rise in personal income as a percent of GNP which occurs during recessions.

On the basis of his results, Thurow estimated that a decrease in the unemployment rate from 7 to 3 percent would increase the ratio of nonwhite-to-white median family income from 0.50 to 0.60. This is quite close to the experience of the late 1960s. Between 1966 and 1969, the unemployment rate was between 3.5 and 3.8 percent, and the relative income ratio was between 0.60 and 0.63.

Thurow also estimated, using 1960 census data by state on the proportion of families with income under $3,000, and holding constant differences in education, farm population, the proportion of families with no one in the labor force, the proportion of population engaged in full-time work, and the industrial structure of the state, that an elimination of discrimination would reduce the percentage of families in poverty by one percentage point.

Guthrie (1970) estimated the long-run secular growth rates of nonwhite and white family income at several points of the distributions of income, and the effects of unemployment on these rates. Guthrie used black and white family income at each of the first four quintiles, and at the 95th percentile, as dependent variables. After adjusting for the cyclical effects as measured by the rate of unemployment, Guthrie found that black family income increased faster than white between 1947 and 1968 at each pair of corresponding points on the income distributions. Unlike Wohlstetter and Coleman who did not adjust for cyclical effects, Guthrie found that the difference between the rates of growth for nonwhites and whites is greatest at the highest percentiles and smallest at the lowest quintile. Guthrie also found that the effects of unemployment on black income relative to white income vary over the income distribution. At every percentile under consideration, the coefficient for the unemployment rate is negative and larger in absolute value for nonwhites than for whites, implying that nonwhites are affected more severely than whites over the entire distribution of income by unemployment. The racial diffference in the effect of unemployment is also larger the higher the percentile. This might account for Wohlstetter and Coleman's finding that improvement, unadjusted for cyclical effects, had been less at the upper end of the income distribution.

Chapter 12 by Horowitz in this part estimates the long-term secular changes between 1954 and 1971 in the inequality within the distributions of nonwhite and of white family income after adjusting for changes in the rate of unemployment, the unemployment rate of nonwhites relative to that of whites, and the rate of growth of GNP. The long-term trends in the degree of inequality within each of these distributions, as well as the difference between the medians of the two distributions, changed after 1964. Inequality of the nonwhite distribution was greater than that of the white distribution over the entire time period, and until 1964 nonwhite inequality was increasing while white inequality was decreasing. After 1964, the inequality of both distributions was decreasing at about the same annual rate. The rate of unemployment had a greater effect on the inequality displayed by the nonwhite distribution than it did on the inequality of the white distribution causing nonwhite inequality to increase relative to white, but the unemployment rate affected the medians of the two distributions about equally. The biggest change in the nonwhite distribution resulting from an increase in unemployment occurred at the lower tail where a 1 percent increase in the unemployment rate increased the percent of nonwhite families with income under $3,000 by nearly 2 percentage points.

The Effects of Age, Education, and Migration on the Ratio of Nonwhite to White Income

Changes in the income of nonwhites relative to that of whites over time may be due in part to changes in the education and age composition of the nonwhite and white populations. The lower level of earnings of nonwhites compared to whites is in part due to lower levels of schooling. Schiller (1973) estimated that in 1969, for example, black male workers earned 70 percent as much as whites with an equal number of years of schooling. Even if an adjustment is made for differences in the quality as well as the quantity of schooling, blacks earn only about 80 percent as much as whites. Several of the studies of secular trend have attempted to adjust their trend estimates for changes in the age and education composition of the nonwhite and white populations. Vroman, for example, controlled for age changes by using fixed age weights. Rasmussen and Ashenfelter both attempted to estimate the portion of the secular trend due to changes in the educational attainment of black relative to white workers.

Gwartney (1970) has performed a detailed analysis of the effects of education on the changes in the ratio of nonwhite-to-white income between 1939 and 1967. Gwartney decomposed the percentage change in the ratio of nonwhite-to-white income between 1939 and 1967 into the percentages due to changes in the educational and age composition of the population, changes in relative income received within education-age cells, and migration.

Between 1939 and 1959 changes in the educational and age composition of the nonwhite and white populations tended to reduce the nonwhite-to-white mean income ratio for urban males. Gwartney asserts this occurred because as the general level of education increased, nonwhites moved into higher education cells where the nonwhite-white income ratio was smaller. Gwartney estimated these changes reduced the percentage growth in the income ratio by about 6 to 7 percent in the North and about 4 percent in the South. He estimated that migration was responsible for increasing the nonwhite-to-white income ratio for the country as a whole by 3 to 4 percent. Most of the large increase in the national ratio was due, however, to increase in relative income within education age groups.

Between 1949 and 1959, the median income ratio of males twenty-five years of age and over increased by only 3.1 percent. Gwartney estimates that changes in education tended to increase the ratio by about 5 percent, while migration tended to increase it by approximately 6 percent. These increases were not realized, however, because relative nonwhite income declined within educational groups. Between 1957 and 1967 the median income ratio increased by 8 percent, largely due to increases in relative income within educational groups. Migration increased the ratio by close to 4 percent, but the effects of changes in education were small. For the entire 1949-1967 period, migration was the primary cause of the increase in relative nonwhite income.

For women, Gwartney found that relative income changes within education cells were the major cause of the large increases in the median income ratio between 1959 and 1967. Changes in educational composition had only a small effect. Between 1949 and 1959, however, relative changes within educational cells and changes in the educational composition of the nonwhite and white female population were about equally responsible for the increase in the relative median income of nonwhite women. Migration was responsible for about 6 percent of the increase in the earlier period and about 4.5 percent in the later period.

Other studies have attempted to estimate the return from schooling by race. While increased schooling increases income for both whites and nonwhites, several studies based on 1960 census data found that the return to education was substantially less for nonwhites than for whites, and to such an extent that nonwhite income as a percent of white income by education level tended to decline as education increased. Welch (1967), for example, found this to be the case for southern rural blacks. Hanoch's (1967) estimates of median income by age and education level for nonwhites and whites also show a general decline in relative income with increasing education in both the North and South. Furthermore, Thurow found the elasticity of income with respect to schooling was smaller for nonwhite males than for white males for every education level (less than 8, 9-12, and more than 12 years of schooling) in both the North and the South. Finally, the difference in elasticities was substantially larger for the college educated.

The tendency for the nonwhite-to-white income ratio to decline with increasing education was not monotonic, however, and in recent years the ratio has increased more rapidly at higher than at lower education levels. Hanoch's estimates show that the income ratio was higher at the graduate school level than at lower education levels. Moreover, Formby's (1968) calculations of the difference between nonwhite and white income as a percent of white income for

1959 imply that the ratio fell with increasing education only for men in the South. For women in the South, the relationship between the ratio and education was U-shaped, with the income of nonwhite relative to white women reaching its peak for those with sixteen or more years of school. In the North, the relationship followed an inverted U-shape for men and was rising for women. In a recent study, Gwartney (1972) found that after adjusting for achievement, the nonwhite to white income ratio was higher for college graduates than any other education group.

Several recent studies suggest that during the 1960s educational returns to blacks increased sharply at all education levels with the greatest increases occurring at the higher educational levels. Recent work by Weiss and Williamson (1972), for example, suggests that there has been a substantial increase in the return from schooling for blacks at all education levels in both the North and the South. Using data from the 1967 Survey of Economic Opportunity, Weiss and Williamson found that in both the North and the South, the elasticity of income with respect to schooling for black males in 1967 exceeded that for white males in 1959. Weiss and Williamson also found that the elasticity of income with respect to years of experience has increased dramatically for younger blacks. Weiss and Williamson observe that the full-employment conditions of 1967 may explain some of these changes, but they suggest that the changes may represent a decrease in discrimination at all education levels possibly due to passage of the Civil Rights Act of 1964 and to passage of Fair Employment Laws by twenty states between 1960 and 1968.

Weiss and Williamson also found that contrary to popular belief a black educated in the South did not have a lower return to education in 1967 than a black educated in the North. Except for those educated in the largest southern SMSAs, people educated in the South received higher earnings in 1967 than those educated in the North. Furthermore, the disadvantage of being educated in large cities, North and South, appears to be greater for younger than for older blacks. The primary determinants of labor and self-employment income of black males in 1967, however, were age, education, and region of residence.

Welch (1973) in his Chapter 13 in this part provides us with further evidence that there has been a shift in the return to schooling for nonwhites, and that the return for younger nonwhites is now greater than that for whites. Using the same data source as Weiss and Williamson, and data from the 1960 census, Welch estimated the return to schooling by race for urban males entering the labor force between 1959-1965, 1955-1958, and prior to 1955. Welch discovered that the finding of earlier studies—that the ratio of nonwhite to white income declines with additional schooling—is not valid for those entering the labor force after 1955-1958. In fact, he finds for those entering the labor force during the 1960s that the direct return from an additional year of schooling is greater for blacks than for whites; for those entering during 1955-1958, the direct return is approximately the same for blacks and whites, and only for those entering prior to 1955 is the direct return greater for whites than blacks. If the indirect effects resulting from the increase in the number of weeks worked as a result of additional schooling are included, the greater return for blacks than whites begins with those entering the labor force in 1955-1958. By utilizing a cohort comparison, Welch shows that the return does not attenuate as experience increases; thus the greater return for "younger" blacks is indeed due to vintage. Welch suggests that the vintage effect is due to an improvement in the quality of schooling received by blacks. He presents statistics suggesting that not only has the quality of schooling improved for both blacks and whites, but there has been a relative improvement for blacks.

The lower level of schooling of nonwhites has been ascribed in part to the lower average rate of return and in part to an alleged greater "risk aversion" on the part of nonwhites compared to whites. Chiswick's Chapter 14 in this part finds that even if there were no difference in the degree of risk aversion, a lower level of schooling is to be expected because nonwhites experience a greater variance in the rate of return from schooling than do whites. Chiswick estimates that the variance in the rate of return is one-third larger for nonwhites than whites, both for the country as a whole and within regions. Because the average rate of return is lower for nonwhites, the coefficient of variation of the rate of return for nonwhites exceeds that of whites by even more, being approximately twice as large. As Chiswick shows, some of this difference may be due to greater variation in weeks worked by nonwhites, but it is unlikely that all of it is. Chiswick's findings, therefore, provide an alternative explanation for the lower level of schooling of nonwhites, since the greater uncertainty of return would induce nonwhites to invest in less schooling than whites.

Concluding Remarks

After remaining roughly stable during the 1950s and early 1960s, both family and individual income increased rapidly for nonwhites relative to whites during the 1960s. Although the increase was largely due to a tight labor market, the evidence suggests that improvement occurred for many segments of the population *net* of the benefits from the tight labor market. The evidence also suggests that the income gains have been greater for younger blacks, probably due to the substantial increase in the return to schooling for younger blacks.

Very large disparities still exist, however, between nonwhite and white income both for families and for males. Although the differentials are reduced when we control for age, education, and region of residence, the disparities remain sizeable. Furthermore, these disparities exist at all positions in the income distribution.

The empirical studies reviewed in this chapter were based on data through 1971 at the latest. The 1972 figures, which are now available, show that black family income was only 59 percent of white family income, down 2 percentage points since 1970. Within regions, the declines are even more substantial, ranging from 6 to 7 percentage points below the 1970 level for regions outside the South. For males, the percentage has not fallen for the country as a whole but in the Northeast and North Central it is down 7.6 and 5.3 percentage points, respectively, since its peaks of 1967-1968.

It is not at all clear, therefore, that the gains of the late 1960s are here to stay. The sizeable post-1964 increases in relative nonwhite income that remain after adjusting for cyclical effects, along with the evidence of both a relative and absolute increase in the return to schooling for blacks, suggest that other factors such as passage of the Civil Rights Act of 1964 and of fair employment laws by a large number of states, the War on Poverty programs and the programs to aid the urban ghettos of the mid-to-late 1960s, and perhaps a greater awareness of racial inequities on the part of the public, were at least partly responsible for the improvement in the relative income of nonwhites. This suggests that the poverty and antidiscrimination programs of the 1960s succeeded in at least partially increasing the income of blacks relative to whites. The conclusion seems apparent. We cannot afford to allow the decline revealed by the figures for the first few years of the 1970s to become the pattern of this decade. Programs designed to alleviate poverty and to provide blacks with opportunities identical to those of whites must be maintained.

References

Ashenfelter, O. (1970) "Changes in Labor Market Discrimination Over Time." *Journal of Human Resources* 5, pp. 403-30.

Batchelder, Alan. (1964) "The Decline in the Relative Income of Negro Men." *Quarterly Journal of Economics* 78, pp. 525-48.

Becker, G.S. (1957) *The Economics of Discrimination.* Chicago: The University of Chicago Press.

Chiswick, B.R. (1974) "Racial Differences in the Variation in Rates of Return from Schooling," Ch. 14, this volume.

Fein, R. (1965) "An Economic and Social Profile of the Negro American." *Daedalus* 94, pp. 815-46. Reprinted in T. Parsons and K. Clark,, *The Negro American.* Boston: Houghton Mifflin Co., 1966, pp. 102-33.

Fein, R. (1966) "Relative Income of Negro Men, Some Recent Data." *Quarterly Journal of Economics* 80, p. 336.

Formby, J.P. (1968) "The Extent of Wage and Salary Discrimination against Non-White Labor." *Southern Economic Journal* 35, pp. 140-50.

Gilman, H.J. (1965) "Economic Discrimination and Unemployment." *American Economic Review* 55, pp. 1077-96.

Guthrie, H.W. (1970) "The Prospects of Equality of Incomes between Black and White Families under Varying Rates of Unemployment." *Journal of Human Resources* 5, pp. 431-46.

Gwartney, J.D. (1970) "Changes in the Non-White-White Income Ratio, 1939-1967." *American Economic Review*, 60, pp. 872-83.

Gwartney, J.D. (1972) "Discrimination, Achievement, and Payoffs of a College Degree." *Journal of Human Resources*, 7, pp. 60-70.

Hanoch, G. (1967) "An Economic Analysis of Earnings and Schooling." *Journal of Human Resources* 2, pp. 310-29.

Iliestand, D. (1964) *Economic Growth and Employment Opportunities for Minorities.* New York: Columbia University Press.

Horowitz, A.R. (1974) "Trends in the Distribution of Family Income within and between Racial Groups." Ch. 12, this volume.

Rasmussen, D.W. (1970) "A Note on the Relative Income of Nonwhite Men: 1948-1964." *Quarterly Journal of Economics* 84, pp. 168-72.

Rayack, E. (1961) "Discrimination and the Occupational Progress of Negroes." *Review of Economics and Statistics* 43, pp. 209-14.

Raymond, R. (1969) "Changes in the Relative Economic Status of Nonwhites, 1950-1960." *Western Economic Journal* 7, pp. 57-70.

Schiller, B.R. (1973) *The Economics of Poverty and Discrimination.* Englewood Cliffs, N.J.: Prentice-Hall, Inc.

Terrell, H.S. (1971) "The Data on Relative White-Nonwhite Income and Earnings Re-examined: A Comment on Papers by Guthrie and Ashenfelter." *Journal of Human Resources* 6, pp. 384-91.

Thurow, L.C. (1969) *Poverty and Discrimination*. Washington, D.C.: The Brookings Institution.

von Furstenberg, G.M. (1974) "The Interrelation Between Labor and Capital Components of Racial Income Differences." *Journal of Political Economy*, 82, forthcoming.

Vroman, W. (1974) "Changes in Black Workers' Relative Earnings." Ch. 11, this volume.

Weiss, L., and Williamson, J.G. (1972) "Black Education, Earnings and Inter-regional Migration: Some New Evidence." *American Economic Review*, 62, pp. 372-83.

Welch, F. (1973) "Black-White Differences in Returns to Schooling." *American Economic Review* 63, pp. 893-907. Reprinted in Ch. 13, this volume.

_____ . (1967) "Labor Market Discrimination: An Interpretation of Income Differences in the Rural South." *Journal of Political Economy* 75, pp. 225-240.

Wohlstetter, A., and Coleman, S. (1972) "Race Differences in Income." In A. Pascal, ed., *Racial Discrimination in Economic Life*. Lexington, Mass.: Lexington Books, D.C. Heath, pp. 3-82.

11

Changes in Black Workers' Relative Earnings: Evidence from the 1960s

Wayne Vroman*

This chapter examines the earnings position of male and female black workers relative to white workers of the same sex with particular attention to trends in the 1960s. Multiple regressions are used to test for both long-run trends in relative earnings and for accelerated upward trends in the late 1960s. Included in the regressions are measures of labor-market tightness to hold constant effects of the business cycle on the relative earnings position of black workers. Two data sources are used in this analysis; the Census Bureau's Current Population Survey and the Continuous Work History Sample of the Social Security Administration.

The analysis leads to five main statistical findings. (1) The relative earnings of black men were strongly affected by labor-market demand conditions. Low unemployment rates were consistently important in raising black-white earnings ratios. (2) Black women realized much larger relative earnings gains than did black men. (3) Younger blacks, both men and women, experienced earnings increases that were proportionately much larger than those of older blacks. (4) There was evidence of a post-1964 acceleration of earnings gains for blacks with black women and southern blacks realizing the largest of these gains. (5) For black men working in the North, no evidence was found of a sustained upward trend in relative earnings. Most of these findings are based on regressions using the Social Security data, but the aggregate data for all blacks and whites from the Current Population Survey yield similar results.

There are four main sections in the chapter. The first section briefly surveys the strengths and weaknesses of the major sources of data useful for studying changes in the relative economic status of blacks. In the second section, nonwhite-to-white income ratios from the Current Population Survey for the period 1948 to 1971 are analyzed using multiple regression techniques, and the results are compared to earlier studies. Section three contains a similar analysis using data from the Social Security Continuous Work History Sample for the period 1957 to 1969 both in aggregate form and disaggregated by age, region, and position in the earnings distribution. The fourth section briefly considers the policy implications of the findings and concludes that relative educational advancements and manpower training programs were not mainly responsible for the upward trends observed in the late 1960s. Reduced racial discrimination in employment was probably responsible for much of the upward trend that occurred in the South after 1964.

---

*Economist, Policy Research Division, the Office of Economic Opportunity.

167

The Major Data Sources

The relative economic position of blacks in the United States can be analyzed with data from a number of sources. Here three sources will be compared and evaluated: (1) decennial census data, (2) data from the U.S. Census Bureau's Current Population Survey (hereafter referred to simply as the CPS) and (3) the Social Security Administration's Continuous Work History Sample (CWHS). Although there are many other sources,[1] these three are especially important for a study of black-white differences over a reasonably long data period.[2]

The decennial censuses provide the most detailed data for analyzing changes in the relative position of blacks in such socioeconomic dimensions as population, family size and composition, labor force and employment status, income, housing, and education. By comparing similar tabulations from successive censuses, one can study changes over ten-year intervals in the relative status of blacks.[3] Batchelder [5], for example, concluded from a comparison of 1950 and 1960 census data that the relative income of black men declined in the 1950s.[4] Several researchers including Duran Bell and Barbara Bergmann are currently analyzing the 1960 and 1970 censuses to determine what changes occurred in the decade of the 1960s.

Large sample sizes and richness of detail make these data an invaluable source. Decennial census data have the drawbacks, however, of generating only one observation per decade, and of possibly occurring at different points in the business cycle so that income and employment changes over ten-year intervals may be obscured by cyclical factors. As an example, the decennial censuses reveal that between 1959 and 1969 the ratio of median family income for blacks relative to whites rose from 0.51 to 0.61.[5] With annual observations one might be able to statistically analyze and isolate the effects of such factors as overall labor-market demand, increased educational achievement by blacks, and reduced labor-market discrimination on relative black-white family incomes.

Beginning with 1948, the Census Bureau's Current Population Survey provides annual tabulations of the distribution of income for families and for persons fourteen and older by race (white and nonwhite), based on a current sample size of 50,000 households of whom about one-tenth are nonwhite.[6] The data for persons display both personal income for all individuals with income and the earnings of wage and salary workers.[7] For recent years the CPS income data are cross-classified by age, region, education, occupation, industry, type of income and labor-force status. These cross classifications must be used with some care, however, because of the small number of nonwhites in the sample. About 2500 nonwhite families were included in the CPS from 1956 to 1965 and only 1500 in earlier years when the total sample was smaller.[8] These small numbers cause the sampling errors for nonwhites to be quite large and to grow with detailed disaggregations.[9]

These relatively large standard errors make it difficult to observe statistically significant changes in income ratios by race. For example, the standard error for the male nonwhite-to-white median personal income ratio was 0.02 in 1971. Only eleven of the annual first differences in this ratio exceeded 0.03 between 1948 and 1971. Much of the year-to-year change in the ratios, then, could be just noise. This situation limits the usefulness of the CPS in analyzing short-run income dynamics by race. Despite this shortcoming, however, the CPS is the only generally available data base for studying annual changes in the relative income position of nonwhites.

The Social Security Continuous Work History Sample (CWHS) data are collected from employer reports for 1 percent of all persons with earnings subject to Social Security contributions.[10] Two attractive features of these data are the large size of the sample and the fact that the sample is longitudinal. If a worker is selected for inclusion he or she will appear in the CWHS in all later years when he or she has covered earnings. In 1969 the CWHS had over 820,000 wage and salary workers of whom 52,600 were black men and 39,200 were black women.

These data with both race and employer detail are available annually since 1957.[11] Lags in processing of the wage records, however, cause delays of up to three years in publication of the data for the most recent years. In addition to detail by race, sex, and age of worker, the employee-employer CWHS records note the employer's location (state and county) and industry. Because an employer identification number is kept as well as the worker's Social Security number, it is possible to study the firm and industry stability of employment patterns using these data.[12]

The larger sample size for the CWHS means that black-white earnings ratios have much less sampling variability than in the CPS. For example, the ratio at the median for civilian male wage and salary workers aged 16 to 64 in 1969 was 0.592 and the standard error for the ratio was 0.007. Significant changes are also more easy to detect in these data because the sample is longitudinal. The year-to-year overlap in the CWHS exceeds 90 percent whereas for the CPS the year-to-year overlap of persons is slightly less than 50 percent. This overlap introduces a negative covariance term that reduces the variance of year-to-year income changes.[13] Further, these overlaps are present for periods longer than two years in the CWHS whereas they are completely absent in the CPS.

The CWHS has some serious weaknesses for analyzing income changes. Social Security coverage is pervasive in the economy but by no means universal. Nearly all federal civilian employees are excluded as are many state and local government employees and small farmers. The reporting of wages for domestic workers is also very incomplete. A second limitation is that actual earnings are known only up to the taxable wage ceiling. Earnings in excess of the ceiling are estimated, and this may cause large errors for individuals with high earnings and/or fluctuating earnings. Another limitation is the absence of information on education, occupation, and family status as well as weeks worked and hours worked per week. Additionally, information on transfer payments, income from capital, and property income is not present in the CWHS.

This brief survey of the decennial censuses, the CPS, and the CWHS has not shown any of the three to be uniquely superior for all purposes. For studying changes in the relative economic status of black Americans, each is useful but each has limitations. Some limitations are common to all three. For example, none of the three include hourly wage rates, cumulative lifetime work experience or the quality of education received.[14]

If we are to better understand how and why the relative position of blacks is changing, it would seem that all three of these data sources (and others like the SEO and EEOC data) need to be analyzed extensively. Comparing results from the different data bases should improve our understanding of how to devise and implement policies to ensure that blacks can obtain a more equitable share of the economic rewards in our society.

Reducing discrimination, eliminating poverty and raising the relative status of blacks and other minorities were important objectives of domestic social policy in the 1960s. Because the CPS and CWHS are annual in nature, they will be examined in the next two sections to identify exactly how much, if at all, the relative position of black workers has increased recently. The emphasis will be on the CWHS since the CPS has been analyzed extensively by others. A major focus with both will be the timing and size of the changes that took place in the 1960s.

Trends in CPS Income Data:
1948-1971

The relative income position of nonwhite men and women showed statistically significant increases between 1948 and 1971 with women realizing much larger gains than men. For nonwhite men, the trendwise increase in both personal income and in wage and salary income was confined largely to the post-1964 period. Nonwhite women, on the other hand, realized a statistically significant increase in relative income continuously throughout the 1948 to 1971 period. Their rate of increase, however, was much faster after 1964 than in the earlier years. These findings are based on multiple regressions using CPS data.

Many researchers have used the CPS for time-series analysis of changes in the relative income of nonwhites. The most comprehensive of these efforts is the work of Wohlstetter and Coleman [28] for the period 1948 to 1967. Their analysis of personal income data covered not only relative income at the medians of the white and nonwhite distributions but at other decile points as well. Using CPS information they estimated the effects of age, occupation, and education on observed racial differences in income. All three were found to contribute to the lower position of nonwhites. Over the 1948-1967 period Wohlstetter and

Coleman noted some relative gains for nonwhites in both tails and at the median of the income distributions.

This section examines changes in relative income and earnings measured at the medians of the white and nonwhite distributions.[15] Of the considerable literature in this area we note specifically the papers by Ashenfelter [3] and Rasmussen [16]. Both have a similar orientation, namely the use of multiple regressions to test for a statistically significant upward trend in the income position of nonwhites after holding constant the effects of labor-market demand. Their specifications differ mainly in the measurement of labor-demand conditions. Rasmussen used real GNP growth and the lagged unemployment rate while Ashenfelter used the current unemployment rate and the ratio by sex of the nonwhite to the white unemployment rate. One interesting difference in their results is that Rasmussen found a statistically significant upward trend for the nonwhite-white income ratio for men while Ashenfelter did not.

Similar equations were fitted for the 1948-1971 period to personal income ratios and to wage and salary income ratios by sex. The results appear in Table 11-1. The independent variables are defined as follows:

U = the current year's unemployment rate for the civilian labor force

Table 11-1
CPS Income Ratios, 1948-1971

Equation	Dependent Variable	Constant	U	U_{-1}	RELU	T	R^2	Se
11-1.1	Male wage and salary ratio	0.620	−1.235 (1.86)	−0.288 (.42)		0.00371 (3.89)	0.487	0.0321
11-1.2	Male personal income ratio	0.597	−1.462 (2.78)	−0.701 (1.32)		0.00336 (4.47)	0.620	0.0254
11-1.3	Female wage and salary ratio	0.458	−0.877 (0.80)	−2.315 (2.07)		0.01890 (11.99)	0.880	0.0532
11-1.4	Female personal income ratio	0.416	0.499 (0.66)	−1.606 (2.11)		0.02103 (19.52)	0.951	0.0363
11-1.5	Male wage and salary ratio	0.726	−1.183 (2.13)		−0.0594 (1.98)	0.00407 (4.55)	0.567	0.0295
11-1.6	Male personal income ratio	0.714	−1.556 (3.88)		−0.0711 (3.28)	0.00378 (5.85)	0.731	0.0213
11-1.7	Female wage and salary ratio	0.735	−1.903 (2.28)		−0.2136 (3.76)	0.02230 (13.74)	0.915	0.0449
11-1.8	Female personal income ratio	0.570	−0.212 (0.34)		−0.1237 (2.90)	0.02299 (18.86)	0.958	0.0337

Note: All variables are defined in the text. The numbers in parentheses beneath the coefficients are t ratios. The standard errors of estimate, Se, appear in the last column.

$RELU$ = the ratio by sex of the nonwhite to the white unemployment rate
T = a linear trend, 1948 = 1

The first four equations in the table are the same as Rasmussen's except that real GNP growth has been replaced by the current unemployment rate.[16] Equations 11.1.5-11.1.8 differ from Ashenfelter's only in the use of actual income ratios rather than logarithms of the ratios.[17]

The linear trend is positive and statistically significant at the 0.01 level in all equations. Of the eight t ratios, the smallest is 3.89. The trend coefficients are five or six times larger in the female equations than in the male equations. Table 11-1 shows that the relative income of nonwhite men as well as women exhibited a statistically significant upward trend between 1948 and 1971. This finding contrasts with Ashenfelter's results and is caused by the addition of more recent data points as well as observations for 1948 and 1949.

The results in Table 11-1 indicate that the trends in the two income ratios (personal income and wage and salary income) were quite similar over the 1948-1971 period. Equations 11.1.5-11.1.8 have a better fit than 11.1.1-11.1.4. Differences in R^2 are especially noticeable in the equations for men, 11.1.1 and 11.1.2 versus 11.1.5 and 11.1.6. The better fit of the last four equations may mean that relative unemployment mirrors closely changes in average weeks worked by race, and that weeks worked is an important determinant of annual earnings.

The overall unemployment rate generally has a higher t-value in the male equations.[18] Since men form the majority of both employment and unemployment, movements in the male unemployment rate dominate movements in the overall rate. Thus one might expect the overall rate to be more important in the male equations while the ratio of unemployment rates by sex would be more important in the female equations. This is roughly what is observed in Equations 11.1.5 to 11.1.8.

Although Table 11-1 reveals a statistically significant upward trend in the relative income of nonwhites, the equations assume constancy in the year-to-year increases except for changes in labor-market demand conditions. Much of domestic social policy in the 1960s was aimed at reducing discrimination and raising the relative incomes of blacks and other minority groups. If antidiscrimination and antipoverty policies were successful to any large extent, evidence might be found in the CPS income data. Specifically, one would look for an acceleration in the rate of increase of nonwhite incomes in the late 1960s.

To test for an acceleration in nonwhite income gains, a second trend variable was added to the regressions of Table 11-1. This trend variable (T 65) was assigned a value of zero from 1948 to 1964, then 1 in 1965, 2 in 1966, up to 7 in 1971.[19] One possible way to interpret this trend is that it assumes discrimination decreased gradually and uniformly between 1964 and 1971 and that its coefficient estimates the impact of reduced discrimination on nonwhites' incomes. Using such a trend is admittedly a crude procedure. Yet the importance of determining whether discrimination decreased and of measuring by how much nonwhite incomes rose makes it necessary to formulate tests. This needs to be done even though precise quantification of the effects of discrimination on the earnings and social status of blacks is obviously a most difficult measurement problem.[20]

Table 11-2 shows the results of adding T 65 to the equations in Table 11-1. In five of the eight equations, T 65 is statistically significant at the 0.01 level. The exceptions are three of the equations explaining the personal income ratios: Equations 11.2.4, 11.2.6, and 11.2.8. All eight coefficients for T 65 are positive with the ones in the wage and salary equations larger than those in the personal income equations. Thus there is strong statistical evidence of a post-1964 acceleration in nonwhite earnings gains and weaker evidence of an acceleration in personal income gains. From the regression coefficients it appears that male earnings converged at an increased rate of about 0.017 per year after 1964, while for women the increased convergence was in the range of 0.032-0.036 per year. The point estimates of accelerated personal income convergence are lower for both sexes.

Other interesting results also are revealed in Table 11-2. First, the lagged unemployment rate and the relative unemployment rate are no longer statistically significant. The current unemployment rate retains roughly the same level of statistical significance, increasing in Equations 11.2.1 and 11.2.2 while decreasing in 11.2.5, 11.2.6, and 11.2.7. Second, the coefficient for T, the original trend variable, is no longer statistically significant in the male equations although it is still highly significant in the female equations.[21] One can infer from Table 11-2 that all of the statistically significant trendwise increases in the male wage and salary ratio occurred after 1964. For women, on the other hand, there was a statistically significant trend for the entire period, but the rate of increase accelerated sharply after 1964. Finally, reduced labor-market discrimination against nonwhites should show up more strongly in wage and salary data than in personal income data since the latter includes transfer payments and income from capital as well as wages and salaries. Furthermore, some transfers such as State Unemployment Insurance and AFDC benefits are lower when annual wages and salaries are higher. Both considerations lead us to expect the post-1964 trend to be larger for wage and salary income than for personal income. The results in Table 11-2 conform to this expectation.[22]

These results suggest that discrimination decreased after 1964, but this is not conclusive. Reasonable people could dispute either the assumption that discrimination decreased markedly in the late 1960s, or that annual reductions followed the smooth path posited by the trend variable T 65. In either case, the interpretation of the T 65 coefficient would be called into question. To try to shed more light on this matter we examined the Social Security CWHS data. The similarity in findings lends support to the results presented in Table 11-2 and,

Table 11-2
CPS Income Ratios, Post-1964 Trend Added, 1948-1971

Equation	Dependent Variable	Constant	Independent Variables					Summary Statistics	
			U	U_{-1}	RELU	T	T65	R^2	Se
11-2.1	Male wage and salary ratio	0.595	-1.095 (2.29)	0.826 (1.52)		-0.00054 (0.47)	0.01780 (4.46)	0.749	0.0231
11-2.2	Male personal income ratio	0.580	-1.371 (3.14)	0.025 (0.05)		0.00059 (0.55)	0.01160 (3.18)	0.752	0.0210
11-2.3	Female wage and salary ratio	0.405	-0.591 (1.11)	-0.039 (0.06)		0.01020 (7.89)	0.03638 (8.17)	0.974	0.0257
11-2.4	Female personal income ratio	0.396	0.606 (0.89)	-0.755 (0.98)		0.01778 (10.68)	0.01360 (2.40)	0.962	0.0327
11-2.5	Male wage and salary ratio	0.573	-0.813 (1.74)		0.0225 (0.64)	-0.00057 (0.36)	0.01744 (3.30)	0.725	0.0241
11-2.6	Male personal income ratio	0.646	-1.391 (3.54)		-0.0345 (1.18)	0.00171 (1.28)	0.00779 (1.76)	0.769	0.0203
11-2.7	Female wage and salary ratio	0.511	-0.769 (1.66)		-0.0684 (1.91)	0.01237 (7.74)	0.03191 (7.33)	0.978	0.0235
11-2.8	Female personal income ratio	0.491	0.189 (0.30)		-0.0724 (1.51)	0.01948 (9.17)	0.01127 (1.93)	0.964	0.0316

Note: All statistics are defined as in Table 11-1.

perhaps, to the conclusion that racial discrimination decreased after 1964. Since the CWHS has a larger data base, it permits more detailed analysis of recent patterns of change in the relative earnings of black workers.

Earnings Trends in Social Security
Data: 1957 to 1969

An examination of the Social Security earnings data indicates that in some segments of the black population quite rapid earnings advances occurred between 1957 and 1969. In other segments, particularly for prime-age men residing in the North, practically no statistically significant changes were observed during this same time span. A major conclusion to be drawn from this analysis of disaggregated data is that undifferentiated assertions about recent changes, or the lack of change, in the relative status of black workers are apt to be only partially correct.

Detailed findings as to recent changes in the economic status of blacks are based on multiple regressions explaining time-series variation between 1957 and 1969 in ratios of black earnings to white earnings. From these regressions we can list five main findings. (1) Black male earnings are much more cyclically sensitive than the earnings of white men. Further, this sensitivity was found to be relatively greater for younger blacks, for blacks in the North, and for blacks at lower points in the earnings distribution. (2) Black women realized much larger earnings gains than black men between 1957 and 1969. (3) Younger blacks of both sexes experienced much larger gains over this period than older blacks. For women, statistically significant increases occurred in nearly all age groups, while for men the gains were confined to younger persons. (4) Most interestingly, there was evidence of a statistically significant acceleration in the relative earnings of many blacks after 1964. Black women in both the North and South experienced these gains as did black men in the South. Furthermore, these post-1964 gains were generally larger at the lower parts than at the upper parts of the earnings distributions. (5) For black men in the North there was no measurable statistically significant trendwise improvement in relative earnings between 1957 and 1969. No evidence was found of either a gradual long-run upward trend or of an accelerated post-1964 trend. Although earnings ratios for these men rose somewhat in the late 1960s, all of the increases can be attributed to the strong labor-market demand conditions of this period.

Age-Earnings Profiles in 1964

Because the 1 percent CWHS is such a large data base it can be disaggregated in a number of ways. Figure 11-1 displays age-earnings profiles for men and women

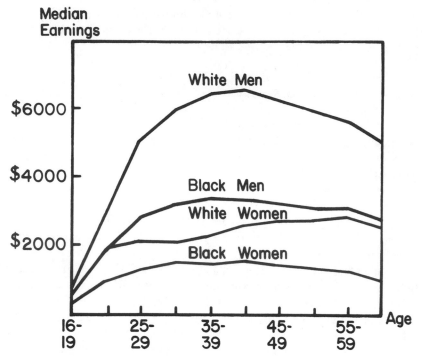

Figure 11-1. Age-Earnings Profiles by Sex and Race for 1964 (Data are Medians from the Social Security Continuous Work History Sample.)

of the two races in 1964. Median earnings are shown for civilian workers in the ten age groups from 16-19 to 60-64. The most obvious feature of the graph is the height of the white male profile in comparison to the other three. The white male profile also shows much more curvature than the others. Thus the ratio of black male to white male median earnings in 1964 was lowest for workers aged 40-44 and 45-49, equaling 0.514 and 0.517 respectively.

For white women, the profile dips at ages 30-34. Because of the flatness of the white female profile at younger ages, the black-white ratio does not show a large decrease until older ages. The ratio decreases for older women, however, both because white female earnings are rising and because black female earnings are declining relative to the earnings of younger female workers. It is interesting to note that the white female profile peaks at ages 55 to 59. Differences in the two female profiles are largely due to the tendency for white women to withdraw from the labor force when they have children. Black women with small children are much more likely to keep working than are whites.[23]

Age-earnings profiles constructed from other data sources, particularly decennial census data, have very similar shapes.[24] Before leaving Figure 11-1, two observations should be made. First, all four profiles exhibit substantial curvature when the entire 16-64 age range is considered. Consequently, measures of average earnings will change when the age distribution of employment changes. Specifically, an increase in the proportion of young workers who typically have low wages will slow the growth in average earnings. This is especially relevant for black workers because they tend to enter the labor force at younger ages than whites. In CWHS data the age distribution can be held constant. This cannot be done with the CPS income data prior to 1965. Second, differences in black-white earnings are small for younger workers. In 1964 the differences for men at ages 16-19 and 20-24 were $211 and $1149, respectively. Figure 11-1 shows that differences were also quite modest in the five youngest female age groups. To anticipate a later finding, it is precisely in these seven age-sex groups that black workers made their largest relative gains between 1957 and 1969.

The Regression Model

The purpose of this analysis is to document changes in the relative earnings status of blacks using time-series multiple regressions. Wage and salary income data from the CWHS were disaggregated by age, sex, and region, and relative status was measured by the ratio of black to white earnings at specific points on the earnings distributions. These ratios were taken not only at the medians but also at the first, third, seventh, and ninth decile points.[25]

In choosing a regression specification, three factors were considered. With only thirteen annual observations, there is a need to preserve degrees of freedom by using relatively few explanatory variables. To make the results comparable with those of the second section, similar specifications were employed. In particular, there is a test for an acceleration in black earnings gains after 1964. Also, the functional form that best fits the data was sought. After some experimentation at the aggregate level, the following equation was chosen.[26] It performed quite well on all three criteria.

$$R = a + b\,RU + cT + d\,T65$$

where

> R = the ratio of black wages and salaries to white wages and salaries at specified decile points
> RU = the reciprocal of the national average unemployment rate for the civilian labor force
> T = a linear trend, 1957 = 1
> $T65$ = a post-1964 trend. It equaled zero from 1957 to 1964, and then 1 in 1965, 2 in 1966, and so forth.

Using the reciprocal of the unemployment rate introduces a nonlinearity into the relationship which would be expected if the labor market behaves like a queue with black workers at the end of the lines.[27] As labor markets tighten up, blacks are apt to benefit increasingly from equal successive reductions in the overall unemployment rate. In the CWHS data, the reciprocal formulation explained more variance than did a linear relationship.

Tables 11-3 and 11-4 show the results of fitting Equation (11.1) to national ratios of median earnings for men and women, respectively, by age group, for all ages, and for all ages weighted by the 1964 employment in each age group. The weighting holds constant the age distributions over time.

The results show that labor-market tightness exerts a statistically significant positive effect on the male earnings ratios for the seven age groups between 20

Table 11-3

Male Earnings Ratios by Age, CWHS Data, 1957-1969

Equation	Age Group	Constant a	RU	T	T65	R^2	Se
			Independent Variables			Summary Statistics	
11-3.1	16-19	0.672	−0.00354 (0.77)	0.00796 (1.54)	0.02772 (1.79)	0.792	0.0373
11-3.2	20-24	0.402	0.00735 (4.43)	0.00903 (4.81)	0.01638 (2.92)	0.985	0.0135
11-3.3	25-29	0.406	0.00600 (5.05)	0.00409 (4.09)	0.00392 (0.98)	0.971	0.0097
11-3.4	30-34	0.432	0.00388 (6.16)	0.00227 (3.19)	0.01252 (5.89)	0.991	0.0051
11-3.5	35-39	0.457	0.00354 (3.86)	−0.00051 (0.49)	0.01171 (3.78)	0.967	0.0075
11-3.6	40-44	0.436	0.00380 (5.98)	0.00012 (0.16)	0.01160 (5.41)	0.986	0.0052
11-3.7	45-49	0.490	0.00224 (3.05)	-0.00299 (3.61)	0.01645 (6.63)	0.971	0.0060
11-3.8	50-54	0.505	0.00243 (2.11)	−0.00343 (2.64)	0.01219 (3.14)	0.885	0.0094
11-3.9	55-59	0.549	0.00099 (0.94)	−0.00349 (2.93)	0.01490 (4.19)	0.884	0.0086
11-3.10	60-64	0.605	−0.00082 (0.55)	−0.00568 (3.37)	0.01782 (3.53)	0.679	0.0122
11-3.11	16-64	0.443	0.00360 (2.83)	0.00063 (0.43)	0.00479 (1.11)	0.902	0.0104
11-3.12	16-64 Fixed Age Weights	0.463	0.00363 (5.15)	0.00027 (0.34)	0.01220 (5.13)	0.984	0.0057

Note: All statistics are defined as in Table 11-1.

Table 11-4
Female Earnings Ratios by Age, CWHS Data, 1957-1969

Equation	Age Group	Constant a	Independent Variables			Summary Statistics	
			RU	T	T65	R^2	Se
11-4.1	16-19	0.663	−0.00461 (1.02)	0.00733 (1.43)	0.04012 (2.64)	0.857	0.0367
11-4.2	20-24	0.366	0.00068 (0.28)	0.01226 (4.58)	0.04282 (5.35)	0.981	0.0193
11-4.3	25-29	0.589	−0.00440 (2.13)	0.01458 (6.23)	0.04367 (6.25)	0.983	0.0169
11-4.4	30-34	0.563	−0.00065 (0.27)	0.01728 (6.33)	0.03506 (4.30)	0.981	0.0197
11-4.5	35-39	0.660	−0.00375 (1.43)	0.00640 (2.15)	0.05489 (6.19)	0.969	0.0214
11-4.6	40-44	0.593	−0.00299 (1.94)	0.00570 (3.28)	0.04103 (7.91)	0.982	0.0125
11-4.7	45-49	0.526	−0.00120 (0.97)	0.00260 (1.85)	0.03567 (8.53)	0.983	0.0101
11-4.8	50-54	0.526	−0.00282 (1.62)	0.00064 (0.32)	0.03415 (5.82)	0.946	0.0142
11-4.9	55-59	0.408	−0.00036 (0.22)	0.00651 (3.50)	0.00869 (1.56)	0.914	0.0134
11-4.10	60-64	0.420	0.00186 (2.14)	−0.01091 (10.58)	0.03167 (10.28)	0.969	0.0074
11-4.11	16-64	0.579	−0.00304 (2.02)	0.00471 (2.77)	0.03666 (7.22)	0.977	0.0122
11-4.12	16-64 Fixed Age Weights	0.550	−0.00189 (1.86)	0.00700 (6.09)	0.03993 (11.63)	0.993	0.0083

Note: All statistics are defined as in Table 11-1.

and 64 as well as for the entire male population, weighted or unweighted by the age distribution. Furthermore, the adverse effect of unemployment tends to decrease with age.

The coefficient for T shows that between 1957 and 1969 there was a secular increase in the relative earnings position of young black men. This coefficient is positive for the four youngest age groups and statistically significant for all except the very youngest. In these age groups, black gains in the number of years of school completed have been quite large. Probably the education gains contribute to the size and statistical significance of these trend coefficients.

For the four oldest male age groups the long-run trend coefficients are negative and statistically significant. This may be due to a more rapid decrease in the number of weeks worked by older black men than by white men between

1957 and 1969.[28] The positive trends for younger workers and negative trends for older workers roughly balance out in the aggregate with the long-run trend coefficients in Equations 11.3.11 and 11.3.12 not differing significantly from zero.

The positive and mostly significant coefficients for the post-1964 trend variable support the finding in the CPS data of an acceleration in the relative earnings of blacks after 1964. The eight statistically significant coefficients for the specific age groups range between 0.011 and 0.018. The coefficient for T 65 for the population as a whole is much smaller and not statistically significant when the estimates are not adjusted for changes in the age of employed men.[29] With the appropriate adjustment, the coefficient for T 65 equals 0.012 which is consistent with the estimates for the individual age groups. Furthermore, Equation 11.3.12 has considerably less error variance than 11.3.11, because there is less noise from the changing age weights in the dependent variable.

In contrast to the male equations most of the unemployment coefficients in the female equations have negative signs, but very few are statistically significant. One interpretation of this finding is that women of both races experience roughly similar variations in median earnings over the business cycle. If anything, the earnings of white women are the more volatile of the two.

Evidence of a long-run uptrend in the relative earnings of black women is quite strong. The coefficients for T are nearly all positive and most are statistically significant. There is also a pronounced pattern by age with the coefficients increasing up to the 30-34 age group and decreasing thereafter. The preponderance of positive trends shows up in the two aggregative equations of Table 11-4 where T has positive and statistically significant coefficients. In contrast to black men, there is a measurable long-run upward trend in the relative earnings of black women.

Table 11-4 also displays strong evidence of an acceleration in black female earnings after 1964. All of the coefficients for the post-1964 trend are positive and only one is not statistically significant. The range of coefficients for the ten age groups is from 0.009 to 0.055 with eight lying between 0.032 and 0.044. These results suggest not only an acceleration in black female earnings but also a much faster acceleration in comparison to black male earnings.

The aggregate results for women are shown in Equations 11.4.11 and 11.4.12. The unexpected sign persists for the unemployment coefficients, and both trend coefficients are positive and statistically significant. Age weighting again turns out to be important in using the aggregate data. The unexplained sum of squares is roughly twice as large in Equation 11.4.11 as in 11.4.12 where the racial age distributions of female employment are held constant. Also, the trend coefficients are larger and more statistically significant in 11.4.12 than in 11.4.11. For black women, as for black men, changing age weights tend to lower the estimated rate of earnings convergence in aggregate CWHS data.

Earnings Trends by Region for
Selected Decile Points

Since about half of the black population resides in the South,[30] it seems important to examine the CWHS data by region. To further increase the detail of the analysis, black-white ratios at the first, third, seventh, and ninth deciles—and the mean as well as the median—were examined.

Because of the large number of equations in an analysis by age, sex, and region for six distribution points—288 altogether—the age dimension was collapsed. From the results in Tables 11-3 and 11-4, however, changing age weights are known to influence parameter estimates in aggregate equations. Consequently, the earnings ratios analyzed in this section all used earnings data with fixed age weights. The weights were 1964 regional employment by race and sex for the ten age groups appearing in Tables 11-3 and 11-4.

The regional decile ratios were regressed against the same explanatory variables as in Tables 11-3 and 11-4 except that separate unemployment rates were used for the North and South. The results are presented in Tables 11-5 and 11-6. The unemployment rates were very similar for both regions with the average in the South being somewhat lower, but the regional rates gave a slightly better fit than the national rate.[31]

Generally speaking, the fit of the equations in Tables 11-5 and 11-6 is quite good, nineteen of the twenty-four R^2's exceed 0.90, and many coefficients are statistically significant. Within each set of six equations the pattern of coefficients seems to be quite consistent, and generally similar to results for the national medians.[32] The reciprocal of the unemployment rate has the expected positive sign in the male equations while in the female equations its coefficient sign is again negative. For the North the fit is better in the middle of the distribution than in the tails. For the South, on the other hand, the standard errors of estimate are somewhat smaller at the ninth decile than at the median for both men and women. For both sexes and in both regions the first decile ratio displays the worst fit. Since the first deciles contain the most marginal workers, these ratios may be strongly influenced by movements into and out of earnings status over the business cycle. The estimates of the first decile points may also contain relatively large interpolation errors.

For men in the North the unemployment rate is the only consistently important explainer of the earnings ratios. Furthermore, the size of the unemployment coefficient is smaller for higher deciles suggesting that black men with relatively high earnings are more isolated from the business cycle than blacks with low earnings. The trend variables are not statistically significant except in the equation for the third decile. In the North, then, the relative position of black men between 1957 and 1969 depended only on overall labor-market demand conditions.

Table 11-5
Male Black-White Earnings Ratios by Region for Selected Decile Points, 1957-1969

Equation	Decile Point	a	Independent Variables			Summary Statistics	
			RU	T	$T65$	R^2	Se
			NORTH				
11-5.1	First	0.224	0.00792 (4.98)	0.00216 (1.14)	−0.00663 (1.19)	0.891	0.0137
11-5.2	Third	0.415	0.00690 (8.41)	0.00454 (4.63)	−0.00538 (1.88)	0.975	0.0071
11-5.3	Fifth	0.596	0.00474 (10.53)	0.00012 (0.22)	0.00191 (1.22)	0.983	0.0039
11-5.4	Seventh	0.645	0.00413 (8.42)	−0.00059 (1.00)	0.00019 (0.11)	0.962	0.0042
11-5.5	Ninth	0.642	0.00233 (1.20)	−0.00078 (0.34)	0.00445 (0.66)	0.548	0.0167
11-5.6	Mean	0.545	0.00435 (7.13)	0.00113 (1.55)	−0.00144 (0.68)	0.958	0.0052
			SOUTH				
11-5.7	First	0.400	0.00153 (1.14)	−0.00722 (4.75)	0.01911 (4.02)	0.858	0.0109
11-5.8	Third	0.403	0.00214 (3.34)	0.00022 (0.30)	0.01950 (8.59)	0.990	0.0052
11-5.9	Fifth	0.475	0.00201 (2.36)	−0.00041 (0.43)	0.01441 (4.82)	0.971	0.0069
11-5.10	Seventh	0.506	0.00175 (2.54)	−0.00071 (0.91)	0.01446 (5.90)	0.978	0.0056
11-5.11	Ninth	0.527	0.00113 (1.47)	−0.00056 (0.64)	0.00879 (3.21)	0.928	0.0063
11-5.12	Mean	0.471	0.00167 (3.34)	−0.00068 (1.19)	0.01226 (6.93)	0.984	0.0041

Note: All statistics are defined as in Table 11-1.

Quite a different situation held for black men in the South after 1964. In each of the last six equations of Table 11-5, the post-1964 trend is statistically significant and has a positive coefficient. Also there is a pronounced tendency for the $T65$ coefficient to be larger in the lower parts of the earnings distribution. It is twice as large at the first and third deciles as it is at the ninth decile.

Although the unemployment coefficients have the expected positive signs and four of the six have t ratios of at least two, they are much smaller in the South than in the North. This could mean that the employment of black men in the

Table 11-6

Female Black-White Earnings Ratios by Region for Selected Decile Points, 1957-1969

Equation	Decile Point	a	Independent Variable			Summary Statistics	
			RU	T	$T65$	R^2	Se
			NORTH				
11-6.1	First	0.814	−0.00014 (0.03)	0.00175 (0.27)	0.00402 (0.21)	0.092	0.0467
11-6.2	Third	0.746	−0.00300 (1.62)	0.00895 (4.05)	0.03188 (4.94)	0.968	0.0160
11-6.3	Fifth	0.720	−0.00109 (1.01)	0.01143 (8.93)	0.02268 (6.06)	0.989	0.0093
11-6.4	Seventh	0.720	−0.00105 (1.67)	0.00953 (12.71)	0.02291 (10.46)	0.996	0.0054
11-6.5	Ninth	0.763	−0.00087 (0.60)	0.00875 (5.03)	0.01155 (2.28)	0.954	0.0125
11-6.6	Mean	0.723	−0.00052 (0.70)	0.01037 (11.65)	0.01652 (6.38)	0.993	0.0064
			SOUTH				
11-6.7	First	1.068	0.00119 (0.24)	−0.02562 (4.52)	0.00547 (0.31)	0.883	0.0406
11-6.8	Third	0.549	−0.00291 (2.14)	0.00094 (0.61)	0.03614 (7.51)	0.961	0.0110
11-6.9	Fifth	0.516	−0.00381 (3.93)	0.00007 (0.07)	0.05163 (15.10)	0.992	0.0078
11-6.10	Seventh	0.496	−0.00204 (2.24)	0.00593 (5.76)	0.04093 (12.71)	0.994	0.0074
11-6.11	Ninth	0.556	−0.00002 (0.03)	0.01102 (12.24)	0.01809 (6.41)	0.994	0.0065
11-6.12	Mean	0.559	−0.00214 (3.50)	0.00561 (8.13)	0.03353 (15.52)	0.996	0.0050

Note: All statistics are defined as in Table 11-1.

South is less concentrated in cyclically sensitive industries than in the North. Perhaps the South should be further divided into SMSA and non-SMSA counties to test whether this lower cyclical sensitivity is related to the greater representation of southern blacks in rural and other non-SMSA counties.

From Table 11-5 it appears there was no long-run upward trend in the relative earnings of black men in either the North or the South from 1957 to 1969. In the South, however, relative earnings did move up sharply after 1964 at an average rate of from 0.009 to 0.019 per year, depending upon where in the distribution earnings ratios are measured, with the ratio of mean earnings rising at the rate of 0.012 per year after 1964.

Turning to the female equations, Table 11-6 shows different patterns of earnings convergence for black women in the North and South. Both trend coefficients are statistically significant at the 5 percent level for all of the northern equations except 11.6.1. The coefficients for the long-run trend are all of about the same size and indicate per decade increases in the earnings ratios of from 0.09 to 0.11. Equations 11.6.2-11.6.6 also reveal an acceleration in earnings gains after 1964 with the rate of acceleration being larger in the lower portions of the earnings distributions. Equation 11.6.6 shows a per year gain for black women of 0.010 between 1957 to 1964 and 0.027 between 1965 and 1969.

In the South the long-run upward trend was statistically significant only at the upper points of the earnings distributions, specifically for the seventh and ninth deciles.[33] An acceleration in earnings gains after 1964 was generally observed for southern black women. The coefficient for T 65 was statistically significant at the 1 percent level in all equations except 11.6.7. From Equation 11.6.12, we conclude that southern black women's relative mean earnings increased 0.006 per year before 1965 and 0.039 per year between 1965 and 1969. Compared to northern black women this was a slower rate of increase until 1964 and more rapid after that date.

The unemployment coefficients for women are negative in all twelve equations. In the South, four of the six coefficients have t ratios of two or larger while none of the coefficients in the North are statistically significant. The results for the South are similar to those based on national data shown in Table 11-4. This suggests that white women, especially in the South, experienced larger cyclical earnings changes between 1957 and 1969 than did black women.

Concluding Discussion

In the aggregate the results from the CWHS and CPS data agree quite closely. Both sources of data show that black earnings gains accelerated after 1964. Neither show evidence of an upward trend prior to 1965 for men of all age groups taken together but both indicate a rapid increase in black male relative earnings after 1964. For black women, both show an upward trend prior to 1965 as well as the rapid acceleration in trend after 1964. The CWHS data permit a more detailed description of the recent changes in relative black earnings which reveals sharp contrasts in the trends by age of worker, by region, and by position in the earnings distribution.

A question arises, however, as to the effects of collinearity of the independent variables on the estimated coefficients in Tables 11-3 through 11-6. Because the latter part of the 1957-1969 data period was characterized by generally falling unemployment rates, the three explanatory variables RU, T and T 65 are highly correlated.[34] These intercorrelations undoubtedly raise the standard errors of the regression coefficients, but they do not necessarily lead to biases.[35] The fact that the trend coefficients agree quite closely in the aggregate CPS and CWHS equations may be evidence against any strong biases in Tables 11-3 through 11-6. Until CWHS data from 1970, 1971, and 1972 become available, questions about the effects of collinearity on the point estimates will remain. The higher unemployment rate in these years will reduce the collinearity between unemployment and the trends.

The regression analysis found that unemployment and the two time trends were frequently statistically significant in accounting for changes in the earnings ratios. Statistical significance and importance (that is, aggregative impact), however, are not the same thing. Statistically significant trend coefficients may be found but, if they are not large or if they do not persist, large black-white earnings differences may be expected to continue for many years or indefinitely.

Earnings ratios at the medians by sex, age, and region for 1959, 1964 and 1969 are displayed in Table 11-7. The ratios show how far from equality black men still were in 1969. The relative position of blacks in the South was considerably lower than in the North in 1969, even though the post-1964 trend toward convergence was more rapid in the South after 1964. For each age group, the 1959 to 1964 increases were generally much smaller than the 1964 to 1969 changes. The female ratios increased quite rapidly over the decade. It is interesting to note that the ratios exceeded unity for northern women aged 30-34, 35-39, and 40-44 in 1969. This serves as a good illustration of how much the relative position of black women has increased recently, but large differences are still observed in the South where ratios of less than 0.5 existed in the three oldest female groups in 1969.

One can follow cohort changes as well as changes for fixed age groups in Table 11-7. For example, workers aged 20-24 in 1959 were 25-29 in 1964 and 30-34 in 1969. The cohort ratios for men were generally stable, some even declining, between 1959 and 1964. Between 1964 and 1969 the ratios for all cohorts increased, with larger increases occurring in the South than in the North. The cohort ratios for women show greater changes took place after 1964 with the younger and middle age groups gaining the most.

Table 11-7 also shows the effect of differing age distributions of workers by race on the aggregate black-white earnings ratios. The ratio for all men aged 16-64 (0.592) is lower than every one of the ratios for specific age groups in 1969. In addition, the fixed age weight ratios grew more rapidly between 1964 and 1969 than did the aggregate unweighted 16-64 year-old ratios due to the rapid growth in black teen-age employment in the late 1960s.

To obtain an idea of how quickly the aggregate male ratio might approach unity, the 1969 cohort earnings ratios were projected to 1999. Even under very optimistic assumptions the aggregate black-white ratio is only 0.90 in 1999.[36] Equality of earnings for black women is a much more plausible short-run prospect. Since black men earn much more on the average than black women,

Table 11-7
Ratios of Median Earnings by Age, Sex, and Region

Age	U.S. Total			North			South		
	1959	1964	1969	1959	1964	1969	1959	1964	1969
MEN									
16-19	0.609	0.694	0.802	0.753	0.780	0.790	0.633	0.688	0.840
20-24	0.548	0.623	0.803	0.660	0.703	0.860	0.541	0.612	0.801
25-29	0.536	0.566	0.651	0.645	0.670	0.713	0.504	0.536	0.652
30-34	0.516	0.531	0.635	0.646	0.637	0.705	0.475	0.509	0.606
35-39	0.525	0.530	0.613	0.653	0.675	0.699	0.481	0.477	0.565
40-44	0.510	0.514	0.607	0.660	0.663	0.714	0.483	0.496	0.557
45-49	0.524	0.517	0.604	0.683	0.680	0.723	0.515	0.504	0.561
50-54	0.539	0.525	0.599	0.726	0.708	0.764	0.532	0.515	0.575
55-59	0.564	0.555	0.609	0.754	0.733	0.760	0.562	0.558	0.611
60-64	0.577	0.569	0.596	0.778	0.794	0.764	0.560	0.526	0.619
16-64	0.515	0.528	0.592	0.657	0.671	0.702	0.501	0.519	0.597
16-64 Fixed Age Weights	0.533	0.544	0.633	0.685	0.692	0.742	0.507	0.519	0.608
WOMEN									
16-19	0.581	0.661	0.806	0.716	0.821	0.883	0.573	0.711	0.827
20-24	0.397	0.509	0.767	0.515	0.667	0.863	0.336	0.391	0.706
25-29	0.550	0.615	0.853	0.759	0.828	0.960	0.420	0.463	0.755
30-34	0.560	0.707	0.958	0.773	0.987	1.147	0.450	0.474	0.826
35-39	0.624	0.641	0.925	0.840	0.884	1.111	0.512	0.470	0.750
40-44	0.548	0.602	0.803	0.787	0.845	1.010	0.425	0.446	0.643
45-49	0.508	0.526	0.718	0.726	0.780	0.904	0.447	0.420	0.559
50-54	0.466	0.495	0.629	0.649	0.729	0.864	0.404	0.416	0.487
55-59	0.409	0.460	0.546	0.626	0.652	0.765	0.358	0.370	0.421
60-64	0.409	0.373	0.482	0.555	0.559	0.703	0.418	0.349	0.385
16-64	0.530	0.574	0.759	0.728	0.797	0.940	0.456	0.455	0.622
16-64 Fixed Age Weights	0.526	0.582	0.794	0.723	0.804	0.964	0.445	0.454	0.645

Note: Data are from the Social Security Continuous Work History Sample.

their earnings are the major income source for black families. The slow rate of convergence of black male earnings implies that family income will also converge rather slowly despite the rapid gains realized by black women.[37] Even if earnings equality is achieved, equality of family incomes for blacks will not be assured because whites derive relatively more of family income from sources other than earnings.

Although the regressions in the first and second sections do not include policy variables, the statistical results do have policy implications. The list of policies for reducing racial discrimination and raising the earnings of black Americans includes education, manpower training, affirmative action programs, job quotas for employers, and guaranteed employment by governments. Of these policies, manpower training and affirmative action programs were in effect after 1964 and might be reflected in the coefficients on $T\,65$.

Relative educational gains for blacks occurred continuously throughout the 1957-1969 period.[38] If education were responsible for trendwise increases for blacks we would expect the trend variable T to have larger and statistically more significant coefficients for the youngest workers. This was found to be the case for men but not for women. Although there were undoubtedly educational gains for black women aged 25-29 and 30-34 over this period, much of the size and statistical significance of the trend coefficients for these ages must be due to changes in hours worked and to occupational changes, for example, an exodus from domestic service into clerical jobs. At least for black women we have to question how much of the trendwise earnings gains can properly be attributed to increases in relative educational achievement between 1957 and 1969.

From results in Tables 11-3 and 11-4, it also does not seem likely that manpower training programs were responsible for the acceleration of black earnings gains observed after 1964. The manpower training programs grew rapidly after that date and many of the trainees were black. One might therefore expect the coefficients of $T\,65$ to reflect partly the positive effects on black earnings of these programs. The pattern of coefficients in Tables 11-3 through 11-6 does not lend support to this conjecture. Considering the whole gamut of programs, the enrollees had a large representation of younger northern black men who reside mostly in cities.[39] Yet the coefficients for $T\,65$ were neither large nor statistically significant in the equations for younger men in the North.[40] In fact, the large statistically significant coefficients for $T\,65$ were in the equations for women in the South. Furthermore, in moving down the age distributions in Tables 11-3 and 11-4 there is no marked tendency for the $T\,65$ coefficients to become smaller.

The results in Tables 11-1 through 11-6 seem to reflect a gradual opening of certain jobs to blacks after 1964. Black men and women may have faced improved job opportunities, especially in the South, both at former jobs and in industries and occupations previously not open to them. Probably some part of the increased demand came from governments as well as from private industry. Documenting these changes requires a much more disaggregated analysis than was possible in the present chapter.[41] The patterns of statistical significance in the $T\,65$ trend coefficients do suggest an increase in demand for black workers after 1964. The increases appear to have been larger in the South and to have had more effect on the relative earnings of black women.

Appendix 11A

Comments on Vroman's "Changes in Black Workers' Relative Earnings: Evidence from the 1960s"

Richard L. Pfister*

The disaggregations that are possible with the Continuous Work History Sample (CWHS) of the Social Security Administration provide a fertile area for additional research. Vroman provides us with a useful beginning in analyzing relative earnings by sex, age group, region, different distribution points, and so on. Such disaggregated data will enable researchers to provide sounder policy recommendations. They can suggest areas where policies might be more effective, and they can monitor the effectiveness of previous policies more accurately.

Vroman's chapter does, however, have some problems with respect to interpretation of his statistical results. These problems stem primarily from his use of the catchall trend variable which is necessary because of the small number of observations. At one point Vroman suggests that the trend variable is a proxy for discrimination against blacks; in his earlier oral presentation of the chapter he suggested that it is a proxy for relative educational achievement of blacks. In fact the trend variable incorporates everything else that is not in the unemployment variable. It includes factors from both the supply side and the demand side in the labor market. One should be cautious about claiming the trend variable as a proxy for any particular factor.

Vroman provides reasonable explanations or hypotheses for some of his findings. But frequently other hypotheses are equally plausible. In Table 11-3, for example, Vroman finds a negative relationship between nonwhite-white earnings ratio and the trend variable among all but the four youngest age groups. He suggests that weeks worked decreased more rapidly for older blacks than for whites. I would suggest that the negative coefficient may simply be the result of blacks bumping up against barriers to further advancement or promotion such that their earnings over time do not rise as rapidly as the earnings of whites. Vroman cites Figure 11-1 to argue that the ratio of black earnings to white earnings actually increases for the ages beyond forty-five. But the data in Figure 11-1 are for just one year (1964), and the negative coefficient for the trend variable in Table 11-3 suggests to me that over time the gap between black and white earnings for the older men is widening. Figure 11-1 presents a static picture and does not tell us anything about the trends reported in Table 11-3.

*Professor of applied urban economics and director of Division of Research, Graduate School of Business, Indiana University.

Vroman also notes in Table 11-3 that the older age groups among males are less affected by unemployment than the younger age groups. He suggests that the older black males are less affected relatively by cyclical fluctuations. But this statement is not an explanation. A reason for this finding might be that the older blacks have more seniority and have worked up, because of their seniority, to jobs that are less sensitive to the cyclical fluctuations of the economy. Blacks might not gain relative to whites during periods of upswings in business activity because, after having been on the job for a number of years, they encounter barriers to further promotion. In other words, they have reached the end of their advancement in any particular occupation or job classification.

In Table 11-5, Vroman notes that neither trend variables was significant in explaining the earnings ratio in the North. He does not provide an explanation or a hypotheses for this finding. One might interpret this result to reflect the elimination of the easy-to-remove discrimination against blacks in the North. There could have been a "creaming" process in removing obstacles for the blacks so that the remaining obstacles are hard-core ones which showed no tendency to decline over the period of 1957 to 1969. By contrast, the earnings ratio in the South showed some acceleration after 1964. Perhaps the South has not yet completed this creaming process of eliminating discriminatory practices.

Not only are alternative explanations generally as plausible as some provided by Vroman, but many of his findings cry out for explanations or further investigation. He has written a long chapter, so I can hardly criticize him for not providing hypotheses for all of his findings. To provide more complete explanations or more hypotheses would require that he write a book. Still, the disaggregation of the data in using the Continuous Work History Sample does reveal many interesting relationships that need more research.

Notes

1. A partial list of other important sources includes the 1966 and 1967 Surveys of Economic Opportunity (SEO), the Michigan Longitudinal Study, the National Longitudinal Survey (NLS) conducted for the Manpower Administration by the Center for Human Resource Research at Ohio State and data collected by the Equal Employment Opportunity Commission (EEOC).

2. Data from the EEOC could also be used to examine changes over time in the relative position of blacks. For example, changes between 1966 and 1970 have been studied by Ashenfelter and Heckman [4]. These data, however, are available only from 1966, are restricted to larger firms (100 or more employees) in the private sector, and do not include wage rate and earnings information.

3. Before the 1970 census, the racial breakdown in most of the published census data was for whites and nonwhites only. Since blacks constitute over 90 percent of all nonwhites, the distinction between blacks and other nonwhites is

not crucial for many black-white comparisons. For a comparison of the change in detail between 1960 and 1970, see [20] and [21].

4. Prior to Batchelder, both Becker [6] and Rayack [17] had examined changes between 1940 and 1950. Because personal income data by race were not available in the 1940 Census, their comparisons were made using indices that weighted white and nonwhite occupational distributions by average wages and salaries within occupations. Ashenfelter and Heckman [4] and Bergmann and Lyle [9] have used similar indices in their analysis of EEOC data.

5. See Table 16 in [22].

6. Separate tabulations for blacks from the CPS are shown for 1964 and later years.

7. Earnings include proprietors' income (farm and nonfarm) as well as wages and salaries. In this chapter, however, we will often use the term earnings in reference to just wages and salaries. For the years 1955 and later, the CPS has published earnings data for full-time, full-year wage and salary workers as well as for all wage and salary workers.

8. The contrast with the Survey of Economic Opportunity (SEO) is striking. Whereas the CPS breakdown by race is about 45,000 white families and 5,000 nonwhite families, the numbers in the 1967 SEO were 19,700 and 9,600 for whites and nonwhites, respectively.

9. For example, the standard error for a nonwhite population estimate of ten million is 72,000 or 0.7 percent. But for a population estimate of 100,000 the standard error is 12,000 or 12 percent. See Table F of [23].

10. See [24] for a more complete description of the CWHS. Brimmer [10] and McCall [14] are among the few who have used the CWHS to examine earnings differences by race.

11. The race breakdown is blacks, other nonwhites, and whites.

12. To date only Alexander [2] has exploited this employee-employer information in the CWHS data.

13. For example, suppose that mean income in two consecutive years was $5000 and $5200 with a standard error of $50 in both years. Also, suppose the year-to-year covariation in income was 0.8. The standard error for the change in income would be $71 if there were no overlap in the two samples but $37 if the overlap were 0.90. See [13, pp. 462-63].

14. SEO is the only data source mentioned here that includes hourly wage rates.

15. Median earnings by race and sex are from Census Bureau income publications, see Table 59 in [23]. The personal income medians were supplied by my coworkers Fritz Scheuren and Lock Oh who have recomputed the published medians.

16. This change does not affect the substance of the results. With current GNP growth the R^2's are slightly higher and lagged unemployment enters significantly in 11.1.1 and 11.1.2, but the trend coefficients are almost identical in size and in statistical significance to those in Table 11-1.

17. Practically identical results were obtained using the logs of the ratios.

18. Perry's [15] weighted unemployment rate which adjusts for cyclical changes in labor-force participation and for changes in the age-sex composition of the labor force was also used in place of the BLS overall unemployment rate. This caused no major changes in the results in either the first or second sections.

19. The results here and in the third section were very similar when the acceleration was assumed to start in 1964, 1966, or 1967 rather than 1965. Thus the exact beginning of the accelerated earnings trend could not be pinned down to one year. A post-1964 trend was selected to coincide with the civil rights legislation of 1964.

20. Schiller's paper [18] attempts to separate the effects of racial and class discrimination on observed black-white differences in socioeconomic status. A very interesting quantification of discriminatory attitudes appears in the paper by Bergmann and Lyle [9]. Their proxy is the percentage of votes received by Governor Wallace in selected SMSAs in 1968. This variable proved to be important in explaining the relative occupational status of blacks.

21. The coefficient for T was also not statistically significant in Equation 11.2.2 using changes in real GNP as in Rasmussen's specification. The point estimate was -0.0001 with a t ratio of 0.08.

22. Quite similar results were obtained when logarithmetic versions of Table 11-2 were fitted. The trend variable T 65 entered very significantly in all of the wage and salary equations and in Equation 11.2.2.

23. Published data from the BLS monthly labor-force survey show contrasting labor-force behavior for married nonwhite and white women in this age range. See Table B1 in [25].

24. See [20] for male age-earnings data by race in the 1960 census.

25. The decile points were computed from tabular data arranged in fixed income intervals. It was assumed these data came from distributions that could be approximated by a three-point log-normal distribution [1]. Estimates of the decile points were made using procedures developed by Fritz Scheuren and Lock Oh. Their help is gratefully acknowledged.

26. The reader will note that lagged unemployment and the ratio of unemployment rates by race have been omitted from this estimating equation. In CWHS data, these unemployment variables did not contribute importantly to the explained sum of squares.

27. Chapter IV in Thurow [19] discusses the queue theory and presents one test of the theory with respect to nonwhite employment levels.

28. The conjecture that the number of weeks worked decreases more rapidly for black men is based on BLS labor-force participation data for 1957 and 1969 which show the decreases in participation rates for whites were 0.015 and 0.041 in the 45-54 and 55-64 age categories, respectively, while the respective decreases for nonwhites were 0.040 and 0.045. Expressed as percentage reductions in participation rates, these differences are 1.6 percent and 4.6 percent for whites versus 4.3 percent and 5.5 percent for nonwhites.

29. Between 1957 and 1969 black men aged 16 to 24 increased from 18.9 to 28.2 percent of total black employment. The increase for younger white men was from 17.8 to 25.1 percent of the total white employment. This growth was caused both by entrances into the labor force from the post-World War II baby boom and increases in covered employment under Manpower Development and Training Act (MDTA) programs and Neighborhood Youth Corps employment. Its effect is to decrease the median income of both the total black and white populations, with the black being effected more than the white.

30. The Census Bureau's definition of the South as the states south of the Mason-Dixon line and east of the Mississippi River plus Louisiana, Arkansas, Texas, and Oklahoma was used.

31. The regional unemployment rates were constructed from state rates [27, Table D4] weighted by average state employment. At the national level, the average rate was adjusted to agree with the annual averages from the BLS monthly labor-force survey.

32. Exceptions are Equations 11.5.2, 11.5.7, and 11.6.7 where the coefficients for T seems to be out of line in comparison to adjacent equations.

33. This finding illustrates the importance of having data for entire distributions. Results in Table 11-6 differ sharply for the ratios at the medians and at the means. What lies behind the divergent trends at different deciles has not been pursued in the present chapter.

34. The lowest of the three zero-order correlations was 0.75.

35. See Johnston [12], Ch. 7.

36. The assumptions were that 1969 age weights would persist into the future for both blacks and whites, that the shape of the white male age-earnings profile would remain constant, that cohort ratios were unity for all cohorts entering the labor force from 1974 onward, and that cohort ratios did not decline as workers grew older.

37. CPS family income data show that black families with two earners enjoy a much higher relative income than single earner families. See Table 29 in [23].

38. See Table B9 in [27].

39. See Tables F1, F2, F5 and F6 in [27].

40. Regional disaggregations by age groups do not appear in Tables 11-5 and 11-6. These equations have been fitted and are available upon request.

41. One trendwise occupational change that speeded up sharply after 1964 was black women leaving domestic service. This behavior would be predicted (by Bergmann's [8] crowding hypothesis) to follow a reduction in discrimination against black women.

References

[1] Aitchison, J., and Brown, J.A.C. *The Lognormal Distribution.* Cambridge: Cambridge University Press, 1969.

[2] Alexander, Arthur. "Income, Experience, and the Structure of Internal Labor Markets." *Quarterly Journal of Economics,* (forthcoming).

[3] Ashenfelter, Orley. "Changes in Labor Market Discrimination Over Time." *Journal of Human Resources* 5 (Fall 1970), pp. 403-30.

[4] _____ , and Heckman, James. "Changes in Minority Employment Patterns, 1966 to 1970." New York: NBER, 1973, mimeographed.

[5] Batchelder, Alan B. "Decline in the Relative Income of Negro Men." *Quarterly Journal of Economics* 78 (November 1964), pp. 525-48.

[6] Becker, Gary S. *The Economics of Discrimination.* Chicago: University of Chicago Press, 1957.

[7] Bell, Duran. "The Economic Basis of Employee Discrimination." Ch. 8, this volume.

[8] Bergmann, Barbara. "The Effect on White Incomes of Discrimination in Employment." *Journal of Political Economy* 79 (March/April 1971), pp. 294-313.

[9] _____ , and Lyle, Jerolyn R. "The Occupational Standing of Negroes by Areas and Industries." *Journal of Human Resources* 6 (Fall 1971), pp. 411-33.

[10] Brimmer, Andrew. "Regional Growth, Migration and Economic Progress in the Black Community." Paper presented at Bishop College, Dallas, Texas, September 1971.

[11] Johnston, Denis F., and Wetzel, James R. "Effect of the Census Under Count on Labor Force Estimates." *Monthly Labor Review* 92 (March 1969), pp. 3-13.

[12] Johnston, J. *Econometric Methods.* New York: McGraw-Hill, 1963.

[13] Kish, Leslie. *Survey Sampling* (New York: Wiley, 1965).

[14] McCall, John. *Earnings Mobility and Economic Growth.* Rand Report No. R-576-OEO, October 1970.

[15] Perry, George L. "Changing Labor Markets and Inflation." *Brookings Papers on Economic Activity* 1 (3:1970), pp. 411-41.

[16] Rasmussen, David. "A Note on the Relative Income of Nonwhite Men 1948-1964." *Quarterly Journal of Economics* 84 (February 1970), pp. 168-72.

[17] Rayack, Elton. "Discrimination and the Occupational Progress of Negroes." *Review of Economics and Statistics* 43 (May 1961), pp. 209-14.

[18] Schiller, Bradley. "Class Discrimination vs. Racial Discrimination." *Review of Economics and Statistics* 53 (August 1971), pp. 263-69.

[19] Thurow, Lester. *Poverty and Discrimination.* Washington, D.C.: The Brookings Institution, 1969.

[20] U.S. Department of Commerce, Bureau of the Census. U.S. Census of the Population 1960, Subject Reports PC(2)-7B. *Earnings by Occupation and Education.* Washington, D.C., 1963.

[21] U.S. Department of Commerce, Bureau of the Census. U.S. Census of the Population 1970, Subject Reports PC(2)-8B. *Earnings by Occupation and Education.* Washington, D.C., 1973.

[22] U.S. Department of Commerce, Bureau of the Census. Current Population Reports. *The Social and Economic Status of the Black Population in the United States, 1971.* Series P-24, No. 42. Washington, D.C., 1972.

[23] U.S. Department of Commerce, Bureau of the Census. Current Population Reports. *Money Income in 1971 of Families and Persons in the United States.* Series P-60, No. 85. Washington, D.C., 1972.

[24] U.S. Department of Health, Education, and Welfare, Social Security Administration, Office of Research and Statistics. *Workers Under Social Security 1960.* Washington, D.C., 1968.

[25] U.S. Department of Labor, Bureau of Labor Statistics. Special Labor Force Report No. 64. *Marital and Family Characteristics of Workers, March 1965.* Washington, D.C., 1966.

[26] U.S. Department of Labor, Bureau of Labor Statistics. Special Labor Force Report No. 141. *Work Experience of the Population in 1970.* Washington, D.C., 1972.

[27] U.S. Department of Labor, Manpower Administration. *Manpower Report of the President, 1971.* Washington, D.C., 1972.

[28] Wohlstetter, Albert, and Coleman, Sinclair. "Race Differences in Income." In Anthony H. Pascal, ed., *Racial Discrimination in Economic Life.* Lexington, Mass.: Lexington Books, D.C. Heath and Co., 1972.

12

Trends in the Distribution of Family Income within and between Racial Groups

Ann R. Horowitz*

This chapter considers the question of whether the secular increase in the ratio of nonwhite to white median family income, which has been documented in several recent studies, has been accompanied (1) by a decrease in the inequality among nonwhite families, and (2) by a narrowing of the gap between the inequality displayed by the nonwhite income distribution and that displayed by the white distribution. For this purpose, an index of income inequality based on the information theory measure of uncertainty is used. This index enables us to additively decompose the inequality displayed by the income distribution of all families (or individuals) into two components: the inequality between subgroups of the population, such as nonwhites and whites, and the inequality within each of the subgroups.

Trends in Nonwhite-White Income, 1947-1971

Median nonwhite family income equalled approximately 55 percent of the median for whites throughout 1947 to 1965, except for recessionary periods when it was 3 to 4 percentage points lower. Between 1965 and 1967, it increased to 62 percent and has remained close to that level since. Although the ratio remained relatively constant or increased over most of the period 1947-1971, the difference between the two median incomes has widened steadily. In constant dollars, however, the difference seems to have stabilized since 1966, equaling $3,900 in 1971 dollars.

In my previous chapter in this part of the volume, I have summarized the findings by Thurow (1969), Batchelder (1964), Rasmussen (1970), and Ashenfelter (1970) regarding trends in the nonwhite to white income ratio. Suffice it here to note that the above studies compare the progress of whites relative to nonwhites on the basis of changes in median income alone rather than for changes in the entire distribution of income. In fact, scant attention has been given to differences in the distribution of income within the two racial groups. Among those who have considered the entire distribution of family income are Guthrie (1970), Weitzman (1970), and Wohlstetter and Coleman (1972).

*Associate professor of economics, University of Florida.

Wohlstetter and Coleman have calculated the ratio of nonwhite to white income for both families and individuals at various percentiles of the income distributions over the period 1947-1967. They found that substantial nonwhite-white differences exist at all percentiles of the income distribution. In addition, the relative rates of growth differ at various points of the income distribution. For families, Wohlstetter and Coleman found that between 1947 and 1967 roughly equal improvement occurred at the lowest 10 percentiles and the 50th through 80th percentiles, while much less improvement occurred for the 20th through 40th percentiles, so that overall the upper half of the distribution of family income showed greater improvement than the lower half.

Wohlstetter and Coleman conclude that a substantial effort aimed at higher- and lower-middle percentiles is needed to equalize nonwhite and white incomes along the entire distribution. Although Wohlstetter and Coleman note (1) that there are cyclical fluctuations in the rates of change of white and nonwhite median incomes which appear to reflect the tightness of the labor market, and (2) that the pattern of improvement in nonwhite relative to white family income at the various income positions depends on the particular years selected, their analysis is limited to a comparison of the ratio at two points in time and does not attempt to separate the cyclical from the long-run distributional changes.

Guthrie estimated the rates of growth of both white and black incomes at each of the first four quintiles and the 95th percentile after adjusting for the national rate of unemployment using data for the period 1947-1968. Guthrie found that the rate of growth is higher for blacks than whites at each of these percentiles, and that the effects of unemployment vary over the income distribution. In every case the coefficient for unemployment is negative and larger in absolute value for blacks. This indicates that unemployment adversely affects both blacks and whites over the entire income distribution, with blacks being affected more severely than whites. The unemployment rate was not statistically significant for the lowest quintile for either blacks or whites nor for the 95th percentile for whites. From his results, Guthrie concluded that given an unemployment rate of 3.5 percent, equality of the middle sections of the two income distributions would be achieved in twenty-five years. Unfortunately, Guthrie did not hold constant the rate of change in GNP in making his estimates, and he estimated the regressions for each quintile independently when in fact the rates of growth of the various quintiles are correlated.[1]

Weitzman has constructed an index of what he calls the degree of differentiation between the white and nonwhite income distributions. Weitzman describes the index of differentiation as "a composite measure describing the departure from equality and the contribution of each income class interval to the departure from equality." The index is defined as one-half the sum of the absolute differences between the proportion of whites and nonwhites in each income interval. If the proportion of whites is equal to the proportion of nonwhites in every income interval, then the index equals zero. If all whites have higher incomes than the highest nonwhite, the index equals unity.

Weitzman found that the index of differentiation between white and nonwhite family incomes declined fairly steadily between 1947 and 1968 from 0.384 to 0.271. Weitzman also compared the distribution of family income for nonwhites in 1967 with that of whites in selected earlier years, after adjusting for price changes. He found that the differentiation between the 1967 nonwhite distribution and the white distribution twenty years earlier was 0.136. Weitzman concluded, therefore, that the lag between the nonwhite and white distributions is in excess of twenty years.

Weitzman's measure is actually equivalent to the percent of nonwhites who are worse off than whites, assuming that all individuals in the same interval are equally well off. One problem with the measure is that it does not take into consideration *how much* worse off the nonwhites are than the whites so that rather drastic changes can occur in one distribution without changing the index of differentiation. Furthermore, in addition to being ambiguous, the index (and similarly its complement, the index of integration) is nonadditive in that if three distributions are considered, the differentiation between 1 and 3 does not equal the differentiation between 1 and 2 plus the differentiation between 2 and 3. Thus the differentiation between the nonwhite distribution in 1967 and the white distribution in 1947, adjusted for price changes, is approximately the same as the differentiation between the 1967 nonwhite distribution and the 1957 white distribution, although the white distribution changed during this time span. In interpreting his measure, Weitzman considers only the extreme cases of perfectly identical and completely nonoverlapping distributions. As a measure of changes over time in the degree of inequality between the income distributions of two overlapping distributions it actually may be misleading.

An alternative measure of the distribution of income is based on entropy, the index of uncertainty or disorder used in information theory to measure the information content of a message.

Redundancy as a Measure of Income Inequality

Information theory is concerned with measuring the information content of a message or equivalently with measuring the uncertainty as to what a message contains. For this purpose an index of uncertainty based on the probabilities of the various possible messages is used. It turns out that this index known as entropy has many applications in economics.[2] In particular Theil (1967) has suggested its use as a measure of income inequality.

Assume there are N individuals each earning some fraction y_i of total income. Entropy is defined as:

$$H = \Sigma \, y_i \log \frac{1}{y_i} \qquad\qquad (12.1)$$

H equals zero if one individual receives all the income and the others get nothing. It equals its maximum of log N if all individuals receive an equal share of total income. In information theory, logarithms to the base 2 are ordinarily used, but for the purpose of calculating the income inequality measures we shall use natural logarithms.

H can, therefore, be regarded as a measure of equality. A measure of *inequality*, which turns out to have more desirable properties than entropy in working with income distributions, is obtained by subtracting H from its own maximum value:

$$I = \log N - H = \Sigma y_i \log N y_i. \tag{12.2}$$

This measure varies from zero when there is perfect equality to log N when there is perfect inequality. In information theory log $N - H$ is known as *redundancy*; here we shall refer to it simply as inequality or I.

This measure is a weighted average of log NYyi with the weights equalling the individuals' shares of total income. If the individual's share equals what he would receive with perfect equality, his contribution to the inequality measure is zero because y_i will equal $1/N$ and log Ny_i will, therefore, equal zero. If one receives double an equal share, his unweighted contribution to the inequality index is +1 (assuming logarithms to the base 2 are used). A person receiving four times an equal share will have an unweighted contribution of +2, while one receiving one-half or one-fourth of a "fair" share will have an unweighted contribution of −1 or −2, respectively. In general, if one receives k times an equal share, his unweighted contribution to the index is log k. Thus those with above-average income are assigned a positive contribution to inequality and those below average are assigned a negative contribution, with the unweighted contribution increasing (or decreasing) by one unit for each doubling (or halving) of the individual's income share. The contributions are then weighted by the individual's income share so that a positive contribution of log k receives k^2 times as large a weight as a negative contribution of the same magnitude.

Theil evaluates redundancy as a measure of income inequality on the basis of three "tests":

1. The measure does not change if all incomes change proportionally.
2. It will be noted that the upper limit of I varies with the size of the population. Theil argues that an increasing limit is desirable. As an illustration, he notes that in a society of two persons we have maximum inequality when all income goes to one person and the other one gets nothing. With two million people, maximum inequality occurs when one gets all and the other 1,999,999 people get nothing. Theil argues that the second society shows greater inequality than the first and, therefore, should be assigned a higher value on the inequality scale. Redundancy has the property of assigning the same value to two societies when the same proportion in each has everything. In Theil's example, half the people in

the first society have everything and I equals log 2. I will equal log 2 for the second society also if total income is divided equally among half of the people.

3. If one individual is poorer than another individual and his income increases at the expense of the richer one, all others remaining the same, then I decreases up to the point where the two individuals have equal income, and increases thereafter.

The greatest advantage of I over other inequality measures such as Gini's concentration ratio is that it can be decomposed into the inequality within subgroups of the population and the inequality among the subgroups. The latter, called the between group inequality, equals zero when each group has the same average income.[3] It is a measure of inequality of the *average* income of the various groups. Differences in within-group inequality reflect differences in the *shapes* of the income distributions of the various groups as opposed to differences in central tendency.

The decomposition feature means that the inequality among all individuals or families in the population can be calculated directly from the distribution for all families, or it can be calculated as the sum of the inequality between subgroups of the population plus a weighted average of the inequality within the subgroups. This enables us to attribute changes in overall inequality to changes in the distribution of income within certain groups and to changes in the distribution between groups.

The decomposition feature of redundancy also may aid us in recognizing changes in the patterns of discrimination. In the absence of discrimination and of differences in the average productivity of various subgroups of the population, we would expect the between-group inequality to be zero. Furthermore, if, in addition, there are no differences in the distribution of skills *within* the various subgroups, we would expect the within-group inequality to be the same for all groups. Thus trends in both between and within-group inequality are of interest.

Published statistics usually do not give the share of total income received by each individual, but instead give the percent of the population in each of several income brackets. It is possible to approximate I from this type of data by assuming every individual in a given bracket receives the same income. This approach will necessarily *underestimate* the degree of inequality since we do not allow for dispersion within brackets. The wider are the brackets, the less satisfactory is the approximation.

Changes in Within- and Between-Group Inequality, 1954-1971

The income inequality measures for the period 1954-1971 are presented in Table 12-1. These measures were calculated using the percentage distribution of

Table 12-1
Inequality within and between Racial Groups, 1954-1971

Year	IW	IN	IWITH	IBET	ITOT	I	IN-IW	IN/IW
1954	0.219	0.251	0.221	0.010	0.231	0.227	0.032	1.15
1955	0.207	0.240	0.209	0.011	0.221	0.220	0.032	1.16
1956	0.201	0.243	0.203	0.011	0.214	0.215	0.042	1.21
1957	0.198	0.252	0.201	0.011	0.212	0.210	0.054	1.27
1958	0.199	0.269	0.203	0.010	0.213	0.217	0.070	1.35
1959	0.203	0.272	0.207	0.010	0.217	0.217	0.069	1.34
1960	0.207	0.280	0.219	0.011	0.222	0.218	0.072	1.35
1961	0.208	0.289	0.214	0.015	0.229	0.222	0.080	1.39
1962	0.202	0.269	0.206	0.011	0.217	0.216	0.067	1.33
1963	0.202	0.266	0.206	0.010	0.216	0.215	0.064	1.32
1964	0.199	0.261	0.203	0.008	0.211	0.210	0.062	1.31
1965	0.191	0.259	0.195	0.008	0.203	0.206	0.067	1.35
1966	0.184	0.242	0.187	0.007	0.194	0.197	0.058	1.32
1967	0.183	0.249	0.187	0.006	0.193	0.195	0.066	1.36
1968	0.176	0.239	0.180	0.006	0.186	0.186	0.063	1.36
1969	0.172	0.230	0.176	0.006	0.182	0.182	0.058	1.34
1970	0.177	0.243	0.182	0.006	0.188	0.188	0.066	1.37
1971	0.176	0.246	0.181	0.006	0.187	0.190	0.070	1.40

Note: See text for definitions of symbols.

white and nonwhite families among seven income brackets, all defined in 1971 dollars.[4] These brackets are: (1) under \$3,000; (2) \$3,000 to \$4,999; (3) \$5,000 to \$6,999; (4) \$7,000 to \$9,999; (5) \$10,000 to \$11,999; (6) \$12,000 to \$14,999; and (7) \$15,000 and over. The brackets were defined in constant rather than current brackets to eliminate the effects of inflation on the percentages in the various brackets. If current dollars were used, it would be necessary to redefine the brackets periodically.

The symbols used in Table 12-1 are defined as follows:

IW: Inequality among white families
IN: Inequality among nonwhite families
IWITH: Average inequality within the two groups
IBET: Inequality between whites and nonwhites
ITOT: Total inequality calculated as sum of *IWITH* and *IBET*
I: Total inequality calculated directly from the distribution for all families.

It is clear that inequality within the nonwhite group (column 2) is greater in every year than the inequality within the white group (column 1). Furthermore, the within-white inequality declined steadily over the period, while the nonwhite inequality increased up to 1961, after which it declined until 1970, when it again reversed itself. The steady decline in white inequality, accompanied by essentially no change in the nonwhite inequality between 1954 and 1971, has resulted in a doubling of the gap between white and nonwhite inequality (column 7) and an increase in the inequality of nonwhites relative to that of whites by 25 percentage points (column 8).

Column 3 shows the weighted average of the inequality within the two groups weighted by the percent of total income going to each group. This average fell over the period, reflecting the decline in inequality within the white group. The between-group inequality reflecting changes in the per capita income of the two groups is given in column 4. Except for 1961, the between inequality remained roughly constant at 0.010 and 0.011 until 1963, after which it declined, reflecting a narrowing of the gap in the average income of the two groups.

The total inequality among all families, obtained by summing the average within and between inequalities, is given in column 5. Column 6 contains the inequality for all families calculated directly from the percentage distribution of income for all families. The minor discrepancies are due to approximating income by the midpoint of each interval and the use of \$22,500 and \$20,000 as the average income of the open-ended interval of whites and nonwhites, respectively.

In order to distinguish cyclical effects from the secular trends, each of the inequality measures was regressed against the unemployment rate, the rate of growth of GNP (in both constant and current dollars), and the ratio of the nonwhite unemployment rate to the white rate as well as a time variable. The results are presented in Table 12-2.

The new symbols in Table 12-2 are defined as follows:

T: Time
U: Rate of unemployment
RU: Ratio of the nonwhite unemployment rate to the white unemployment rate
RG: Real rate of growth of GNP.

Neither the rate of growth of GNP, nor the relative unemployment rate of nonwhites and whites had a significant effect on the inequality measures when U and T are held constant. Accordingly, these variables were eliminated from the regressions. The results for the inequality measures regressed against U and T alone are also shown in Table 12-2.

The unemployment rate is positively related to the degree of inequality among both white and nonwhite families. Inequality among whites increases with unemployment, but at a slower rate than does inequality among nonwhites. Thus the difference between IN and IW increases with the unemployment rate. In addition, high unemployment also significantly increases $IBET$, the inequality

Table 12-2
Least-Squares Estimates of the Effects of Cycle and Trend on Income Inequality

Dependent Variable	T	U	RU	RG	R^2	$\bar{R}^2$	D.W.
IW	-0.0022^b (6.60)	0.0046^b (3.26)	-0.0060 (0.40)	0.0009 (1.59)	0.893	0.860	1.26
IW	-0.0021^b (8.25)	0.0042^b (3.20)	$-$	$-$	0.869	0.852	0.77
IN	0.00004 (0.06)	0.0139^b (5.04)	0.0277 (0.97)	0.0008 (0.72)	0.702	0.610	1.37
IN	-0.0003 (0.72)	0.0118^b (4.60)	$-$	$-$	0.628	0.578	0.68
IBET	-0.0003^b (3.18)	0.0011^a (2.82)	0.0039 (0.93)	0.0004 (0.26)	0.772	0.702	1.86
IBET	-0.0004^b (5.15)	0.0009^a (2.52)	$-$	$-$	0.741	0.707	1.60
ITOT	-0.0023^b (6.14)	0.0063^b (3.98)	-0.0002 (0.01)	0.0009 (1.41)	0.895	0.863	1.32
ITOT	-0.0022^b (7.99)	0.0056^b (3.82)	$-$	$-$	0.872	0.855	0.82
IN-IW	0.0022^b (3.96)	0.0093^b (3.86)	0.0337 (1.35)	-0.0001 (0.12)	0.666	0.564	1.06
IN-IW	0.0017^b (4.10)	0.0076^b (3.49)	$-$	$-$	0.605	0.552	0.56
IN/IW	0.0140^b (5.35)	0.0373^b (3.26)	0.152 (1.28)	-0.0021 (0.46)	0.758	0.683	0.98
IN/IW	0.0118^b (6.12)	0.0312^b (3.07)	$-$	$-$	0.726	0.689	0.58

Note: The figures in parentheses are the t-ratios. The coefficients marked a and b are significantly different from zero at the 5 and 1 percent levels of statistical significance, respectively. The symbols are defined in the text.

between white and nonwhite average income. Thus, higher unemployment rates both widen the discrepancy between the average income of whites and nonwhites and increase the dispersion of nonwhite family income relative to that of whites.

White families have experienced a downward trend in inequality over this period, but the regression of *IN* on *U* and *T* discloses that inequality among nonwhites has not changed significantly over time. Both the difference between *IN* and *IW* and their ratio have accordingly increased significantly over time. The inequality *between* the two groups, however, shows a significant decline even after eliminating the effects of falling unemployment. Thus the increasing discrepancy between *IW* and *IN* indicates that the shapes of the nonwhite and white income distributions have tended to differ more and more over time while the decline in *IBET* indicates that the discrepancy between the average incomes of the two groups has fallen.

Although the nonwhite inequality has not changed significantly over the 1954-1971 period, the inequality measures for both whites and nonwhites declined steadily between 1961 and 1969, the period of the war on poverty programs and of a growing awareness of the problems and rights of nonwhites. In order to determine whether there was a shift in the secular trend of the income inequality measures in the 1960s, dummy variables were added to the regressions.

A dummy variable D was defined, such that D equals zero for the years 1954-1963 and one for the years 1964-1971. The cutoff point of 1964 was chosen because that was the year of the Civil Rights Act, and it was felt that by that time the civil rights marches of the early 1960s had permeated the consciousness of the American public.

The addition of this variable to a regression allows for a shift in the intercept between the two periods. We are also interested in whether there was a shift in secular trend between the two periods, that is, in the value of the regression coefficient for the time variable. To test for such a shift, it is necessary to introduce the product of D and T as an explanatory variable. DT will equal zero for the earlier period and T for the latter period. Therefore, the coefficient of T estimates the trend for the 1954-1963 period and the sum of the coefficients for T and DT estimates the trend after 1964.

Since the 1964-1969 period was a period of falling unemployment rates, it is necessary to hold unemployment constant in order to distinguish the secular from the cyclical effects. The regressions were also run including RU and RG, but the coefficients for these variables again were not significantly different from zero. The results obtained by regressing the within-group inequality measures against D, T, DT and U are shown in Table 12-3.

The results show that there was a significant positive trend in inequality among nonwhite families between 1954 and 1963, a period during which inequality among white families was decreasing. During the post-1964 period, however, this positive trend was reversed with the nonwhite inequality index declining at a rate of 0.0033 per year, almost as rapidly as the white index, which by then was falling at an annual rate of 0.0036. This shift from a tendency for nonwhite inequality to increase to a tendency for it to decrease at approximately the same rate as white inequality is particularly striking because it occurred during a time when the downward trend in white inequality increased significantly—from −0.0013 to −0.0036 per year. The sharp reversal in trend is also noticeable in the regression for $IN-IW$. This difference increased significantly at an annual rate of 0.0039 during the 1954-1964 period, but decreased at a rate of 0.0036 during the later period.

The unemployment rate continues to have a significantly larger effect on nonwhite inequality than on white, even after allowing for the shift in trend.

The dummy variables were not significant in the regression of $IBET$, which suggests that the shift in trend affected only the rate of change in the dispersion of both white and nonwhite income, but not the difference in the mean incomes of the two groups.

Table 12-3
Least-Squares Estimates of the Effects of Unemployment and Pre- and Post-1964 Trends on Income Inequality

Dependent Variable	Intercept	D	T	DT	U	R^2	$\bar{R}^2$	D.W.
IW	0.1896 (28.76)	0.0238[a] (2.33)	−0.0013[a] (2.36)	−0.0023[a] (2.60)	0.0038[a] (2.78)	0.914	0.888	1.05
IN	0.2024 (19.87)	0.0484[b] (3.30)	0.0026[b] (3.30)	−0.0059[b] (4.68)	0.0090[b] (4.54)	0.869	0.829	1.50
IN-IW	0.0128 (1.13)	0.0247 (1.51)	0.0039[b] (4.45)	−0.0036[a] (2.58)	0.0518[a] (2.34)	0.763	0.690	0.84
IN/IW	1.082 (18.32)	0.0666 (0.78)	0.0200[b] (4.40)	−0.0119 (1.62)	0.0210 (1.81)	0.792	0.728	0.76
ITOT	0.1988 (26.24)	0.0247[a] (2.26)	−0.0010 (1.74)	−0.0027[a] (2.93)	0.0046[b] (3.13)	0.924	0.900	1.18
MEDW	7632 (52.01)	−522[a] (2.47)	233.9[b] (20.68)	46.5[a] (2.56)	−186.3[b] (6.49)	0.996	0.995	2.38
MEDN	4525 (22.6)	−1526[b] (5.28)	126.5[b] (8.18)	165.8[b] (6.68)	−183.3[b] (4.67)	0.990	0.988	1.71
MEDN/MEDW	0.58 (26.4)	−0.11[b] (3.40)	−0.0004 (0.22)	0.0130[b] (4.76)	−0.009 (1.97)	0.920	0.895	1.63

Note: See Table 12-2.

The median incomes of both groups also were regressed against the cyclical and secular variables. These results are presented in Table 12-3 with the medians for the white and nonwhite groups symbolized by *MEDW* and *MEDN*, respectively. The medians also display a significantly higher trend after 1964, with the increment in the nonwhite trend being much larger than the increment in the white trend. In fact, the trend in the median income of nonwhite families more than doubled after 1964, so that it actually increased faster than the median white income in the latter period. Furthermore, when the regressions differentiate between the trend before and after 1964, changes in unemployment have essentially the same effect on the median family income of both racial groups.

When we consider the ratio of nonwhite to white median family income, we find that it was not significantly affected by the unemployment rate, did not change significantly prior to 1964; but did increase significantly after 1964. The differences in the findings for the ratio are due to the fact that white median income is so much higher than nonwhite that the absolute difference between the two medians can increase while their ratio remains relatively constant.

Changes in the Proportions of Families within Income Brackets

The results of the preceding section show that the unemployment rate is positively related to the degree of inequality within each racial group and, furthermore, that the adverse effects of rising unemployment affect inequality among nonwhite families more severely than inequality among white families. The effects of U, RU and T on the proportion of whites and nonwhites falling into each of the seven income brackets under consideration were also estimated in order to determine how the various parts of the income distribution have varied cyclically and over time. The results are presented in Table 12-4.

Some care should be taken in interpreting these regression coefficients. The coefficients are estimates of the *net* change in the proportion of families in each

Table 12-4
Least-Squares Estimates of the Effects of Trend and Cycle on the Fraction of Families in Each Income Bracket

Fraction of Families in Income Bracket	T	U	RU	R^2	$\overline{R}^2$	$D.W.$
		Whites				
1	−0.0059[b] (19.56)	0.0027 (1.90)	−0.0259 (2.11)	0.978	0.973	0.94
2	−0.0042[b] (19.46)	0.0027[a] (2.62)	0.0234[a] (2.67)	0.978	0.973	1.55
3	−0.0073[b] (18.41)	−0.0001 (0.05)	−0.0478[a] (2.95)	0.972	0.966	1.09
4	−0.0034[b] (4.59)	0.0065 (1.85)	0.0651 (2.14)	0.826	0.789	1.05
5	0.0024[b] (9.93)	0.0004 (0.38)	0.0319[a] (3.25)	0.899	0.878	1.51
6	0.0062[b] (20.46)	−0.0028 (1.94)	0.0313[a] (2.54)	0.979	0.975	1.05
7	0.0122[b] (22.30)	−0.0092[b] (3.54)	−0.0309 (1.39)	0.986	0.982	1.30
		Nonwhites				
1	−0.0146[b] (28.52)	0.0187[b] (7.75)	0.0113 (0.54)	0.992	0.990	2.37
2	−0.0032[b] (4.21)	0.0036 (0.99)	0.0553 (1.76)	0.780	0.733	0.88
3	−0.0015[b] (5.32)	−0.0009 (0.68)	0.0043 (0.38)	0.776	0.727	2.15
4	0.0046[b] (9.33)	−0.0059[a] (2.52)	0.0160 (0.79)	0.920	0.903	1.97
5	0.0038[b] (14.51)	−0.0039[a] (3.12)	−0.0058 (0.53)	0.967	0.960	2.55
6	0.0045[b] (12.41)	−0.0060[b] (3.51)	−0.0227 (1.55)	0.960	0.952	2.01
7	0.0063[b] (9.93)	−0.0057 (1.88)	−0.0573[a] (2.20)	0.941	0.928	1.02

Note: See Table 12-2.

bracket. Thus the coefficient may indicate no net change when in fact there were substantial but offsetting entries into, and exits from, a given bracket. Nevertheless, the results provide information on how the distributions of white and nonwhite family income have changed with the overall unemployment rate, the ratio of nonwhite to white unemployment rates, and over time. It might also be noted that for either group the sum of the coefficients of each explanatory variable must equal zero since the seven dependent variables for each race sum to one. That is, if rising unemployment leads to a positive net change in the fraction in one income bracket it must lead to a negative change in some other brackets. This means that in both sets of equations, the coefficients of one equation can be inferred from the other six.

The unemployment rate has little effect on the proportion of white families in the various income brackets. The proportion in the $3000-$5000 bracket increases by less than 0.01 and that in the over $15,000 bracket decreases by approximately 0.01 for each 1 percent increase in the unemployment rate, while the proportion in other brackets does not change at the 5 percent level of statistical significance.

For nonwhites, rising unemployment significantly increases the proportion of families in the first bracket and significantly decreases the proportion in the three upper-middle brackets ranging from $7,000 to $15,000, but the decrease in the proportion in the over-$15,000 bracket is not statistically significant at the 5 percent level. The estimates of the unemployment coefficients for the first bracket indicate that the percent of black families with incomes under $3,000 increases by nearly 2 percentage points, and the percent in the upper-middle income brackets by approximately 1.6 percentage points, for every 1 percent increase in the unemployment rate.

Although the ratio of the unemployment rates for nonwhites and whites was not statistically significant in the regressions for the inequality within the two racial groups, this variable is statistically significant at the 5 percent level for the proportion of white families in several income brackets. The statistically significant results indicate that the higher is the relative rate of nonwhite unemployment, the lower is the fraction of white families in the $3,000 to $5,000 and $5,000 to $7,000 brackets, and the higher is the fraction of white families in the $10,000 to $12,000 and $12,000 to $15,000 brackets.

Rather surprisingly, the relative unemployment rate does not have a statistically significant effect at the 5 percent level on the proportion of nonwhites in the various income brackets except for the over-$15,000 bracket. The signs, however, indicate that a rising ratio of nonwhite to white unemployment rates tends to cause a shift of the nonwhite population from high to low brackets.

The proportion of whites and nonwhites in each income bracket has changed significantly over time. There has been a net reduction slightly in excess of 2 percent in the proportion of white families in the four lower income brackets (<$10,000) compared to a net reduction of slightly less than 2 percent in the three lower brackets (<$7000) for nonwhite families. The largest absolute change for nonwhites occurred in the lowest income bracket whose population declined by 1.5 percent per year, given U and RU. The percent of whites in the lowest bracket fell at a rate of 0.6 percent per year, given U and RU. For whites the largest change occurred in the over-$15,000 bracket whose population has been increasing at a rate of 1.2 percent per year. For nonwhites, the uppermost bracket changed at a rate of 0.6 percent per year, given U and RU.

Concluding Comments

This chapter has considered the question of whether the decrease in inequality between white and nonwhite families as measured by the difference in mean or median incomes has been accompanied by a decrease in the difference between the historically higher inequality displayed by the nonwhite income distribution and the inequality displayed by the white distribution. The conclusion here is that while the difference between the means and medians of the two groups has declined over time, particularly since 1964, there is no evidence of a decline in the difference in overall inequality within the two groups. In fact, after adjusting for cyclical effects, the evidence is that this difference increased prior to 1964 and remained roughly stable after 1964.

Looking at the period as a whole, it appears that there was a turnaround in the trend in nonwhite family income inequality during the 1960s. Throughout the 1950s, inequality among nonwhite families was increasing while inequality among white families was decreasing. Since 1964, however, both nonwhite and white inequality have decreased at essentially the same rate. Although the rate of decrease of nonwhites now roughly equals that of whites, the nonwhite inequality is still substantially higher than the white. In fact, nonwhite inequality has merely returned to its level of the mid-1950s. Furthermore, both nonwhite and white inequality are positively related to the rate of unemployment, but unemployment affects nonwhite inequality substantially more than white.

The results by income bracket revealed some further differences in the distributions of income for white and nonwhite families. In particular, the proportions in the upper two income brackets are increasing more rapidly for whites than nonwhites; the number of lower income brackets displaying a net decrease is larger for whites than nonwhites; and the unemployment rate is statistically significant for more brackets for nonwhites than whites, with a tight labor market sharply reducing the proportion of nonwhites in the lowest bracket and increasing the proportion in the upper-middle income brackets. Further, the relative rate of nonwhite-white unemployment is not statistically significant over most of the nonwhite distribution, but the signs of the regression coefficient indicate that it has the expected effect of increasing the proportion of nonwhite families in the lower half of the distribution.

The differences in results based on the median income and those based on the distribution demonstrate the importance of considering the entire distribution of income in measuring progress toward equality of the white and nonwhite distributions. Looking at the medians alone, we would conclude that prior to 1964 there was no statistically significant change in relative nonwhite-white inequality, that after 1964 this inequality decreased, and that after allowing for the time trends, the unemployment rate had no statistically significant effect on the ratio of nonwhite to white median income. The inequality measures show, however, that prior to 1964 the inequality among whites was decreasing while the inequality among nonwhites, which already exceeded that of whites, was increasing. Furthermore, after 1964 the difference between the overall inequality within the white and within the nonwhite groups remained roughly constant. Also, both the inequality measures for the two income distributions and the analysis of the distributions by income brackets show that unemployment affects the distribution of nonwhite income differently from the distribution of white income.

Notes

1. For a critique of Guthrie's work, see Atkinson and Bergmann (1972).

2. See Theil (1967) for a wide variety of economic applications.

3. Between-group entropy assumes its maximum when each group has the same total income. Since the number of individuals may vary from group to group, this would not represent equality in the usual sense. This is why redundancy rather than entropy is the preferable income inequality measure.

4. The data are from the U.S. Bureau of the Census, *Current Population Reports*, Series P-60, No. 85, p. 31.

References

Ashenfelter, O. (1970) "Changes in Labor Market Discrimination Over Time." *Journal of Human Resources* 5, pp. 403-30.

Atkinson, L.C., and Bergmann, B.R. (1972) "The Prospect of Equality of Incomes Between Black and White Families under Varying Rates of Unemployment: A Comment." *Journal of Human Resources* 7, pp. 545-47.

Batchelder, A. (1964) "The Decline in the Relative Income of Negro Men." *Quarterly Journal of Economics* 78, pp. 525-48.

Guthrie, H.W. (1970) "The Prospects of Equality of Incomes between Black and White Families under Varying Rates of Unemployment." *Journal of Human Resources* 5, pp. 431-46.

Rasmussen, D.W. (1970) "A Note on the Relative Income of Nonwhite Men: 1948-1964." *Quarterly Journal of Economics* 84, pp. 168-72.

Theil, H. (1967) *Economics and Information Theory*. Amsterdam: North-Holland Publishing Company.

Thurow, L.C. (1969) *Poverty and Discrimination*. Washington, D.C.: The Brookings Institution.

U.S. Bureau of the Census. (1972) "Income in 1971 of Families and Persons in the United States." *Current Population Reports*. Series P-60, No. 85.

Weitzman, S.M. (1970) *Measures of Overlap of Income Distributions of White and Nonwhite Families*. U.S. Bureau of the Census, Technical Paper No. 22.

Wohlstetter, A. and Coleman, S. (1972) "Race Differences in Income." In Anthony H. Pascal, ed., *Racial Discrimination in Economic Life*. Lexington, Mass.: Lexington Books, D.C. Heath and Co.

13

Black-White Differences in Returns to Schooling*

Finis Welch†

Investments in schooling in the United States have earned high returns in the aggregate, but at the same time estimated returns to blacks have been low. This chapter updates previous estimates, showing that underlying the low averages reported for cross-sections of the black population there is a strong upward drift. Returns to blacks schooled in the 1920s and 1930s were so low that, relative to whites, black income fell as school completion levels rose. Recent evidence shows, on the other hand, that returns, as a fraction of earnings, for blacks schooled in the 1950s and 1960s exceed returns to whites. These estimates imply that those income gains, which were earlier realized by whites as average educational levels increased, are now being realized by blacks.

Earlier Estimates

In 1967, I observed that to a southern rural black, schooling was a poor investment: "A non-white with no schooling will receive 81 percent of the income of a similar white. Yet, for non-whites, school attendance increases income at a rate which is only 28 percent of the corresponding increases for whites" [Welch p. 235]. This estimate was based on the 1960 census, for earnings in 1959. Relative earnings of around 80 percent for blacks with no schooling, fall to less than 50 percent for college graduates. Using the same data, Giora Hanoch observed that "internal rates of return for Non-whites are generally low and relatively erratic ..." [Hanoch p. 325], and William Landes estimated that outside the South, schooling returned only about 20 percent as much to nonwhites as to whites.

These are three of several income studies showing similarly pessimistic results, that the educational route to economic and social mobility was apparently closed to blacks. More recently this cloud of pessimism has been expanded to hover over quality of schooling as well. Christopher Jencks and others argue that family background factors dominate measures of academic achievement, leaving

*©*American Economic Review*. Reprinted by permission.

†Professor of economics, City University of New York; National Bureau of Economic Research.

little room for attributes of schools to have an effect. And in any case, measured academic achievement (as distinguished from years of attendance) has little effect upon earnings. That this link between school traits and income is twice filtered through the screen of measured achievement seems not to matter. This, even though Herbert Gintis, one of Jencks' coauthors, has argued that existing achievement tests are capable of explaining only between 10 and 20 percent of the observed earning power of schooling. The view offered here is no more direct than that of Jencks. I simply compare very broad trends in school characteristics to trends in the return to schooling. It seems, on the basis of this comparison, that there may be an important relationship between schooling quality and income, or at least that the possibility that such a relation exists should not be dismissed without further research.[1]

In reference to the early estimates, I think we erred by not considering the full implications of secular changes in schooling quality. The estimates are based on observations around 1960, and at that time the majority of the black adult population would have been in school in the decades of the 1920s and 1930s. During those periods, blacks attended school only about two-thirds as many days as whites. Furthermore, approximately one-third of all black students enrolled in public elementary and secondary schools in the segregated South were enrolled in the *first* grade. There were typically more than twice as many first as second graders—suggesting that retardation rates exceeded 100 percent, that is, the average black pupil spent something more than two years in the first grade. Also, southern schools spent a little more than three times as much on white as on black pupils. In this context, it should not be surprising that schooling contributed much less to black than to white income. Given the substantial improvement in the relative quality of the schools attended by blacks in the past few decades, it should not be surprising that vis-à-vis the return to schooling, young blacks—more recent graduates—fare better in comparison to whites. And that, pure and simple, is what the data show.

Reexamination

In this chapter, the contributions of schooling to earnings are compared between blacks and whites for two bodies of data. The first is the 1 in 1000 sample from the 1960 census and the second is the Survey of Economic Opportunity (SEO). Census income refers to earnings in 1959, and SEO refers to 1966 earnings. Comparison is restricted to urban males (Negro or white) who are not in the military, are not enrolled in school, and are not working without earnings. In the subsamples drawn, the census contains 14,918 whites and 1,749 Negroes, and SEO contains 6,879 whites and 3,442 Negroes.[2] The SEO data are potentially the richer source for making black-white earning comparisons because the sampling procedure insured a larger proportion of blacks. The SEO increased the percentage of blacks by adding to a national random sample of about 30,000 individuals, a companion sample including about 20,000 persons from "poverty" areas. It is unfortunate that stratification was based upon an income correlate, for this carries the potential of introducing biases via "creaming" of the economic successes.[3]

The point of departure for the income comparisons is the stratification of the individual observations by race and an estimate of the time of entry into the labor force. This estimate was expressed as years of work experience.[4] The census experience classes are 1-4, 5-12, and 13-25 years. These workers would have entered the labor force approximately between 1955-58, 1947-54, and 1934-46, respectively. Their schooling would presumably have occurred in the years prior to entry into the work force. The SEO sample is comfortably partitioned into experience classes of 1-3, 4-7, 8-11, 12-19, and 20-32 years. Since SEO refers to 1966 income, the last three classes correspond to the 1959 census cohorts. The first two classes represent entry into the labor market between 1963-65 and 1959-62, respectively.

The estimated earnings equations are of the form:

$$\log Y = a_o + a_1 S + a_2 \log W + a_3 ZY + a_4 F + a_5 SF + u. \tag{13.1}$$

Observations are of individuals and variables are defined as follows:

Log Y is the natural logarithm of annual earnings when earnings are positive; it is set equal to zero when earnings are zero.

S refers to years of school completed. The coefficient estimate, $\hat{a}_1$, is thus an estimate of the proportional increase in earnings associated with an extra year of schooling (when other independent variables are held constant).[5]

Log W is the natural logarithm of weeks worked in the year for which earnings are reported. The coefficient $\hat{a}_2$ estimates the elasticity of earnings with respect to time worked.

ZY is a dummy variable that takes the value one when earnings are zero, and is zero otherwise.[6]

F is a dummy variable that equals one if the individual is a federal employee and zero otherwise.

SF is a measure of the federal government's share of the industry in which the individual is employed. The share is equal to one for federal employees.

Thus ($\hat{a}_4 + \hat{a}_5$) estimates the proportional increase in earnings associated with direct federal employment (as opposed to working in the private nongovernmental sector) and $\hat{a}_5$ estimates the proportional increase in income associated with indirect federal employment. In a period of civil rights activism one might expect the earliest effects to appear for federal employees and in private firms in which the government has the most obvious control. These variables are included to try to identify such effects.

Regression estimates appear in appendix Tables 6 and 7 (not published here) and are summarized. The tables are available upon request.

The return to schooling is broken into two components, a direct and an indirect effect. Empirically we observe that not only do persons with more schooling receive higher wages per unit of time spent on the job but, in addition, these persons devote more time to their jobs: they work more hours per week and more weeks per year.

The direct wage effect is measured by $\hat{a}_1$. It estimates the proportional increment in annual earning associated with an extra year of schooling *holding weeks worked and the probability of zero earnings constant*. It is this component of the return to schooling which is most closely linked to productivity and therefore is most obviously affected by trends in quality of schooling. When education received in a school year is of higher quality, the coefficient is expected to be higher.[7] This coefficient (plus one) is the relative wage of a person with an extra year of schooling and can be taken in a competitive market as an estimate of the marginal rate of substitution of a worker with given schooling for a worker with an extra year. As such, it is sensitive to factor proportions and in the aggregate may fall as average schooling levels rise.

The second component in measuring the earnings gain from schooling is the compounding of earning differentials that result from comovement between wage rates and time devoted to work. Here the indirect effect refers to proportional increments in earnings related to the increased number of weeks worked and the reduced probability of having zero earnings that are associated with increased schooling. This effect is measured as:

$$\hat{a}_2 \left. \frac{d \log W}{d S} \right|_E + \hat{a}_3 \left. \frac{dZY}{dS} \right|_E \tag{13.2}$$

The terms $\left. \dfrac{d \log W}{dS} \right|_E$ and $\left. \dfrac{dZY}{dS} \right|_E$ are auxiliary regression coefficients on schooling holding experience constant. Two auxiliary regressions are estimated, one in which the dependent variable is log W so that the coefficient is the proportional increase in weeks worked associated with an added year of schooling. In the other, the dependent variable is the ZY dummy and the schooling coefficient is an estimate of the change in the probability of having zero earnings associated with an extra year of schooling. These coefficients are reported in appendix Tables 6 and 7 (available upon request) with estimates of the earnings equation. For computing variances of estimates, these auxiliary coefficients are treated as constant.

A complete specification of factors determining the indirect return of schooling is beyond the scope of this chapter, but I will note a few of the more obvious possibilities. First, if unemployment is involuntary, the auxiliary relation between time worked and schooling may refer to statistical screening of employees. Schooling reduces job-search time. Insofar as this phenomenon is important, we expect a contracyclical component in the indirect return. In a period like 1959 of relatively high unemployment, the impact of involuntary unemployment is greatest for the less schooled. We also expect this auxiliary correlation between schooling and time worked to attenuate over the working career as better measures of worker quality emerge. The second alternative is that the auxiliary relation between work and schooling (the indirect effect) is simply a labor supply response to the direct or wage rate effect (see C.M. Lindsay).

If the supply of labor is positively sloped, we then expect the direct effect, which captures the wage increment, to be positively related to the indirect effect, which embodies the resultant work response.[8]

Table 13-1 reports estimates of the total, direct, and indirect returns to schooling. The sum of the direct and indirect effects is not constrained to equal the total effect, because a provision for federal employment is also included. The covariance between federal employment and schooling is consistently positive, both for blacks and whites, but the contribution to the return to schooling is numerically trivial even though it occasionally is "statistically significant."

Several patterns in the coefficients reported in Table 13-1 are of interest. The most obvious is the attenuation in the cross-section of both direct and indirect returns as experience increases or as "vintage" decreases. In 1959, a year of fairly high unemployment, the indirect effects actually exceed the direct effects at lower levels of work experience, although the pattern quickly reverses itself as experience increases. Further, the share of the indirect in the total effect is larger for blacks than for whites. This adds support to the hypothesis of involuntary unemployment, with the heavier burden falling upon blacks and upon persons with little experience, that is, persons for whom the years of school completed represents an important part of the information available for assessing productivity.

In the 1959 data, the evidence is that for persons with 1-4 years of experience, black earnings rise relative to white earnings as school completion levels increase. This point has not been noted previously. For persons with 5-12 years of experience, the black/white earning ratio is insensitive to schooling, and for persons with 13-25 years of experience relative earnings of blacks fall as schooling increases.

The 1966 data present patterns that are generally similar to those found for 1959. At low levels of experience, the black/white earnings ratio rises with schooling, but at higher levels of experience, the opposite is true. Interestingly enough, the share of the indirect in the total return to schooling is similar between blacks and whites in the relatively tight labor market that prevailed in 1966.

Table 13-1
Proportional Increment in Income Associated with One Additional Year of Schooling

Experience Class	White			Black		
	Total	Direct	Indirect	Total	Direct	Indirect
Census (1959)						
1-4	0.208	0.095	0.111	0.317	0.079	0.231
5-12	0.134	0.081	0.052	0.149	0.065	0.077
13-25	0.099	0.064	0.035	0.059	0.040	0.015
SEO (1966)						
1-3	0.306	0.146	0.157	0.519	0.230	0.289
4-7	0.191	0.106	0.084	0.256	0.142	0.111
8-11	0.149	0.082	0.067	0.192	0.078	0.109
12-19	0.143	0.090	0.053	0.130	0.062	0.065
20-32	0.110	0.069	0.041	0.096	0.049	0.042

Note: Standard Errors are not reported, but were typically small relative to the coefficients. For total returns, t-ratios ranged between 5.2 and 33.0, between 14.6 and 32.0 for direct returns, and for indirect returns, between 2.3 and 11.7 for whites and 1.8 to 5.0 for blacks.

Because the indirect effect is likely to contain important life-cycle and business-cycle influences, a comparison of the effects of secular trends in the relative quality of black schooling is more safely founded in comparisons of direct effects alone.

The first panel of Table 13-2 presents t statistics for black-white differences in the direct return to schooling in 1959 and 1966 within experience classes. Panel II gives t statistics for the black and white cohorts for differences in direct returns between 1959 and 1966. These statistics simply confirm what is obvious in Table 13-1. For those with 1-4 years of experience in 1959 or 8-11 years in 1966, there is no significant black-white difference. As experience extends to encompass persons who entered the labor force before the mid-1950s, the difference cumulates becoming "significantly" higher for whites especially in the 13-25 and 20-32 experience classes. But, for persons entering the work force in the 1960s, the evidence is that returns are significantly greater for blacks. That is, viewed as a proportional contribution to earnings, schooling yields more to blacks than whites when comparisons are restricted to recent vintages. The earlier vintage comparisons yield the opposite conclusion.

That this effect is primarily one of vintage—not a life-cycle effect in which schooling initially offers more to blacks but quickly peters out—is evidenced in the cohort comparisons. Of six comparisons, the direct returns to schooling are remarkably similar in a numeric sense and statistically they change "significantly" in only one case of six as the cohorts add seven years of experience.

Table 13-2
Student T-Statistics for Comparisons of Differences in Direct Returns to Schooling

I. Black-white differences (coefficient difference relative to standard error).

Census (1959)		SEO (1966)	
—		1-3	+11.83
—		4-7	+ 2.37
1-4	−0.69	8-11	−0.39
5-12	−1.74	12-19	−3.47
13-25	−3.81	20-32	−3.45

II. Cohort differences 1959-1966.

Approximate Year of Entry into Labor Force	Black			White		
	Direct Schooling Coefficient		t-ratio on Coefficient Difference	Direct Schooling Coefficient		t-ratio on Coefficient Difference
	1959	1966		1959	1966	
1955-58	0.079	0.078	0.04	0.095	0.082	+1.96
1947-54	0.065	0.062	0.27	0.081	0.090	−1.86
1934-46	0.040	0.049	−1.15	0.064	0.069	−1.39

More generally, the twelve equations on which the six cohort comparisons are based were "stacked" into a single regression equation for which it is possible to jointly impose the constraints of cohort equality for the schooling coefficients in 1959 and 1966. The computed F (6,24705) statistic on this constraint is 1.73 with a 0.05 critical level of 2.10.

This is not to say that there are no life-cycle effects associated with the return to schooling,[9] but if such effects exist they are swamped in these data by the general "tightening" of the labor market that occurred between 1959 and 1966. To summarize, the evidence is that, viewed as a proportional contribution to earnings, returns to schooling have increased for blacks relative to whites. For those entering the work force in the 1930s and early 1940s (who were schooled over the ten to fifteen years preceding entry to the market), returns for blacks were significantly less than for whites. Yet the opposite is true for those entering the labor market in the 1960s. Furthermore, in the cohort comparison this return does not attenuate as experience increases. Since rapid attenuation occurs in each of the cross-sections, the implication is that vintage is an important explanation. This interpretation is also presented by Leonard Weiss and Jeffrey G. Williamson in a separate analysis of the SEO data.[10]

This vintage effect could be interpreted as changes in labor-market conditions with changing attitudes toward discrimination. Suppose that the labor market is such that a person's career profile is largely determined by conditions that exist at the time he enters the work force and that "taste for discrimination" has been falling over time. This would predict the improving relative position of blacks, but would not explain the obvious vintage effect for whites. As an alternative, consider the effects of quality of schooling. The evidence is that real inputs into predominantly white schools have increased through time and that black schools have improved relative to white schools. This is sufficient to explain the observations reported in Tables 13-1 and 13-2. Given this possibility, we turn to evidence of schooling's quality.

Schools for Blacks

Until we are more knowledgeable about the technology of learning and about exactly what it is that schools produce that allows more schooled persons to earn more, comparisons of schooling quality will be superficial at best. Nonetheless, we do have fragmentary evidence that both in terms of the facilities schools offer to students and in terms of measured achievement, blacks are gaining relative to whites. This is not to say that we have achieved parity, but only that trends are in the "right" direction.

In Table 13-3, summary statistics are offered for segregated southern schools for selected years between 1919/20 and 1953/54. With the Supreme Court decision of 1954, the publication by the federal government of segregated school system statistics stopped. It is difficult to say how seriously these comparisons should be taken. Clearly, not all blacks attended school in the South. Less clearly, the relative quality of school offerings may have been better outside the South. Nonetheless, the data of Table 13-3 indicate a very strong upward trend in virtually every measure of schooling quality I could find, and it is this trend I want to stress.

The change that may have been of greatest importance, in terms of total learning in this century, has been the convergence in the length of school terms between urban and rural areas and between the South and other parts of the country. Because blacks were concentrated in the rural South prior to World War II, they may have been most penalized by the shorter school terms, and may have gained most by the general trend to equality of the term. As is indicated in the third row of panel I, in 1919/20, blacks attended school only two-thirds as many days each year as did whites. Differences in days attended were more the result of differences in the length of the school term than in attendance rates. By 1953/54, black-white differences in days attended had virtually disappeared. The overwhelming difference between black and white schools in the 1920s and 1930s was in the composition of enrollment. In this period, typically one-third

Table 13-3

Comparison of Trends in Enrollment, Attendance, and Expenditures for Segregated Black Public Elementary and Secondary Schools in the Southern United States to Trends for All Schools, 1919-1954

I. School Term and Attendance

Characteristic:	1919-20	29-30	39-40	49-50	53-54
1. Average number of days schools were in session					
a) Black Schools	119	132	156	173	177
b) All Schools	162	173	175	178	179
2. Percentage of pupils enrolled in average daily attendance					
a) Black Schools	67.3	72.1	80.4	85.3	85.1
b) All Schools	74.8	82.8	86.7	88.7	88.9
3. Average days attended per pupil enrolled					
a) Black Schools	80	97	126	148	151
b) All Schools	121	143	152	158	159

II. Enrollment and Grade Level

Characteristic:	1919-20	29-30	39-40	49-50	53-54
4. Percentage of pupils in public elementary and secondary school who are enrolled in the first grade					
a) Black Schools	36.8	34.4	26.0	19.5	16.5
b) All Schools	22.9	16.2	11.9	12.6	12.7
5. Percentage of pupils in public elementary and secondary schools who are enrolled in secondary school					
a) Black Schools	1.6	4.9	10.5	14.1	16.2
b) All Schools	10.2	16.1	26.0	22.7	21.8

III. Salaries and Instructional Expenses

Characteristic:	1919-20	29-30	39-40	49-50	53-54
6. Average salary per member of instructional staff					
a) Black Schools	—	—	$601	$2143	$2861
b) Southern White Schools	—	—	1046		3384
c) All Schools	$871	1420	1441	3010	3825
7. Current expenditure per pupil in average daily attendance					
a) Black Schools	—	15[a]	19	—	110[b]
b) Southern White Schools	—	49[a]	59	—	181[b]
c) All Schools	—	87	88	209	265

[a]Refers to 1931-32 instead of 1929-30.

[b]Instructional expenses only.

Source: Various issues of Biennial Survey of Education and David Blose, "Statistics of the Education of Negroes," U.S. Office of Education, Federal Security Agency, circular No. 215, June 1943.

of all black elementary and secondary school pupils were enrolled in the *first* grade. Retardation rates appear to have been phenomenal in both the first years of elementary and secondary school. For example, prior to 1940 there were consistently more than twice as many black pupils enrolled in the first as in the second grade, and about one and one-half as many in the first as in the second year of high school. Since school enrollment was increasing at only 1 or 2 percent per year, the bulk of this discrepancy is retardation between grades one and two, and in high school it is a combination of retardation and "dropping out."[11]

By 1953/54, the ratio of first to second graders had fallen to 1.45 and the number in the first year of high school, relative to the second, had fallen to 1.30. Another important trend in the composition of enrollment was the rapid increase in the proportion attending secondary school. In 1919/20, only 1.6 percent of all black pupils in public schools were enrolled in high schools (in comparison to 10.2 percent of white pupils); by 1953-54 this proportion increased to 16.2 percent.

Expenditures on the black schools appear to have lagged behind the increases in attendance, enrollment, and the reductions in retardation, but the trend between 1940 and 1954 is impressive. Teacher salaries increased from a relative level of 57.5 percent of the salaries of southern white teachers to 85.0 percent in the later year. Similarly, expenditures rose from 31 percent of southern white levels in 1931/32 to 61 percent in 1953/54. Perhaps the levels of relative expenditures were a social crime at the time of the segregation decision, but the trend had been upward and had apparently accelerated after the beginning of World War II. And it is this upward trend that is an outstanding candidate for explaining the substantial trend in the value of schooling to blacks in comparison to whites. Recall that those in the experience class 13-25 years in 1959 would have last attended school between 1933 and 1945. Maybe the question of why returns were so low should have been reversed: If expenditures by school systems are the norm, then the relative value of black schooling is only slightly less than expected.

There is scattered evidence that the southern story of separate but unequal schools was partly true of the North—slightly less separate and slightly less unequal. Harold Baron offered some evidence for Chicago in 1961, 1963, and 1966. He argues that in 1961 there were significant differences in expenditures within the city's educational system which favored white students. By 1966, this expenditure difference had disappeared.

The Board of Education in New York City annually gives nationally standardized reading tests to third, sixth, and eighth grade pupils, and school average scores are available. Table 13-4 summarizes estimates of black-white differentials for selected years between 1957 and 1969. The technique used for measuring these differences is based upon the identification of *de facto* segregated schools, since only school averages, not individual scores, are available.

Table 13-4

Comparison of Black-White Reading Score Differentials by Grade Level. De Facto Segregated New York City Schools, Selected Years, 1957-1969

| | Grade in which Test Administered | |
	3rd	6th
Norm		
(National Average)	3.5	6.5
New York City Schools		
1957		
Black	2.67	4.88
White	4.07	7.81
1960		
Black	2.87	5.22
White	4.14	8.10
1965		
Black	3.19	5.67
White	4.53	8.13
1969		
Black	3.31	5.38
White	4.37	7.60

Note: These data are weighted averages of school reading score averages within each class. Third and sixth grade scores refer to elementary schools. The scores are normalized to allow for year-to-year variation in the time the test is administered. The criterion for selecting schools for these computations varied from year-to-year as data availability permitted. *Black Schools:* The object was to select a modest number of reasonably large schools with the largest proportions of black students. The third grade data refer to from twenty-one to twenty-eight schools, each having 700 or more pupils, with at least 90 percent black. The sixth grade data are for the same schools, except that in 1965 and 1969 only eleven of these elementary schools had sixth grades. *White Schools:* The number of elementary schools ranged between twenty-three and twenty-seven with enrollment exceeding 800, at least 97 percent white.

Source: The Board of Education of New York City, unpublished data.

Once again, the story of reading-score differentials is pretty much the same as for income differences and for the segregated southern schools of an earlier period.

Viewed in absolute terms, there are very large black-white differentials, and these differences compound as years completed increase. Whatever forces result in differences by the third grade, appear to continue to operate at the sixth grade. The important evidence of Table 13-4 lies in the trend between 1957 and 1969. For third graders, a 1.40 years reading deficit eroded to 1.06. In twelve years, black third graders in New York City improved an average of 0.64 years in reading achievement. This is reason for optimism. The reduction in the deficit for the sixth grade is a little more ambiguous. The deficit falls from 2.93 years to 2.22—a larger absolute improvement, but about the same fraction (25 percent) of the original deficit as for third graders. Certainly the gain for blacks from 4.88

to 5.38 is important, but the norm is 6.5, and the deficit remains large. Notice that children in the sixth grade in the spring of 1969 would have entered school no later than fall of 1963, and would therefore have missed the Headstart programs. Also, given the rapid rise in black school completion levels, the average education levels of parents of black third graders in 1969 would have exceeded the average schooling of parents of black sixth graders so that these increments may refer more to changes in home than in school environment. For purposes of this analysis, the important point is that the "knowledge" associated with given school completion is rising for blacks relative to whites. The question of why these changes occur is not relevant.

The fragments of evidence tell a consistent story: schools for blacks may be inferior to those for whites and much improvement is still in order, but the record is undeniable. Improvement has occurred.

Earnings and Returns to Schooling

Table 13-5 reports average earnings and the associated earning increment from a single year of schooling, estimated from the earning equation when schooling is held constant at twelve years.

Table 13-5
Estimated Average Annual Earnings and the Value of an Extra Year of Schooling by Race and Experience (Schooling = 12 Years)

Experience Class:	Annual Earnings			Return to Schooling (Direct Component Only)		
Census (1959)	Black	White	Black/White	Black	White	Black/White
1-4	$1500	$2620	0.57	$120	$250	0.41
5-12	2510	4700	0.53	160	380	0.43
13-25	2360	5830	0.41	90	370	0.25
SEO (1966)						
1-3	2830	3160	0.90	650	460	1.41
4-7	3880	5024	0.77	550	530	1.03
8-11	4160	5968	0.70	330	490	0.67
12-19	4420	6800	0.65	270	610	0.45
20-32	4300	6690	0.64	210	460	0.46

Note: Average income is predicted from the regression equations of appendix Tables 6 and 7 (not published here but available upon request). Where an auxiliary structure is estimated between schooling, S, and another independent variable, x, the mean level of that variable is adjusted to $S = 12$, according to $\bar{x}(s = 12) = \bar{x} + b(12 - \bar{s})$, where b is the auxiliary regression coefficient. Mean income is estimated as the antilog of the predicted mean log of earnings plus one-half of the residual variance. The variance adjustment results from an assumption that the residuals are log-normal and increases the income predictions by 15 to 30 percent. The estimated return to schooling is the schooling coefficient (the direct return) times estimated mean income at twelve years of schooling.

Between 1959 and 1966 there was a sharp rise of the relative earnings of blacks in each of the cohorts such that relative earnings increased by 0.12 to 0.13 within each of the two less experienced cohorts and by 0.23 in the third. This suggests the possibility that much of the gain experienced over this seven-year period may be serendipity of the business cycle and subject to erosion as labor-market conditions weaken. It seems reasonable to predict that had the 1966 observations occurred alongside the 1959 labor market, the earning ratios would decline to their 1959 levels. If so, then instead of relative earnings between 0.77 and 0.90 for those beginning work in the 1960s, the ratios would have been something like 0.64-0.77. This is to point out that although vintage effects appear to be pushing toward earnings parity, the gap remains large.

To try to disentangle the effects of activities of the federal government on relative black earnings, the variables for direct and indirect governmental employment were added to the regression equations. The results are that, although these variables are statistically "significant," the total effect, allowing for employment shares, is numerically small. Direct governmental employment increased average black earnings relative to the white average by 1 to 2 percent in both 1959 and 1966, and the effects of indirect governmental employment are similar. Blacks who work for the government (directly or indirectly) gain relative to whites, but the proportions so employed are small enough that the total effect remains small. Nonetheless, since the earning differential between private and governmental employment is large for blacks, there is an apparent incentive to acquire these jobs.

Summary

This is an empirical attempt to identify some of the structural components of the observed rapid rise in the relative earnings of blacks in the United States between 1959 and 1966. It is clear that much of the gain is associated with tightening labor markets: In 1959 white high school graduates in all experience classes worked 15 to 20 percent more "weeks" than blacks, whereas the discrepancy fell to about 2 percent in 1966. But, even though this cyclic component is important in accounting for the rise in relative earnings, there is also a vintage effect to be considered. In comparison to whites, blacks who have entered the work force in recent periods fare better than earlier entrants.

Part of this gain results from a convergence of school completion levels. For example, in the census, blacks with 1-4 years of experience average 11.1 years of schooling as compared to a white average of 12.8. Yet for those with 13-25 years of experience the black average was 8.8 years and 11.4 for whites. Clearly, part of the gain in relative earnings of younger blacks comes from this relative increase in average school completion, but a more important part of the gain comes from the combined effect of increased schooling and an increased return to schooling. For example, based upon the direct returns to schooling (holding constant weeks worked and the probability of zero earnings) for the cohort with 13-25 years work experience in 1959, the rise in black average school completion would have resulted in an increase in earnings of 9.2 percent, and taking the increase in white schooling into account, relative earnings would have increased by only 0.2 percent. Yet based upon the direct returns realized for the cohort with 1-4 years of experience, the increase in black earnings resulting from increased average schooling would have been 18.2 percent and earnings, relative to whites, would have risen by 5.0 percent.

Clearly, the complete picture of relative black earnings cannot be obtained from a reference to quality of schooling, but examination of the data suggests that schooling quality is important. For both blacks and whites the cross-sectional evidence is that the proportional contribution of schooling to annual earnings declines sharply as experience increases, or, since these are cross-sections, as vintage decreases. Yet in comparing six cohorts (three experience classes for blacks and whites separately) this attenuation does not occur in the seven-year interval between 1959 and 1966. The direct return to schooling is remarkably constant over this period, suggesting that the experience—vintage effect of the cross-section is really only a vintage effect: More recent entrants into the work force enjoy higher returns to schooling than do those persons schooled in an earlier period. Further, this upward trend is stronger for blacks, such that the percentage contribution of schooling to earnings is larger than for whites in comparing persons who entered the labor force in the 1960s but is significantly lower for those who entered in the 1930s and 1940s.

To get a feel for the underpinnings of this change, I turned to a comparison of black-white differences in statistics of schools. There, the data are clear: Through time the relative quality of black schooling has risen rapidly. In the segregated South there were important differences in enrollment, attendance, and expenditure patterns at the time of the 1954 desegregation decision, but these differences are dwarfed in comparison to those of the 1920s and 1930s. Since 1954, partial evidence of continuing convergence in schooling quality is offered by referring to a study of the Chicago schools that found black-white expenditure differences vanishing by 1966. For New York City schools, reading score data for *de facto* segregated schools indicate that about one-third of the discrepancies existing in 1957 had disappeared by 1969.

There are, of course, many explanations for the vintage effects of rising relative black income with a downward drift in market discrimination being the simplest and most obvious alternative. It seems reasonable to expect that whatever social, political, and judicial forces allowed convergence in offerings to black and white students also have allowed convergence in offerings to black and white workers. The role of alternative hypotheses is confounded because most would not be exclusive of the quality phenomenon, but would be supplementary to it. It would be helpful to be able to identify the partial effects of the several forces that have been operative, but I doubt that available data are capable of such fine distinction. Certainly the data reported here are not.

In behalf of the quality of schooling hypothesis let me summarize the trends revealed here with which alternatives must contend. First, not only have relative black incomes increased but the gain has been greatest for higher school completion levels. Second, the phenomenon of rising returns to schooling is not only true in comparing black relative to white incomes but holds within the races as well: Young blacks fare better in comparison to young whites than do older blacks in comparison to older whites *and* schooling contains more of an income boost for young blacks and young whites than for older generations of their own races.

Appendix 13A

**Comments on Welch's "Black-White
Differences in Returns to Schooling"**
Samuel Gubins*

We know that returns to schooling for blacks have been far below those for whites, in part from previous work by Finis Welch. In the present chapter Welch offers us two new elements to consider—one a fact, the other a hypothesis. The fact is that returns to schooling for more recent black entrants to the labor force are higher than for older black workers. And it appears that the gap in returns to schooling as between blacks and whites is narrowing. This welcome news we owe to Welch's scrutiny of the 1960 census and the 1967 Survey of Economic Opportunity. By breaking down the census and SEO samples into age-group cohorts which reflect different periods of entry into the labor force, Welch shows that while returns for blacks were significantly less than for whites among those educated during the 1920s and 1930s, the opposite is true for those educated during the 1940s and early 1950s. This is an important finding to which several alternate hypotheses may apply.

The hypothesis that Welch offers is that the quality of education for blacks has been improving relative to that for whites. In consequence, black workers whose education is of more recent vintage embody a higher quality of education than do older black workers.

This hypothesis is supported not only by the evidence of a narrowing of the gap in returns to schooling between young blacks and young whites, but by the clear evidence that certain school characteristics have changed over time. By several measures, schools for blacks are improving relative to schools for whites. Almost twenty years since the Brown case we know that schools are still separate, but they are less unequal.

I have no quarrel with the facts about the relative improvement of black school characteristics. What I would like to raise are a few questions about what this improvement signifies. In particular, I think that what Welch measures is not really increases in the quality of education but increases in quantity. And I am very uncomfortable with the explanation that improvements in school characteristics—whether we call these improvements in quantity *or* quality—are what account for improvements in relative earnings.

What we would like to measure and to compare are the rates of return on black and white education. Presumably differences in rates of return for equal education, holding ability constant, reflect in part labor-market discrimination and housing discrimination which result in denial of access to employment. In past studies, a year's education in a predominantly white school was considered

*Professor of economics, Haverford College.

equal to a year's education in a predominantly black school. Even as these earlier studies were being conceived, we strongly suspected that the educations were not comparable. Yet, for want of a good measure of quality, we could not substantiate this belief empirically. What Welch claims to offer us is a measure of quality of education. He notes that black schools by 1953-54 had virtually caught up with white schools in average number of days schools were in session, the percentage of pupils in average daily attendance, and the average days attended per pupil enrolled. In addition, he notes that the gap in salaries and instructional expenses per pupil between white and black schools has been closing. What the first three of these measures are actually pointing to is that a school year for black students is beginning to approximate, in length, a school year for white students. This is not, however, a measure of the quality of education. If anything, Welch's evidence in Table 13-3 points only to increases in *quantity* of education. In 1919/20 black schools were in session only 73 percent as long as all schools; by 1953/54 the sessions were virtually equal in length. During the academic year following World War I, average days attended per pupil enrolled in black schools were 66 percent of that for all schools; by the first year of President Eisenhower's tenure there was no difference. Quite simply this means that by 1953/54 a year's schooling for black and white schools were comparable in length, whereas thirty years earlier what we called a year for black schools was actually between two-thirds and three-fourths of a year in a white school.

Welch also points to a narrowing in the gap between expenditures per pupil in southern black schools and southern white schools as evidence of increased quality of the black schools relative to the white schools. First, it should be pointed out that the narrowing of the gap has been far from spectacular. In 1949/50 average salary per member of instructional staff in black schools was 71 percent of that for all schools. Ten years later the percentage had grown to 74 percent. This change may reflect factors other than the increased "quality" of the teachers, such as a trend toward uniformity of pay scales. Future research may yield information on additional or alternate factors.

As others have pointed out, it is far from evident that the quality of education is related directly or indirectly to its cost. It is important to address the issue of whether to focus on inputs or outputs in measuring educational quality. Is the importance of education to be measured by the expenditures per pupil, the level of education of teachers, the size of the classroom, or is the importance of education to be measured by the reading and mathematical achievement of students?

To return to the question of what accounts for improvements in relative earnings, I believe that there may be an additional or alternate explanation of Welch's empirical findings. The hypothesis is the changing social and political climate which has rendered labor-market discrimination less acceptable and therefore more costly: I am proposing a public policy hypothesis.

In the last paragraph of Welch's chapter, the claim is made that the reduced discrimination hypothesis must contend with two facts. The first is that not only have relative black incomes increased but the gain has been greatest for higher school completion levels. My reduced discrimination hypothesis can explain this quite as easily as the Welch quality of education hypothesis. The impact of antidiscrimination measures has been most keenly felt in those occupational levels which have been most effectively antiblack—most entry level jobs have always been open. It is only recently that clerical and higher level jobs have begun to be opened to blacks.

The second fact that Welch claims the reduced discrimination hypothesis must contend with has two facets relating to the young and the old. "Young blacks fare better in comparison to young whites than do older blacks in comparison to older whites." The reduced-discrimination hypothesis can handle this very well. Older blacks are working at jobs below what their education would warrant, but they have been working at those jobs for many years. In consequence, the on-the-job training which would have capitalized on their education was not experienced and these workers have effectively lost the benefits to which their higher education entitled them. Younger workers, in contrast, are now reaping the benefit of the reduced tolerance for discrimination and are being given jobs more closely attuned to their education, and this is reflected in their earnings. In other words, there is no reason, a priori, to think that antidiscrimination policies would affect all workers, regardless of age, equally, and good reasons to believe that such policies favor younger workers.

What does challenge the reduced-discrimination hypothesis, however, is Welch's observation that "schooling contains more of an income boost for young blacks and young whites than for older generations of their own races." What this suggests to me is that the vintage theory *is* a plausible explanation of the returns to schooling regardless of race, and for this we owe Welch a great deal. It is not, however, a complete explanation for the increased returns from schooling for blacks relative to whites. Obviously, what we would like to have is some way of measuring the separate impact of quality/quantity changes and public policy changes. In other words, these hypotheses are complementary, not mutually exclusive.

Perhaps the point I am trying to make may be illuminated by a comparison with another discriminated-against group, women. If, over the next several years, antidiscrimination efforts on behalf of women continue, it seems likely to me that calculated rates of return on women's education should increase, relative to rates of return on men's education. Would it be reasonable to claim that this was the consequence of increased quality of women's education? To be sure, increased emphasis on women's liberation ought to find an outlet in the schools, and young girls *will* be encouraged to think of themselves as career-oriented. In this sense the "quality" of women's education may indeed increase. But the primary explanation for the anticipated increase in returns from education for women will be that social and political pressures are being generated which will result in women being admitted into the labor force at levels commensurate with their education. And this, I would like to believe, partially explains Welch's important finding.

Notes

1. Lewis Solmon has recent evidence linking college traits to earnings. Also, the work of Frank Stafford and George Johnson is relevant.

2. The census contained observations for 56,732 males between 14 and 70 years of age who, if they reported a positive number of weeks worked, reported positive earnings. Of these, 40,065 were eliminated: 6,835 were rural; 26,962 either had "negative" work experience, were in school, or had more than twenty-five years experience; 169 worked without pay; and 529 were neither black nor white.

The SEO sample of males 14 to 70 years contained 28,552 persons. Of these, 18,231 were eliminated: 378 were in the armed forces; 6,000 had rural residence; 10,992 had either negative experience, were in school, or had experience in excess of thirty-two years; 31 worked without pay or were missing information on working class; an additional 230 had race other than black or white.

3. As schooling increases income, it increases the probability that an individual will not be in the sample. Thus, as schooling increases, we observe increasing proportions of those who are "losers" relative to the norm, and systematically understate the increase in "expected" income associated with schooling.

4. In accordance with Hanoch, I assume the following ages of entry into the labor market:

Years of School	0-7	8	9-11	12	13-15	16	17+
Age at First Year Out of School	14	16	18	20	23	26	28

Experience is simply defined as current age less the estimated age at leaving school.

5. The proportional increment actually equals

$$e^{a_1} - 1 = a_1 + \frac{a_1^2}{2!} + \frac{a_1^3}{3!} + \frac{a_1^4}{4!} + \ldots$$

For small values of a_1, the higher order terms disappear so that the proportional increment is approximately a_1.

6. The coefficient $\hat{a}_3$ is the negative value of the average log of earnings, for those who have earnings, adjusted by differences between those with and without earnings in mean levels of other independent variables when these differences are weighted by regression coefficients. In principle, the coefficients on other independent variables are smaller, in absolute value, than they would be if the regression were restricted to those observations with positive earnings. The relationship between the coefficients reported here and those obtained in regressions restricted to positive incomes is straightforward. First, partition total variance of the i-th independent variable into variance about the group (those with and without income) means and variance within each group about its mean. Let f_i represent the fraction of within-group variance attributable to those who have income. Then $\hat{a}_i = f_i \hat{b}_i$, where $\hat{a}_i$ refers to regression coefficients reported here and $\hat{b}_i$ refers to coefficients obtained from restricting the sample to persons with positive income. For the constant or intercept term, the weeks worked, and the government employment variables, a constant is assigned when earnings are zero and for these variables $f_i = 1$. Therefore the schooling coefficient is the *only* parameter estimate that is affected by introducing the zero earnings dummy.

7. As an example, define *education* as "effective" schooling and *quality of schooling* as effective schooling per year of school completion. In the model, log $W = \alpha_0 + \alpha_1 E$, where W is the hourly wage and E is education. With $E = QS$, quantity times quality of schooling, the percentage return to quantity is $\alpha_1 Q$, since $(\alpha_1 Q) S = \alpha_1 E$.

8. In fact, if there is no involuntary unemployment and if schooling is competitively purchased such that there is no income or wealth effect, the ratio of the indirect to the direct effect is an estimate of the substitution component in the labor supply function. The indirect effect is the time worked response to the wage change accompanying increased schooling so that the ratio of this to the wage response to schooling gives an estimate of the rate at which time at work responds to wage increments.

9. In fact, at very low levels of work experience there is good reason to expect a life-cycle component in the direct return as well as in the indirect return. Bear in mind that an extra year of schooling, experience constant, implies that age also increases by one year. In fact, in the estimates used here, the age of entry into the labor market rises something more than a year with an added year of schooling. At relatively young ages this maturation effect, included in the return to schooling, may be important.

10. It is not clear that a distinction between life-cycle and vintage effects is possible using a single cross-section. Weiss and Williamson observed that over the age interval, 20-49 years, and within the schooling interval, 8-12 years, the percentage increment in earnings from schooling falls as age increases. This is not true for persons who have attended college, nor is it true of those who are 50 years old or over.

Weiss and Williamson purport to test the impact of inferior southern schooling by using the variable for residence at age 16 that is available in SEO. Unfortunately, they did not allow interaction between schooling and this early residence variable, so that the marginal value of schooling is assumed independent of location. This formulation is then not a test of quality. In fact, given the evidence of trends through time presented here, I would argue that the appropriate test concerning quality of schooling involves interaction between vintage, early residence, *and* schooling. The introduction of dummy variables for early residence does not adequately specify the role of schooling's quality.

11. Since there were always more students enrolled in the first year of high school than in the last year of grade school, the evidence is for retardation.

References

Baron, Harold M. "Race and Status in Schools' Spending: Chicago, 1961-1966," *Journal of Human Resources* 6 (Winter 1971), pp. 3-24.

Blose, David. "Statistics of the Education of Negroes." U.S. Office of Education, Circular No. 215, June 1943.

Gintis, Herbert. "Education, Technology, and the Characteristics of Worker Productivity." *American Economic Review* 62 (May 1971), pp. 266-79.

Hanoch, Giora. "An Economic Analysis of Earnings and Schooling." *Journal of Human Resources* 2 (Summer 1967), pp. 310-29.

Jencks, Christopher, et al. *Inequality: A Reassessment of the Effect of Family and Schooling for America.* New York: Basic Books, 1972.

Landes, William. "The Economics of Fair Employment Laws." *Journal of Political Economy* 76 (July/August 1968), pp. 507-52.

Lindsay, C.M. "Measuring Human Capital Returns." *Journal of Political Economy* 79 (November/December 1971), pp. 1195-1215.

Solmon, Lewis. "The Definition and Impact of College Quality." Unpublished paper, NBER, June 1972.

Stafford, Frank, and Johnson, George. "Social Returns to Quantity and Quality of Schooling." Unpublished paper, Ann Arbor: University of Michigan, December 1970.

Weiss, Leonard, and Williamson, Jeffrey G. "Black Education, Earnings, and Interregional Migration: Some New Evidence." *American Economic Review* 62 (June 1972), pp. 372-83.

Welch, Finis. "Labor-Market Discrimination: An Interpretation of Income Differences in the Rural South." *Journal of Political Economy* 75 (June 1967), pp. 225-40.

U.S. Department of Labor. *Manpower Report of the President, 1971.* April 1971.

_____. Bureau of Labor Statistics. *Patterns of U.S. Economic Growth.* Bulletin 1672.

U.S. Office of Education. *Biennial Survey of Education in the United States.* "Statistics of State School Systems," various issues. (Earlier editions are by the Bureau of Education in Department of the Interior.)

14

Racial Differences in the Variation in Rates of Return from Schooling

Barry R. Chiswick*

In the last few decades there has been considerable attention paid to differences in earnings between white and nonwhite male workers. The recent literature has focused on racial differences in investments in schooling as an important explanatory variable. Nonwhite males as a group are characterized by both lower levels of schooling and lower average rates of return from schooling than white males.

The lower level of schooling has, in part, been attributed to the lower average rate of return from schooling. In addition, it has been suggested that nonwhites have a greater "risk aversion" than whites, which would also discourage investments in human and nonhuman capital.[1] It should be recognized, however, that even if there were no racial difference in risk aversion or in the average level of return from an investment, a greater uncertainty of the return among nonwhites would result in a smaller investment by nonwhites.

The purpose of this study is the measurement of racial differences in the uncertainty of rates of return from schooling. A wider variation in rates of return is assumed to be associated with greater uncertainty on the part of an individual as to where he (or she) will be in a given distribution of rates of return. A larger variation in rates of return for nonwhite males would imply that young nonwhites face greater uncertainty as to the profitability of schooling. Thus, if we assume equal risk aversion for whites and nonwhites, nonwhites would have a smaller incentive to invest in schooling for the same average rate of return from schooling and the same rate of discount of future earnings into present earnings.

Two measures of this variation are considered the variance and the coefficient of variation in rates of return. The variance in rates of return [Var(r)] is a measure of absolute variation, while the coefficient of variation [CV(r)] is a measure of relative variation.[2]

The first section recapitulates the "human capital earnings function," which relates income to investment in human capital.[3] This function can be used to compute estimates of the variance in rates of return from schooling.[4]

Since individual differences in weeks worked in a given year reflect both long-term and temporary employment differences, the variance in rates of return based on (unknown) long-term or permanent employment patterns cannot be

---

*Senior staff economist, Council of Economic Advisers, on leave from Queens College, C.U.N.Y.

computed directly from observed annual income data. An upper-bound estimate of the variance or the coefficient of variation in rates of return may be obtained by assuming that all interpersonal differences in weeks worked in a given year are permanent. Alternatively, assuming that differences in weeks worked are all transitory permits a lower-bound estimate to be computed from observed weekly income (i.e., annual income adjusted for weeks worked).

In the second section, the upper- and lower-bound estimates of the variance and the coefficient of variation in rates of return are computed for white and nonwhite males for each of the states using data from the *1960 Census of Population*. Whenever a choice of alternative assumptions has to be made, the assumption which biases downward the racial difference in the variance and coefficient of variation in rates of return is selected. The computed upper-bound estimates for the coefficient of variation for nonwhites are twice the white value and the lower-bound estimates for nonwhites are 50 percent larger than for whites. Thus part of the racial difference in the coefficient of variation in rates of return can be attributed to the greater inequality of weeks worked during the year among nonwhite males. The larger variance and coefficient of variation in rates of return from schooling for nonwhites is not due to regional differences; the same patterns exist among the southern and among the nonsouthern states as exist for the states as a whole.

The data suggest that as much as one-half of the greater uncertainty of individual differences in returns from investments in schooling is due to the greater nonwhite instability of employment during the year.[5] The greater uncertainty of returns from investments for nonwhites may make them appear to be less responsive to changes in average returns from human capital. In fact, however, nonwhites may be equally motivated to increase their income through investments in human capital, but face a different opportunity set.

Procedure

The model described in Equations (14.1) to (14.7) has been developed elsewhere, but is repeated here for the convenience of the reader.[6]

If earnings were due only to investment in training, there would exist a simple relation between earnings and training parameters. If Y_0 were the earnings of an individual with no training, and if he invested (direct and opportunity costs) $100k_1$ percent of his potential income in year 1, his earnings in year 2 and in all subsequent periods would be

$$Y_1 = Y_0 + r_1 k_1 Y_0 = Y_0 (1 + r_1 k_1), \tag{14.1}$$

where r_1 is the rate of return on the investment. If he invested in N periods of training, his earnings after training, are[7]

$$Y_N = Y_0 \prod_{j=1}^{N} (1 + r_j k_j). \tag{14.2}$$

If he does not work the full year, but the rate of return r_j is calculated on the basis of full-period employment, Equation (14.2) can be modified as

$$Y_N = Y_0 \prod_{j=1}^{N} (1 + r_j k_j)(fw)^\gamma, \tag{14.3}$$

where Y_N now means annual earnings, (fw) is the fraction *weeks worked* (WW) divided by 52, and γ is the elasticity of annual earnings with respect to weeks worked. If γ equals unity, weekly wages are independent of the number of weeks worked per year. A γ greater than unity implies that those who work more weeks per year receive higher wages for each week they work.

Taking the natural logarithm (Ln) of both sides of Equation (14.3) and using the relation $Ln (1 + a) \cong a$, when a is small,[8] results in

$$Ln\, Y_N = Ln\, Y_0 + \sum_{j=1}^{N} r_j k_j + \gamma\, Ln \frac{WW}{52}. \tag{14.4}$$

The N years of training can be divided into S years of schooling followed by $N-S$ years of experience or postschooling investment. The term k_j for the schooling years is approximately equal to one, and will be assumed to equal one.[9]

If individual differences are introduced and it is assumed that the rate of return from schooling to an individual is constant for all levels of schooling, Equation (14.4) becomes

$$Ln\, Y_{N,i} = Ln\, Y_0 + r_i S_i + \sum_{j=S_i+1}^{N} r_{ij} k_{ij} + \gamma\, Ln \frac{WW_i}{52} + U_i, \tag{14.5}$$

where a residual term U_i includes the effects of omitted variables such as individual variations in Y_0 and γ. Let us simplify Equation (14.5) by writing it as

$$Ln\, Y_{N,i} = Ln\, Y_0 + r_i S_i + U_i^* \tag{14.6}$$

where $\quad U_i^* = \sum_{j} r_{ij} k_{ij} + \gamma\, Ln \frac{WW_i}{52} + U_i.$

Note that the rate of return r_i is an average, not marginal, rate of return to the individual. If those with greater training ability (i.e., higher marginal rate of return schedule) have lower costs of obtaining funds for investment, the coefficient of variation of average rates of return to individuals can be substantial even if there is equality of marginal rates of return.[10] Even if there were horizontal supply curves of funds for investment and equality of opportunity in the sense that all individuals have the same supply curve, average rates of return would differ due to differences in ability or other dimensions of demand conditions.

Analytically, the relation between r_i and S_i is not clear. Those with greater ability have a stronger incentive to invest in schooling and will have a larger S_i and r_i if the interest cost of funds for investment is upward rising and constant across investors. If the marginal rate of return declines with additional investments and all individuals have the same rate of return schedule (equal ability), those with greater wealth have a lower cost of funds schedule and there will be a negative correlation between S_i and r_i. However, those of greater ability tend to have a lower cost of funds schedule, and therefore the net relation between S_i and r_i is unclear. Empirically, when weeks worked are held constant, the hypothesis of no correlation between the level of schooling and the rate of return to that level cannot be rejected.[11] It shall, therefore, be assumed that r_i and S_i are independent random variables.

If r_i and S_i are independent, and we compute the variance of both sides of Equation (14.6), we obtain,[12]

$$\text{Var}(LnY) = \bar{r}^2 \, \text{Var}(S) + \bar{S}^2 \, \text{Var}(r) + \text{Var}(r) \, \text{Var}(S) + \text{Var}(U^*) \quad (14.7)$$
$$+ 2\text{Cov}(rS, U^*).$$

Rearranging the terms,[13]

$$\text{Var}(r) = \frac{\text{Var}(LnY) - \bar{r}^2 \, \text{Var}(S) - \text{Var}(U^*) - 2\text{Cov}(rS, U^*)}{\bar{S}^2 + \text{Var}(S)}. \quad (14.8)$$

The residual U^* includes the effects of luck, experience, weeks worked, and other variables. If we designate

$$\text{Var}(r)^* = \frac{\text{Var}(LnY) - \bar{r}^2 \, \text{Var}(S)}{\bar{S}^2 + \text{Var}(S)} \quad (14.9)$$

then

$$\text{Var}(r)^* \geq \text{Var}(r), \quad (14.10)$$

if $\text{Var}(U^*) + 2\text{Cov}(rS, U^*)$ is not negative.[14]

Var(r)* is an upper limit estimate of the variance in rates of return from schooling. Equation (14.9) indicates that an upper-limit estimate of the variance in rates of return can be estimated from data on the level and inequality of schooling, the relative inequality of income and the rate of return from schooling. Direct estimates of the rate of return from schooling are not available for many regions. However, the slope coefficient from a linear regression of the log of income on years of schooling can be interpreted as a regression estimate of the rate of return [see Equation (14.6)]. The estimate is unbiased if the rate of return (r_i) is independent of schooling (S_i), and if schooling is uncorrelated with the residual (U_i^*). However, the regression estimate computed from Equation (14.6) is downward biased because of the negative correlation between years of schooling and years of experience.[15] Using a downward biased estimate of the rate of return biases upward the estimated variance in rates of return. The regression estimate of the rate of return ($\bar{r}$) is biased downward more for white males than for nonwhite males because of the steeper white experience-income profile.[16] This biases upward the measured variance in rates of return more for white males than for nonwhite males.

The residual variance (VarU^*) in Equation (14.8) contains the effects of the dispersion of investments in experience and the rate of return from these investments. Because of the lower nonwhite slope of the log income-experience profile, the effect of postschool experience on income inequality is smaller for nonwhites than for whites. Thus the absence of an experience adjustment also biases upward the estimate of the variance in rates of return more for whites than for nonwhites. Since the estimates calculated without the experience adjustment have a larger variance for nonwhites than for whites, a fortiori nonwhites would have a larger variance with the adjustment.[17]

The coefficient of variation in rates of return is calculated as

$$\text{CV}(r)^* = \frac{\sqrt{\text{Var}(r)^*}}{\bar{r}} \tag{14.11}$$

with $\bar{r}$ estimated by the regression rate of return. Even if the numerator were unbiased, since the denominator, the regression estimate of the rate of return, is downward biased, the coefficient of variation calculated from Equation (14.11) would be an upward biased estimate of the true population value. Since $\bar{r}$ is biased downward more for whites than for nonwhites, the estimated coefficient of variation is biased upward more for whites than for nonwhites. Since we find a larger coefficient of variation for nonwhites, a fortiori we would find a larger nonwhite coefficient of variation if unbiased estimates of the level of the rate of return were employed.

The estimate of the variance in rates of return in Equation (14.9) includes the effect of differences in weeks worked on incomes. The variance in rates of return based on long-run employment conditions (i.e., long-run earnings) would be smaller than the variance based on "measured" or current employment (or earnings). The variance based on weekly wages (i.e., on the assumption of no differences in weeks worked across individuals) would be even lower than that based on permanent employment patterns. Permanent employment patterns cannot be quantified, but the variance in rates of return based on the assumption of no differences in weeks worked can be computed by a modification of Equation (14.9) to[18]

$$\text{Var}(r)_p = \frac{\text{Var}(LnY) - \bar{r}^2 \, \text{Var}(S) - \gamma^2 \, \text{Var}(LnWW)}{\bar{S}^2 + \text{Var}(S)}. \tag{14.12}$$

The variance in rates of return among individuals based on long-run employment patterns computed by the technique developed here would be in the interval bounded by $\text{Var}(r)^*$ and $\text{Var}(r)_p$. The coefficient of variation in rates of return adjusted for employment is computed as

$$\text{CV}(r)_p = \frac{\sqrt{\text{Var}(r)_p}}{\bar{r}}. \tag{14.13}$$

Recall that the term γ is the elasticity of earnings with respect to weeks worked. A γ greater than unity implies that those with higher weekly wages work more weeks per year.[19] Mincer estimated $\gamma = 1.2$ for nonfarm white males with earnings but not enrolled in school, and this value is used here.[20] For two reasons the racial difference in the variance in rates of return adjusted for weeks worked cannot be taken at face value. First, part of the uncertainty associated with investment in schooling is due to long-run variations in less than full-year employment. The variance based on long-run employment conditions is in the interval bounded by $\text{Var}(r)^*$ and $\text{Var}(r)_p$. Second the estimate of $\gamma = 1.2$ for white males is also used for nonwhites, but there are theoretical reasons and empirical evidence which support the hypothesis that the elasticity of earnings with respect to weeks worked (γ) is lower for nonwhites than for whites.[21] Using too large a γ biases downward the estimated weeks-worked adjusted variance in rates of return to nonwhites compared to whites.

The estimated variance in rates of return, even when adjusted for long-term employment, contains within it the effects of differences in ability, quality of schooling, investments in postschool training, and pure luck. If individuals know that part of the variation in rates of return is due to factors that are not random, the true measure of risk is smaller than the computed variance in rates of return.[22]

Estimates

The *1960 Census of Population* state data are used to compute the variance and coefficient of variation in rates of return for white and nonwhite males. Separate nonwhite data are published for only thirty-nine of the coterminous states (where the District of Columbia is treated as a state) of which seventeen are southern.[23] Data for white males exist for these thirty-nine states, and in addition for all males in the ten remaining states with few nonwhites.

The model in the first section was developed for the labor-market earnings of adult males. Unfortunately, such data do not exist on a state basis. Data do exist for the income (Y) in 1959 of males aged 25 and over with income, and the earnings (E) in 1959 of labor force males aged 14 and over with earnings. The variance and coefficient of variation in rates of return are computed for both definitions of income. Since the variance of nonlabor income is greater for whites than nonwhites, the inclusion of property income is expected to bias upward the variation in rates of return more for whites than nonwhites.

The schooling and weeks-worked data are for labor-force males aged 25 and over. The rate of return from schooling for each race in each state is the slope coefficient from the linear regression of the natural logarithm of income on years of schooling completed [see Equation (14.6)], using microdata for that race-state.[24]

The data in Table 14-1 indicate that the variance in the rate of return (unadjusted for weeks of employment) is just over one-third larger for nonwhites

Table 14-1

Mean and Standard Deviation of the Variance in Rates of Return from Schooling for Males

| | | | | RACE (Number of States) | | | |
| | | | | Non-South | | South | |
	"White" (49)	White (39)	Nonwhite (39)	White (22)	Nonwhite (22)	White (17)	Nonwhite (17)
Income Data							
Mean	0.0053	0.0055	0.0083	0.0050	0.0070	0.0061	0.0099
S.D.	0.0010	0.0010	0.0024	0.0007	0.0017	0.0010	0.0021
Earnings Data							
Mean	0.0052	0.0052	0.0077	0.0049	0.0064	0.0056	0.0094
S.D.	0.0008	0.0008	0.0023	0.0006	0.0017	0.0008	0.0021

Note: Computed from Equation (14.9): $\text{Var}(r)^* = \dfrac{\text{Var}(Ln\ Y) - \bar{r}^2\,\text{Var}(S)}{S^2 + \text{Var}(S)}$.

Definitions: "White" Males = White males in the thirty-nine states with separate white-nonwhite data and all males in the remaining ten states. The district of Columbia is treated as a state.

White Males = White males in the thirty-nine states with separate white-nonwhite data.

White Males (twenty-two States) = Data for white males in the twenty-two continental nonsouthern states with separate white-nonwhite data.

Sources: *U.S. Census of Population: 1960*, Vol. 1, *Characteristics of the Population*, Parts 2 to 52, Washington, D.C.: Bureau of the Census, Tables 103, 118, 124, 138.

The procedure for computing the rate of return for each race in each state is discussed in Chiswick (1974), Part B.

for the country as a whole and within each region. Because the rate of return from schooling is lower for nonwhites than whites, the relative racial difference in the coefficient of variation in rates of return is even larger (Table 14-2). The white coefficient of variation is approximately 0.70, while the nonwhite coefficient is 1.4, or twice the white magnitude. However, the racial difference in the variance in rates of return computed from income data may be underestimated due to the definition of income. Non-labor-market income is more important for whites than nonwhites and biases upward the variance and coefficient of variation more for whites than nonwhites.

When the adjustment is made for weeks worked, using $\gamma = 1.2$, the picture changes (see Tables 14-3 and 14-4). The variance in rates of return declines for both race groups, but the relative and absolute decline is much larger for nonwhites. For the South, the nonwhite variance is still larger than the white variance, and due to the lower average rate of return from schooling for nonwhites, the coefficient of variation is still larger for southern nonwhites than whites. For the non-South and the country as a whole, the variance in rates of return with the employment adjustment is lower for nonwhites.[25]

As indicated in the first section, the white nonwhite data adjusted for weeks worked cannot be taken at face value. First, part of the uncertainty associated with investment in schooling is due to long-run variations in less than full-year employment. The variance based on long-run employment conditions is the interval bounded by $Var(r)^*$ and $Var(r)_p$. Second, the estimate of $\gamma = 1.2$ for

Table 14-2

Mean and Standard Deviation of the Coefficient of Variation in Rates of Return from Schooling for Males

					RACE (Number of States)			
					Non-South		South	
	"White" (49)	White (39)	Nonwhite (39)		White (22)	Nonwhite (22)	White (17)	Nonwhite (17)
Income Data								
Mean	0.72	0.71	1.41		0.71	1.41	0.70	1.40
S.D.	0.06	0.05	0.27		0.04	0.33	0.07	0.20
Earnings Data								
Mean	0.71	0.69	1.36		0.71	1.35	0.67	1.36
S.D.	0.07	0.06	0.27		0.04	0.32	0.07	0.20

Computed from Equations (14.9) and (14.11): $CV(r)^* = \dfrac{\sqrt{VAR(r)^*}}{r}$.

Definitions and Sources: See Table 14-1.

Table 14-3

Mean and Standard Deviation of the Variance in Rates of Return from Schooling for Males, Adjusted for Weeks Worked during the Year

	RACE (Number of States)						
				Non-South		South	
	"White" (49)	White (39)	Nonwhite (39)	White (22)	Nonwhite (22)	White (17)	Nonwhite (17)
Income Data							
Mean	0.0039	0.0040	0.0036	0.0038	0.0027	0.0043	0.0047
S.D.	0.0007	0.0006	0.0015	0.0007	0.0012	0.0005	0.0012
Earnings Data							
Mean	0.0038	0.0037	0.0030[a]	0.0037	0.0022[a]	0.0038	0.0041[a]
S.D.	0.0006	0.0006	0.0015	0.0007	0.0011	0.0004	0.0011

[a]The estimated variance was negative in Arizona, New Mexico, and North Dakota.
Note: Computed from equation (14.12):

$$\text{Var}(r)_p = \frac{\text{Var}(LnY) - \bar{r}^2 \, \text{Var}(S) - (1.2)^2 \, \text{Var}(LnWW)}{\bar{S}^2 + \text{Var}(S)}.$$

Definitions and Sources: See Table 14-1.

Table 14-4

Mean and Standard Deviation of the Coefficient of Variation in Rates of Return from Schooling for Males, Adjusted for Weeks Worked during the Year

	RACE (Number of States)						
				Non-South		South	
	"White" (49)	White (39)	Nonwhite (39)	White (22)	Nonwhite (22)	White (17)	Nonwhite (17)
Income Data							
Mean	0.61	0.61	0.93	0.62	0.91	0.59	0.96
S.D.	0.05	0.05	0.27	0.04	0.34	0.05	0.15

Notes: Computed from Equations (14.12) and (14.13): $CV(r)_p = \dfrac{\sqrt{\text{Var}(r)_p}}{\bar{r}}.$

Earnings data are not presented because the estimated variance is negative for nonwhites in Arizona, New Mexico, and North Dakota.
Definitions and Sources: See Table 14-1.

white males was also used for nonwhites, but the elasticity appears to be lower for nonwhites than for whites. Using too large a γ biases downward the estimated weeks-work adjusted variance in rates of return to nonwhites compared to whites[26] It is interesting to note, however, that the effect of variations in weeks worked on the dispersion in rates of return appears to be much larger for nonwhites than whites. The larger relative variation in weeks of employment of nonwhite males may be due to lower levels of investment in specific training, discrimination, fair employment laws, and minimum wage laws.

In summary, the variance and coefficient of variation in rates of return from schooling for nonwhites appear to be substantially larger than for whites. Much of this difference may be due to the greater relative variation in weeks worked by nonwhites. This result provides an explanation for a lower level of investment in schooling and other forms of human capital by nonwhites. With an equal distaste for risk, average money return, and discount rate, the greater uncertainty of return would induce nonwhites to invest less than whites. Note, however, that this finding does not indicate whether the alleged greater nonwhite aversion to risk is a correct hypothesis. What it does do is demonstrate that an alternative (though not necessarily mutually exclusive) hypothesis does exist and is consistent with the data.

Notes

1. For example, in his study of migration Bowles concluded that blacks appear to be less responsive to the income gain from moving than whites. He writes that this is consistent with "socially generated attitudes—risk aversion and high rates of time preference, for example—which inhibit black people from taking advantage of those avenues for higher incomes such as education and geographical mobility, ordinarily used by whites from upper and middle income backgrounds." Bowles (1970) p. 362. Although this and similar statements often appear in the literature on racial differences in economic behavior, the hypothesis that nonwhites have a greater distaste for risk has not been subjected to empirical testing.

2. Variants of the coefficient of variation are commonly used in analyses of portfolio and firm profit uncertainty. See, for example, Vickers (1960) pp. 59, 101-102, and Sharpe (1970), pp. 85, 154.

3. For a history of the development of the equation, see Mincer (1970). A detailed development of the function in its most modern form is presented in Mincer (1974).

4. This procedure was suggested to me by Jacob Mincer. He uses a similar procedure to compute the inequality in the rates of return from schooling for white males for the one-in-a-thousand sample of the *1960 Census of Population*.

5. The greater instability of employment may be due to smaller investments

in specific training by nonwhites, minimum-wage laws, fair-employment laws, and labor-market discrimination. See Becker (1964), Part I, Landes (1968), and Kosters and Welch (1972).

 6. A history of the development of the equation is in Mincer (1970).

 7. The net earnings of those still investing in year $N + 1$ is

$$Y_N = Y_0 \prod_{j=1}^{N} (1 + r_j k_j)(1 - k_{N+1}).$$

The equations developed in the text can be modified to include current investment. The level and variance of these investments cannot be estimated empirically. In the empirical analysis, the effects of current investments are included in the residual.

 8. The rate of return, r_j, is likely to be between 0.10 and 0.20, and k_j is not likely to be much greater than unity. Thus rk is small.

 9. This assumes that the direct costs of schooling to the student are approximately equal to his actual earnings during the year.

 10. For an analysis of the supply and demand curves for funds for investment, see Becker (1967).

 11. Mincer (1974), Part II.

 12. If r_i and S_i are independent random variables,

$$\mathrm{Var}\,(rS) = E\,(rS)^2 - [E\,(rS)]^2 = Er^2 ES^2 - \bar{r}^2 \bar{S}^2 = [\bar{r}^2 + \mathrm{Var}\,(r)]$$

$$[S^2 + \mathrm{Var}\,(S)] - \bar{r}^2 S^2 = \bar{r}^2 \,\mathrm{Var}\,(S) + \bar{S}^2 \,\mathrm{Var}\,(r)$$

$$+ \mathrm{Var}\,(r)\,\mathrm{Var}\,(S),$$

where $E\,(r)$ and $E\,(S)$ are symbolized by $\bar{r}$ and $\bar{S}$, respectively.

 13. This manipulation and Equations (14.9) and (14.10) were suggested to me by Jacob Mincer.

 14. Although S is positively correlated with weeks worked, it is negatively correlated with years of experience, and the net effect is a negative covariance term. [See Becker and Chiswick (1966).] The variance is necessarily positive. It seems unlikely that the sum of the residual variance and the covariance term would be substantially negative.

 15. Due to the secular increase in schooling, those with low levels of schooling tend to be older and are receiving their return on earlier investments in postschool training. Thus a regression of the log of earnings on years of schooling in which all age groups are pooled results in a downward biased estimate of the slope coefficient, and hence of the regression estimate of the rate of return. The downward bias would not be eliminated by restricting the regression to a specific age group. For a given age, a higher level of schooling implies fewer years of experience (investments in postschool training). Thus the

omission of experience as an explicit explanatory variable in the regression of log income on schooling biases downward the slope coefficient of schooling.

16. In the equation

$$\text{(i)} \qquad Ln\,Y = b_0 + b_1 S + b_2 (EXP) + U_0,$$

where Y = income, S = Schooling, EXP = years of experience, b_2 = the slope of the log income-experience profile, b_1 = a measure of the rate of return from schooling, $b_1 > 0$ and $b_2 > 0$. If instead we estimate

$$\text{(ii)} \qquad Ln\,Y = a_0 + a_1 S + U_1,$$

we know that

$$\text{(iii)} \qquad a_1 = b_1 + b_2 \frac{\text{Cov}(S, EXP)}{\text{Var}(S)}$$

The term a_1 is the estimate of the rate of return used for whites and nonwhites because it is the only estimate available on a state basis. The flatter experience earnings profile for nonwhites (lower b_2 for nonwhites), and the negative covariance of schooling with years of labor-market experience for both races, results in a smaller downward bias of a_1 for nonwhites than whites.

For an analysis of racial differences in the slope of experience earnings profiles, see Johnson (1970). For an analysis of the regression estimate of the rate of return used here, see Becker and Chiswick (1966) or Chiswick (1974).

17. It has been suggested that social class differences and school quality differences should be explicitly included in the analysis. If, as seems plausible, the inequality of social class and of school quality is greater for whites than for nonwhites, the exclusion of these variables biases upward the estimated variance in rates of return more for white males than for nonwhite males. Since we find a larger variance in rates of return for nonwhites without this adjustment, we would necessarily find a larger variance after the adjustment. For an analysis of the smaller income inequality within states among nonwhites than among whites, see Chiswick (1974). For contrary national evidence, see Horowitz, Ch. 12 of this volume.

18. The implicit assumption of a zero covariance of schooling and log of weeks worked in Equation (14.8) means that $\text{Var}(r)_p$ is biased upward.

19. This can be explained by factors affecting either labor supply or labor demand. On the supply side, workers with higher weekly wages may work more weeks per year because of an upward rising supply curve of labor, a lower quit rate because of greater amounts of specific training, or a shorter duration of unemployment due to the higher opportunity cost of their time. On the demand side, if firms have a larger investment in workers with more training, these workers have a lower rate and duration of layoff. If there were no investment in postschool training and inelastic labor supply curves to the market, γ would be less than unity but still greater than zero as firms which offer fewer weeks of

employment per year provide higher weekly wages and lower annual incomes. For an analysis of the relation between training and turnover rates, see Becker (1964), Ch. 2. An additional factor is the observed positive correlation between hours worked per week and weeks worked per year [see Fuchs (1967), p. 4].

20. Mincer, (1974), Part II.

21. Nonwhites appear to invest in less postschool training than whites (Johnson, 1970). Tests of the hypothesis that $\gamma = 1.2$ using state data result in the acceptance of the hypothesis for white males, but a rejection for nonwhite males. The coefficient is significantly lower than 1.2 for nonwhites. [Chiswick (1974), Part C.]

22. If r_i is the measured rate of return to the ith individual

$$r_i \cong \frac{d_i}{C} = \frac{d_i(\text{predicted}) + d_i(\text{random})}{C} = r_i' + R_i,$$

where d_i is a constant perpetual annual wage differential, C is the cost of schooling, r_i' is the "riskless" rate of return, and R_i is the random "pure risk" rate of return. Then, $\text{Var}(r) \cong \text{Var}(r') + \text{Var}(R)$, since r_i' and R_i are uncorrelated. The measure of risk, $\text{Var}(R)$ is necessarily smaller than the measured variance in rates of return, $\text{Var}(r)$.

23. Alaska and Hawaii are excluded from the nonwhite analysis because of the large proportion of the population which is neither white nor black.

24. The data are obtained from Chiswick (1974), Part C.

25. It is even "negative" for nonwhites for earnings in three states, Arizona, New Mexico, and South Dakota, where American Indians comprise the majority of nonwhites.

26. This is responsible for the computed negative "variance" for nonwhites in three Western states in which most nonwhites are American Indians.

References

Becker, Gary S. *Human Capital*. New York: NBER, 1964.

_____ , and Chiswick, Barry R. "Education and the Distribution of Earnings." *American Economic Review, Proceedings* (May 1966), pp. 358-69.

Becker, Gary S. *Human Capital and the Personal Distribution of Income: An Analytic Approach*. Ann Arbor: University of Michigan, 1967.

Bowles, Samuel. "Migration as Investment: Empirical Tests of the Human Investment Approach to Geographical Mobility," *Review of Economics and Statistics* (November 1970), pp. 356-62.

Chiswick, Barry R. *Income Inequality: Regional Analyses Within a Human Capital Framework*. New York: NBER, forthcoming 1974.

Chiswick, Barry R. and Mincer, Jacob. "Time Series Changes in Income Inequality in the United States Since 1939, with Projections to 1985." *Journal of Political Economy*, Supplement (May/June 1972), pp. 34-66.

Fuchs, Victor. *Differentials in Hourly Earnings by Region and City Size, 1959*. New York: NBER, 1967.

Johnson, Thomas. "Returns from Investment in Human Capital." *American Economic Review* (September 1970), pp. 546-60.

Kosters, M., and Welch, F. "The Effect of Minimum Wages on the Distribution of Changes in Aggregate Employment." *American Economic Review* (June 1972), pp. 323-32.

Landes, William. "The Economics of Fair Employment Laws." *Journal of Political Economy* (July/August 1968), pp. 507-52.

Mincer, Jacob. "The Distribution of Labor Incomes: A Survey," *Journal of Economic Literature* (March 1970), pp. 1-26.

_____ . *Schooling, Experience and Earnings*. New York: NBER, forthcoming 1974.

Sharpe, W. *Portfolio Theory and Capital Markets*. New York: McGraw-Hill, 1970.

United States Census of Population: 1960. Vol. 1, Characteristics of the Population, Parts 2 to 52. Washington, D.C.: U.S. Bureau of the Census, 1963.

Vickers, D. *The Theory of the Firm*. New York: McGraw-Hill, 1968.

Index

About the Editors

George M. von Furstenberg is professor of economics at Indiana University and senior staff economist at the Council of Economic Advisers, Washington, D.C. He is the author of *Technical Studies of Mortgage Default Risk* (Ithaca, N.Y.: Center for Urban Development Research at Cornell University, 1971) and has been a consultant on aspects of federal housing and mortgage credit policy to several government agencies. His other work deals with fiscal policy, taxation, and income redistribution; he has published both in the specialized journals and in the *American Economic Review* and the *Journal of Political Economy* in these fields.

Ann R. Horowitz is associate professor of economics at the University of Florida; she was formerly an assistant professor at Indiana University. She is the author of several articles on industrial organization, public finance, and racial differences in income which have appeared in *The Journal of Industrial Economics, The Southern Economic Journal, Applied Economics*, and other professional journals. Dr. Horowitz is also a member of the board of editors of *The Industrial Organization Review.*

Bennett Harrison is associate professor of economics and urban studies in the Department of Urban Studies and Planning at the Massachusetts Institute of Technology, where he teaches urban economic development, the economics of poverty, and statistics. He is the author of *Education, Training, and the Urban Ghetto* (Baltimore: Johns Hopkins Press, 1972) and a new textbook, *Urban Economic Development* (Washington, D.C.: The Urban Institute, 1974). He is the coauthor, with Harold L. Sheppard and William J. Spring of *The Political Economy of Public Service Employment* (Lexington Books, 1972). Dr. Harrison has been actively engaged as a researcher, consultant, and participant in the fields of community economic development, public service employment, and manpower planning, and has published extensively in all three fields.